THE ZAD AND NOTAV

THE ZAD AND NOTAV

Territorial Struggles and the
Making of a New Political Intelligence

Mauvaise Troupe Collective

Translated and edited
with a Preface by Kristin Ross

VERSO

This English-language edition published by Verso 2018
Originally published in French as *Contrées: Histoires croisées de la zad
de Notre-Dame-des-Landes et de la lutte No TAV dans le Val Susa*
© Editions de l'eclat 2016
Translation and Preface © Kristin Ross 2018

1 3 5 7 9 10 8 6 4 2

Verso
UK: 6 Meard Street, London W1F 0EG
US: 20 Jay Street, Suite 1010, Brooklyn, NY 11201
versobooks.com

Verso is the imprint of New Left Books

ISBN-13: 978-1-78663-496-2
ISBN-13: 978-1-78663-497-9 (UK EBK)
ISBN-13: 978-1-78663-498-6 (US EBK)

British Library Cataloguing in Publication Data
A catalogue record for this book is available from the British Library

Library of Congress Cataloging-in-Publication Data

Names: Ross, Kristin, translator, editor. | Collectif Mauvaise troupe.
Title: The Zad and NoTAV : territorial struggles and the making of a new
  political intelligence / Mauvaise Troupe collective ; translated, edited
  and introduced by Kristin Ross.
Other titles: Contrãees. English
Description: English language edition. | London ; Brooklyn, NY : Verso, the
  imprint of New Left Books, 2017 | Includes bibliographical references. |
  Translation of: Contrãees : histoires croisãees de la zad de
  Notre-Dame-des-Landes et de la lutte No TAV dans le Val Susa.
Identifiers: LCCN 2017022087| ISBN 9781786634962 (pbk.) | ISBN
9781786634986
  (US E-book) | ISBN 9781786634979 (UK E-book)
Subjects: LCSH: Government, Resistance
  to—France—Notre-Dame-des-Landes—History—21st century. | Government,
  Resistance to—Italy—Susa Valley—History—21st century. | Protest
    movements—France—Notre-Dame-des-Landes—History--21st century. |
Protest
  movements—Italy—Susa Valley—History—21st century. | Regional
    planning—Environmental aspects—France—Notre-Dame-des-Landes. |
Regional
  planning—Environmental aspects—Italy—Susa Valley.
Classification: LCC HN425.5 .C65413 2017 | DDC 323/.044094—dc23
LC record available at https://lccn.loc.gov/2017022087

Typeset in Minion Pro by Hewer Text UK, Ltd, Edinburgh
Printed and bound by CPI Group (UK) Ltd, Croydon, CR0 4YY

Contents

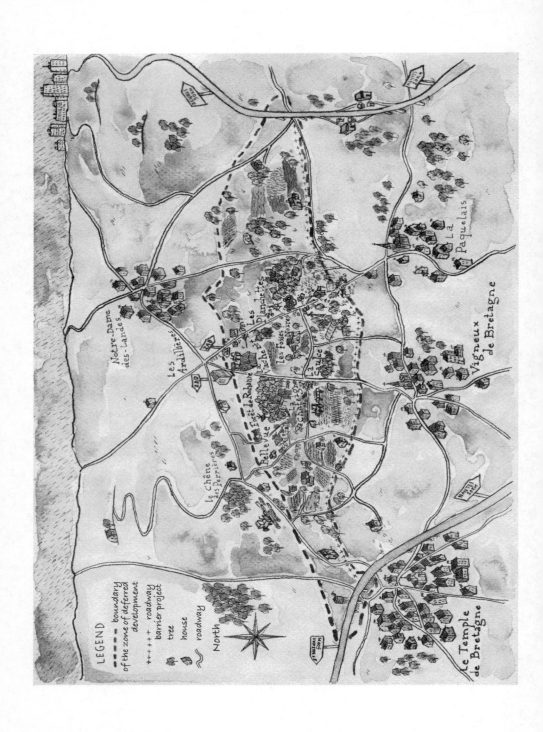

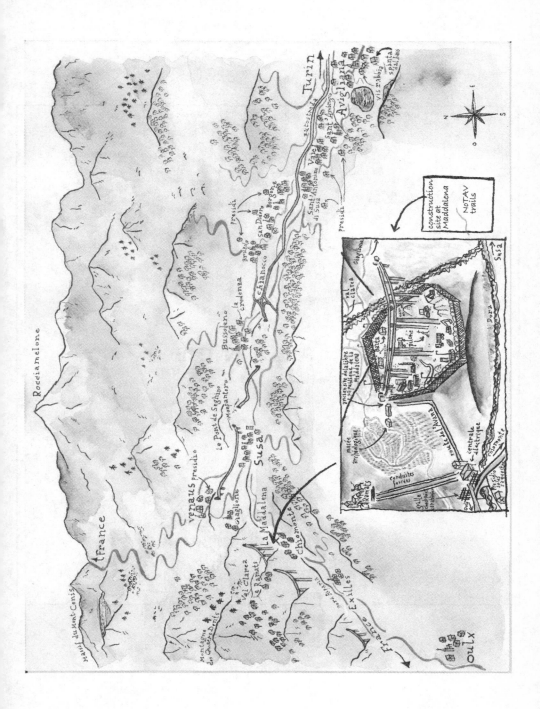

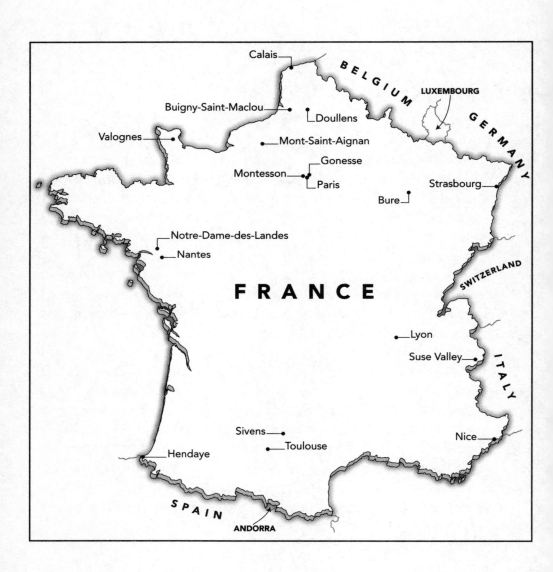

Calais

BELGIUM

LUXEMBOURG

GERMANY

Buigny-Saint-Maclou

Doullens

Valognes

Mont-Saint-Aignan

Gonesse

Montesson

Paris

Bure

Strasbourg

Notre-Dame-des-Landes

Nantes

FRANCE

SWITZERLAND

Lyon

Suse Valley

ITALY

Sivens

Nice

Toulouse

Hendaye

SPAIN

ANDORRA

Preface: Making a Territory

Kristin Ross

In recent years the rise in the number of occupations and attempts to block what have come to be known as 'large, imposed, and useless' infrastructural projects bears witness to a new political sensibility. It is as if some time toward the end of the last century, people throughout the world began to realize that the tension between the logic of development and that of the ecological bases of life had become the primary contradiction ruling their lives. And, in many rural and semirural regions throughout the world – in the Larzac in France, for example, or at Sanrizuka (Narita) in Japan – struggles sprang up against state control of land management. These were movements whose particularity lay in being firmly anchored in a particular region or territory. From the 1988 opposition to a large-scale dam on the Xingu River in Altamira, Brazil, through the Zapatista uprising in Chiapas, to the Standing Rock Sioux's recent resistance to the North Dakota Pipeline, situated movements of this kind in the Americas have tended to be characterized by an indigenous base and leadership.[1] The two most emblematic and ongoing European territorial movements, the zad and NoTAV, however, whose intertwined stories are recounted in this book, differ from the American examples in that each holds together and is held together by people of vastly different cultures and practices, with no one social or ethnic group in charge. But by trying to block what the book's authors call 'the inexorable

---

1 See Arturo Escobar, *Territories of Difference: Place, Movements, Life, Redes* (Durham: Duke University Press, 2008).

extension of a nightmarish world', they unite with their American counterparts in reconfiguring the lines of conflict of an era. In so doing, they make visible the silhouette of a new political grasp on the everyday and a way of managing common affairs. Henceforth, it seems, any effort to change social inequality will have to be conjugated with another imperative – that of conserving the living. Defending the conditions for life on the planet has become the new and incontrovertible horizon of meaning of all political struggle.

The occupation of a small corner of the countryside outside of the village of Notre-Dame-des-Landes in western France is the site of the longest-lasting battle in the country today. For forty years the construction of an international airport on that spot has threatened to destroy 4,000 acres of agricultural land, wetlands, and woods. In the Susa Valley in the Italian Alps, the quasi-totality of a valley inhabited by 70,000 people has battled for over a quarter of a century the construction of a high-speed train line (*Treno ad Alta Velocità* or TAV) through the Alps between Turin and Lyon. While it is frequently said of indigenous peoples that they 'stand in the way' of progress, in each of these regions in Europe a heterogeneous but highly efficient coalition of people has effectively done just that. They have succeeded in delaying, obstructing, and perhaps, ultimately – time will tell – blocking the progress of construction and the destruction of their regions.

In the first chapter of this book readers will find the most thorough chronology of the two movements available in English – here, though, is a brief sketch of the two projects that generated the opposition.

The Airport and the Train

Justifications for, and sponsors of, a new airport on the outskirts of the city of Nantes in western France have changed over the years since their origins in the dreams and magical thinking of a regional bourgeoisie entranced by the booming developmental rhetoric of the peak years of the *Trente Glorieuses*. At one point, the airport was slated to be the departure and landing point for the Concorde, in an attempt to relieve Paris of the massive noise pollution this ill-fated technological wonder produced in its relatively brief life. After this, promoters of the project billed it as the third airport for the Greater Paris region. In recent years, it has been rebranded to become instead the 'Great Airport of the West', a kind of bid for prominence in the fierce regional competition over accessibility, tourism and commercial opportunities. But in the late 1960s and early 1970s, when the project was first floated, one of the earliest (and still worth reading) critiques of the developmental rhetoric promoting it likened the project to the cargo-cults of New Guinea, where simulacra of airport runways were carved out of the brush to attract airplanes. Nantes businessmen believed that 'if you build it, they will come': they had decided the industrial destiny of their region was one that could soon make Germans and Japanese tremble. A new airport would transform the Nantes region into the next 'airian Rotterdam of Europe',[2] The sum spent on studies designed to give a scientific veneer to the project far exceeded the purchase price of the land needed for its realization – an area regularly described as 'almost a desert'. This description could only have been the echo of the familiar colonial trope indicating a perceived scarcity of population preceding invasion, since the area chosen was in fact largely wetlands – an environmental category virtually unrecognized in the 1970s.

And so, an area of some 4,000 acres containing several dozen farms was designated in 1974 as the site for the future airport. The area was decreed by the state to be a ZAD, or 'zone d'aménagement différé', a zone of deferred development. This administrative status allowed the state time to begin buying up land from farmers willing to sell out or, in the familiar pattern of rural exodus, to buy whenever a farmer died and his children sold out. Yet while the slow process of expropriation was continuing, the energy crisis sunk the overall project into one of

---

2   See Jean de Legge and Roger Le Guen, *Dégage! . . . On aménage,* Collection 'La province trahie'. (Les Sables-d'Olonne: Editions le Cercle d'or, 1976). For a critical history of the developmental rhetoric and policies undergirding French postwar economic growth, see Céline Pessis, Sezin Topçu and Christophe Bonneuil, *Une autre histoire des 'Trente Glorieuses': Modernisation, contestations et pollutions dans la France d'après-guerre* (Paris: La Découverte, 2013). Here and elsewhere, translations from the French are mine.

the intermittent long naps that mark its history. This one lasted throughout the 1980s and 1990s – the airport was forgotten, not entirely dead but not entirely alive either. In the meantime, though, the zone profited from what could only be called a secondary gain from the illness of having been destined to be one day covered over in concrete: much like Cuba during the Special Period, it had inadvertently been transformed, de facto, into a protected agricultural zone. Developers were hesitant to build near a future airport and no one wanted to live next door – the suburbanization that was befalling much of the area around Nantes was held at bay in Notre-Dame-des-Landes.

Opposition to the airport by farmers who refused to sell their land, some of whom were active in the Paysans–Travailleurs movement and had supported striking workers during the 1968 insurrection in Nantes, and townspeople living near the zone had gotten underway as soon as the project received administrative approval back in the early 1970s. But it was not until the new century, when the Socialist government under Prime Minister Lionel Jospin pumped life back into the construction agenda, that something resembling the current coalition made up of farmers, townspeople and a new group, squatters and soon-to-be occupiers, began to take shape. With the arrival of the first squatters around 2008, the ZAD (*zone d'aménagement différé*) became a zad (*zone à défendre*) – the acronym had been given a new combative meaning by opponents to the project and the administrative perimeter of the zone now designated a set of battle lines.[3]

One of the most peculiar aspects of the two infrastructural projects is their redundancy vis-à-vis existing services. An international airport exists already in the city of Nantes and a train line already runs through the Alps (usually operating at less than half capacity) between Turin and Lyon, in central France. Nevertheless, in 1991, a new high-speed line was planned in Italy to be added to the current one as a key element of the east–west corridor linking Lisbon to

---

3   The new definition of the acronym has entered the *Grand Robert* dictionary in France: a 'zad' is defined as 'a (frequently rural) zone that militants occupy to oppose a development project damaging to the environment'.

Budapest initially, and ultimately to Kiev. The initial goal of the project, a joint partnership between French and Italian governments and the European Union, was to enhance the movement of passengers and tourists, while also facilitating the integration of managers and corporate executives, between Italy and the Rhône region in France. Subsequently, the future train had been refunctioned to be used mainly for the transport of freight, despite the fact that the flow of goods between France and Italy has declined steadily since the beginning of the new century.[4] The project elicited little opposition on the French side of the Alps. On the Italian side, however, in the Susa Valley, an area with a complex economy based in industry, agriculture, and tourism, and a historically united population known for its anti-fascist resistance and earlier opposition to infrastructural projects, reaction against their valley being transformed into nothing more than a transit corridor was swift, with the first coordinated group of citizen opposition organized in 1994.

Space-specific, geographically defined struggles have a kind of refreshing flat-footedness about them. David Harvey has suggested this is because the fact of being bound to a particular space creates an either-or dialectic – something quite distinct from a transcendental or Hegelian one.[5] Demands, concerns, and aspirations that are place-specific in kind create a situation that calls for an existential and political choice – one is either for the airport or against it. In the words of Marx to Vera Zasulich, writing in the context of an earlier rural battle against the state, 'It is a question no longer of a problem to be solved, but simply of an enemy to be beaten . . . it is no longer a theoretical problem . . . it is quite simply an enemy to be beaten.'[6] A 57 kilometre

4   See Michele Monni, 'Italian Politics and the NoTAV Movement: The Resiliency or Failure of Citizen Activism?' and Lucie Greyl, Hali Healy, Emanuele Leonardi, and Leah Temper, 'Stop That Train! Ideological Conflict and the TAV', in *Economics and Policy of Energy and the Environment*, n. 2 (2012).

5   David Harvey, *Spaces of Hope* (Berkeley: University of California Press, 2000), pp. 164–75.

6   'Marx-Zasulich Correspondence: Letters and Drafts', in Teodor Shanin, *Late Marx and the Russian Road: Marx and the Peripheries of Capitalism* (New York: Monthly Review Press, 1983), p. 116.

tunnel will either be drilled through the Alps or it will not. An airport will either be built on farmland or it will not. Other countries know this well. In the most stirring and significant precedent to Notre-Dame-des-Landes, expropriation of farmland for the Tokyo Narita airport in Japan started in 1966, and by 1971 a decade of murderous battles between the state and farmers who refused to give up their lands, supported nimbly by far-left Zengakuren, had begun.[7] It was these highly exemplary, even Homeric battles, immortalized in the films of Shinsuke Ogawa and Yann Le Masson – what I have come to regard as among the most defining combats of the worldwide 1960s – which, according to the testimony of many French militants of the era, inspired their own frontal and physical clashes with the police in the streets of Paris and other French cities. Breton documentary maker Le Masson's film of the Narita battles, *Kashima Paradise,* screened in Nantes in the early 1970s, brought the Japanese example to the attention of early opponents in Notre-Dame-des-Landes. But the Japanese experience was not singular. A little earlier, an economic boom nourished an urge in Canada to build, outside of Montreal, and in time for the 1976 Olympics, what was destined to briefly become the largest airport in the world. Against the vigorous protest of the 12,000 farmers removed from their land, the Mirabel airport was built. But it was soon judged to be too far from the city and usage faded away in favour of the old Montreal airport. Mirabel was converted to a freight airport, but even that did not prove lucrative – for many years its desolate and empty terminal was used as a film set. Canadian prime ministers attempted to lure evicted farmers back to the region, with little success. In 2014 the terminal building was demolished at a cost of $15 million.

But it is Spain – home of the proliferating 'ghost airport' phenomenon – that provides the best contemporary example of the pillaging of public funds for useless structures.[8] With a population of 47 million people, Spain now houses 52 airports. (Germany, a country with

---

7   See David Apter and Nagayo Sawa, *Against the State: Politics and Social Protest in Japan* (Cambridge: Harvard University Press, 1984).

8   See Christine Delphy, 'B comme Béton', barricades-mots-zad.org/lettre-b.

double the population of Spain, has 39). Out of those 52 Spanish airports over two-thirds are failing – in some, no aircraft ever lands or takes off. Yet the airports are staffed and maintained at enormous expense.

Territories

I did not know much about the zad before I was invited there to participate in a discussion on communal imaginaries, but I knew enough to bring a pair of rubber boots as I had heard the place described, rather unappealingly, as a swamp. When I mentioned this to my hosts they firmly corrected me – I was not in a swamp, I was in a *bocage*. Translating this book, the word 'bocage' posed a problem, mostly because the bocage is, as far as I can tell, a landscape unknown in the Americas, because of our lack of a feudal history. The problem is not unlike that of Antonio Gramsci, who as a young Sardinian student attending school on the mainland, wrote an essay about a woodland animal from his island, a snake-like creature with legs, but could not find the Italian word to name it. There is no name, his teacher told him, because such an animal does not exist. At first I tried 'copse' – obscure to Americans but known to the British – until I finally settled on the English 'bocage' – a little-used, long-ago borrowing from the French to mean 'little woods'. A bocage is actually a mosaic of prairies and cultivated fields of variable shapes and sizes, enclosed and separated by shrubs, hedges and clusters of trees. As Anne Berger points out, it is, by all measures, a modest landscape, one that is on a human scale, or to be less anthropocentric, a scale conducive to humans and smallish animals like rabbits and small deer, or river fish. There is nothing sublime or transcendent about a bocage – the vast vistas needed to unleash soaring sentiments are lacking. The eye is always stopped by a hedge which, even if it limits the gaze, does not block physical entry.[9] You can always jump over a hedge or walk through a wood – in the end, the only way to experience the contours

---

9 See Anne Berger, 'B comme Bocage', barricades-mots-zad.org/lettre-b.

of a bocage is really by moving through it. Geographer-novelist Julien Gracq, close witness to the mutation of the French countryside and a great amateur of the bocages of his native region, wrote that nothing had marked his generation more than the unbelievably *unchanging* nature of the rural and urban landscape in France for more than third of a century – between 1914 and 1950. Everything, it seems, changed at a very rapid pace during the Second Empire, through the Belle Époque, and up until 1914. And everything resumed that chaotic pace again, beginning in the 1950s. In between, though, time was frozen.[10] Yet even during that stationary moment, Gracq foresaw the fragility of the bocage and the sad fate awaiting it. In a radio interview in 1977, he commented:

> I remember when I wrote a little article on the bocage for the *Annales de Géographie* in 1934 where I said that the bocage would soon be gone, that it would die from social transformation. The editor was frightened by that kind of peremptory judgment. But in fact, the bocage did disappear, or is in the process of disappearing, perhaps for reasons other than the ones I predicted.[11]

Anyone who has driven through large swathes of the French countryside in recent years has witnessed, perhaps without realizing it, the forces that destroyed the bocage: a kind of rural reification and aggressive 'redistricting' process familiar to urbanists, which in the countryside is called 'remembrement'. Mobilized most intensively throughout the 1980s and 1990s, 'remembrement' occurs when a territory that allowed subsistence is reoriented and restabilized to maximize profits. With the arrival of large farm machinery, hedges and other natural obstructions were leveled to create vast single-owner agribusiness parcels for mono-cultural cultivation, especially in Brittany. Today, there is a growing recognition of the important

---

10   See Julien Gracq, *Lettrines 2* (Paris: José Corti, 1974).

11   Julien Gracq, radio interview, *France Culture* (1977) cited in Jean-Louis Tissier, 'De l'esprit géographique dans l'oeuvre de Julien Gracq', in *Espace géographique*, p. 58. See also Poirier, Louis (Julien Gracq), 'Bocage et plaine dans le sud de l'Anjou', in *Annales de Géographie*, t. 32, n. 241, 1934, pp. 22–31.

ecological degradation in the form of water pollution and soil erosion that occurs when water-retaining shrubs and trees are destroyed in this way. But the process continues.

Yet the polemic unleashed by Notre-Dame-des-Landes and the Susa Valley cannot be seen simply as one of technology versus nature. Consider the specificity of the two territories in question and the genesis of their landscapes. The Susa Valley is as far from a pristine Alpine 'Heidi' environment as one can imagine. Historically a prime strategic point for conquerors from Hannibal to Caesar to pass through, it is now a highly urbanized area that bears the scars of earlier modernization efforts and transportation construction – the valley is crossed by major motorways leading to the Fréjus tunnel. And nothing in the history of a bocage lends itself to a cult of pure nature or the pastoral dynamic of retreat. What Raymond Williams used to call 'the sweetness of the place' is always a construction – and one made in part out of interventions and influences from the outside.[12] A bocage is, as Gracq points out, an artificial formation, a very human endeavour, or better, the result of neither man nor nature alone but of their alliance. A bocage is not on the side of nature or on the side of humanity against nature. We might see it as an enduring record or testimony to the lives and works of the humans and non-humans who have dwelt within it. The bocage offers a graceful example of the way in which nature is, above all, historical. For it was the peasantry as a form of collective life that fashioned the bocage over centuries, and without the use of machines. And – irony of ironies – in a place like the zad where right now the question of the common use of a territory is the most pressing one of the day, the creation of the bocage, historically, corresponded to the *end* of communal usage of land in Brittany: the hedges were first and foremost enclosures delimiting and attributing land parcels to individuals or groups of peasants who were allowed to farm them in return for a portion of crops given over to the landowner. The bocage was a segmentation of space resulting from the privatization of the commons. And now, in a

---

12 Raymond Williams, cited in David Harvey, *Justice, Nature and the Geography of Difference* (Oxford: Blackwell, 1996), p. 27.

kind of delightful paradox, in the form of the zad it has come to figure as the possibility of restitution, a kind of restitution of the land back to the collective. Where once people fought the bocage to defend the commons, now it is the bocage that is defended as a common good.[13]

Neither can the battles of Notre-Dame-des-Landes and the Susa Valley, as they emerge in the pages of this book, be understood in terms of the usual confrontation between, on the one hand, those who know, the *sujets supposés savoir*, the allegedly neutral technocrats and policy experts, and, on the other, the uninformed who must learn to abandon their narrow and myopic self-interest and submit to 'progress' in the service of the general good. It is a war between two dueling logics, two argumentations, two knowledges, two futures that I will call, for now, the 'airworld' versus the territory. The two knowledges are, of course, not symmetrical in terms of the power behind them. For the airworld, it is the global luxury trade, the third of the world's traded goods – the iPads, Peruvian roses, and farmed salmon now flown by air – which is powering world growth and which is what, in fact, now and in the final determining instance, matters.[14] Market laws, which continue to be as indisputable as they are indemonstrable, still decree that infrastructure equals the modernization that fuels economic growth. The quality prized above all others here seems to be *friction-lessness* – the ability to move people and goods in and out as quickly and effortlessly as possible. To this end, cities need to connect more easily and intensely to each other than to the towns, villages, and countryside just beyond their borders – these last are, of course, now destined to slow or precipitous but, in any case inevitable, decline. As for the cities, these would become nothing more than high-density urban centers linked to intercontinental neighbourhoods. People and things, torn from their living entanglements, are freed to become

---

13   See 'A la lisière du bocage', lundi.am/IMG/pdf/4._brochurelisie_reboca-gea4.pdf.

14   For a vivid enactment of the future according to the 'airworld', see John Kasarda and Greg Lindsey, *Aerotropolis: The Way We'll Live Next* (New York: Farrar, Strauss and Giroux, 2011). See also Will Self's review of *Aerotropolis* in the *London Review of Books*, April 28, 2011, pp. 10–11.

mobile investments in a world where the fungibility of space is taken as a given.

The making of a territory, as this book narrates the process in two very different regions, is the making of a place that, precisely, cannot be exchanged for any other. If what matters for the airworld is a smooth and seamless transit between substitutable spaces, for the territory what matters has everything to do with a logic of difference and possibility, autonomy and self-determination: the perpetuation of the possibilities of common life that place-based social relations can create, even amidst a striking diversity of beliefs. Where once the territory's fight was with the airport or the train-line, it is no longer with high-speed transport per se, but with its world: a world of class-division that identifies human progress with economic growth and defines human needs in terms of markets and the submission of all the world's resources to markets. The high-speed world is one in which the value of any item of earthly life is calculated according to its service to capital. Preventing one's territory from becoming a mere node in a global capitalist system, a space of pure transit where people do nothing more than pass through, is a way of stabilizing in time – and perhaps even, with luck, a lifetime – a way of life that lies at least partially outside of and against the state and the market.

And it is the ability of these movements to have *stabilized in time*, to fashion new and creative ways of inhabiting a conflict, which emerges as one of the most important elements of their stories. For these struggles are what the Maoists used to call 'protracted wars' – children, even grandchildren of early opponents are now implicated in the struggles. Ogawa's filming of the 'Mama's Brigades' during the Narita battles makes this vividly clear. Their sheer duration is a vital factor in creating a different relationship to the territory than shorter-lived occupations like Taksim, Occupy, or Madrid – not coinciden-tally, all urban occupations. As Peter Kropotkin pointed out in his re-writing of the history of the Paris Commune in *The Conquest of Bread*, proximity to and involvement with the means of subsistence is essential not only to the duration of a movement but to establishing a lived intimacy with the territory. At the heart of that relationship is a form of embeddedness that this book's authors describe as the breakdown in daily life of any distinction between dwelling in a territory and defending it. With the passage of time, however, the nature of what is being defended changes. Where once it may have been an unpolluted environment or agricultural land, what is defended as the struggle deepens now comes to include all the new social links, solidarities, affective ties, and lived entanglements that the struggle produced. Any place owes its character to the experiences it affords to those who dwell in it or spend time there, and these include the new physical relation – what Gaston Bachelard called the 'muscular consciousness' of the territory – something that derives in part from the seasonal rhythm of agricultural labour and in part from physical combat during the many skirmishes and battles with the forces of order. And in both the Susa Valley and Notre-Dame-des-Landes these physical battles with the state have been severe. Perhaps for this reason, the new relationship to the territory also includes the reawakening of its past rebel history: the anti-fascist resistance in the Susa Valley, or a vernacular commune-precedent to the zad like the Commune de Nantes in 1968. Defending the territory in a protracted war comes to entail defending the very collective life project that has taken shape there during its defense – a project that, as Escobar suggests, may include the very concept of territoriality itself.[15] To the extent that the concept nurtures a certain autonomy and will to self-determination akin to what Raymond Williams theorized as 'militant particularism', this seems to be the case in the two struggles. The notion of a territory helps create an environment that, in Williams' words, can be 'received and made and remade', actively molded and achieved through work, play and battle.[16] It creates in the dweller an experiential center or standpoint from which to perceive the greater world, a mode of apprehension based on being actively engaged in the

---

15   Escobar, *Territories of Difference*, p. 68.

16   Williams, cited in Harvey, *Justice, Nature and the Geography of Difference*, p. 29. Harvey argues that it is in the novels set in the Black Mountains of Wales that Williams analyzes the productive relationship between local embeddedness or 'militant particularism' and the abstract understanding of the wider realm of global capitalism.

labour, practices, and material details of conducting life collectively at the daily level – cultivating, building, caring for animals, assembling a library.

A smaller-scale and more circumscribed territory like the zad may lend itself more easily to fashioning a productive form of livable secession than the vast Susa Valley. This was what William Morris, for one, believed – direct management of one's own affairs can occur only on a scale small enough that each person 'can take pleasure in all the details of life.'[17] The NoTAV movement numbers in the tens of thousands dispersed throughout a large region, while the zad's residents, whose exact number is unknown since the most recent administrative census could find no volunteers willing to enter the zone to take an official count, are perhaps a couple hundred, only swelling to the tens of thousands on the days of mass mobilization in the face of impending evacuation. Experiments at the zad include, but are not limited to, a weekly 'non-market' to distribute vegetables, collective use of lands, the embrace of what the Parisian Communards called 'communal luxury' – the aesthetic, pleasurable dimension of all labour, in any number of examples.[18] To cite again one of communal luxury's most adept exponents, William Morris: 'the true secret of happiness lies in the taking of interest in all the details of daily life, in elevating them by art instead of handing the performance of them over to unregarded drudges.'[19] This is a version of happiness proven to provoke aggravation and retaliation on the part of the state. 'If it has become so crucial for the political classes to crush the zad, it is because the zad constitutes an insolent demonstration of a life that is possible without them. A better life . . .'[20] Left to its own devices, which is not at all certain to be the case, the zad's future points to a

---

17   William Morris, 'The Society of the Future', in May Morris (ed.) *William Morris: Artist, Writer, Socialist* (New York: Russel and Russel, 1966), p. 459.

18   See Kristin Ross, *Communal Luxury: The Political Imaginary of the Paris Commune* (London: Verso, 2015)

19   William Morris, 'The Aims of Art', in *Signs of Change* (London: Longmans, 1903), p. 137.

20   Mauvaise Troupe Collective, 'Unconditional Vals vs. the Zad' (trans.) Kristin Ross. Editorial, *Le Monde*, October 2016.

becoming-commune. But this book shows militants in the Susa Valley also undergoing a substantial transformation of their daily life by re-owning it, by and through political struggle, and becoming fully accountable for it. Thus, the importance granted to those creative movement-driven inventions and forms of sociability like the *presidii* (protest sites) in the Susa Valley that are at once banquets, meeting places, and shelters.

In both cases, defending a territory from the outset brought together extremely eclectic and diverse groups of people around that goal. The never-ending process of soldering together black bloc anarchists and nuns, retired farmers and vegan lesbian separatists, lawyers and *autonomistas* into a tenacious and effective community is what the authors call 'composition', and the story of its unfolding is, to my mind, the most compelling part of the book. This is the daily drama of unexpected encounters, of co-existing, sharing space, coordinating, recognizing difference, undergoing existential overhaul, and, above all, learning to avoid the temptation of trying to convert others to the superiority of one's practices, whether these be spreading counter information, hunger strikes, the fastidious preparation of legal appeals, nocturnal sabotage, naturalist surveys to document the endangered species among the flora and fauna of the zone, or frontal confrontations with the police. And it is what is meant by the book's subtitle: 'the making of a new political intelligence'. 'In the act of holding diverse elements together', write the authors, 'it is more a question of tact than tactics, passion than sad necessities, and opening up the field than carving up the terrain.'

The phenomenon of solidarity in diversity is mirrored in another 'composition' as well: the formal decisions the authors have made in recounting its achievement almost entirely through the voices of those who built it. This book is not an anti-state manifesto or an abstract treatise. While highly theoretical, very little time is wasted on theoretical edifices or citational strategy. It does not prophesize the coming insurrection but instead recounts – from the inside, for the authors are themselves actively engaged in the struggles they narrate – two insurrections in progress. Telling the two stories together, in a productive entanglement that isolates moments of convergence, while allowing each struggle its own history, poetry and praxis, is not only difficult – it is itself an exemplary exercise in solidarity in diversity. The narrative choice to relate the movements almost entirely in the individual voices of their protagonists mirrors the authors' territorial commitments and it also leads to something quite new in the creation of a tableau of what revolution might look like today. The personal testimonies are not merely called upon to provide context or local colour to the dominant story, as is so frequently the case. They certainly do this, and very vividly, but they also move the plot forward in time, providing key eye-witness depictions of dramatic moments in their sagas; they enact conflicting viewpoints and commentary on strategy debates; they reflect on the reasons behind particular choices made under given conditions – choices that are the very essence of historical change; they theorize their own commitments and conflicts. They show the forceful role of women in every aspect of the struggle – something I have witnessed myself at the zad. Often intensely personal, the voices reach beyond to a common flow. And as such, those who speak are not mere data, illustrations, or foot-soldiers to a pre-existing theory or revolutionary prediction but the flesh, blood and thought of the movements they are making.

Introduction

He speaks, without pausing, for several hours straight. His powerful voice fills the small Italian café in the Susa Valley. He tells us the story of his valley, the forests he has learned how to see, the streams that no longer flow, the Juventus soccer games that no longer interest him. Each word is a reverberation of the territory he resolved to defend, now, some several years ago. Each sentence, each intonation emanates from the deepest part of himself, surprising and touching the heart as much as the mind. He sells fish, and has left his stand to devote the whole morning to three strangers curious about his stories and his reasoning.

> A few years ago, I was what the system wanted me to be. I worked, I thought I was doing good because I wasn't harming anyone. I read the newspaper and I thought it told the truth. But now, I've decided what to do with my life: to fight for this movement that is also the future. If I have one more day to live, I want to use it to wake people up.

She is in front of her cabin, in the sunlight. She tells us the thousands of reasons why she decided to move to the zad at Notre-Dame-des-Landes. She was a pianist, gave lessons to children, and today she points out the places where she imagines hiding if they try to throw her off the territory. A quality shines forth in her artless words:

> I have countless things to do, but earning money is another whole kettle of fish. I could have made 4,000 euros a month working twenty-six

hours a week, but when you feel that your life could be useful for something, when you have causes that are really dear to your heart, you can't just go on giving lessons and only do that. I had to come here.

These are the kind of words that disrupt lives, because they flow from lives that have been themselves disrupted. Poetry can be heard emanating from the ordinary mouths of opponents to an airport on the outskirts of Nantes and to a TAV rail line (Treno ad Alta Velocità – high-speed train) between Lyon and Turin. And a poetry capable of conveying, in simple terms, what is important: lessons and ideas with the capacity to orient and guide future acts, and to make us collectively intelligent just as much as they make us laugh or cry. And all of this was born from a single first word taken to its full consequences: no. Two letters that for years have polarized the lives of thousands of men and women, letters written on barricades, tractors, houses, and that resound in slogans and songs. One syllable that gives birth to others, and that in turn gives rise to dizzying thoughts and questions.

We gathered these hundred or so interviews between the autumn of 2014 and the summer of 2015, walking up and down the muddy paths and twisting mountain roads, the vineyards and the chestnut forests, in the bocage of Notre-Dame-des-Landes and in the Susa Valley. One part of our collective went to the western valley in Piedmont, while another had, for some time already, been engaged in the adventure of the zad, some of us living there. We write from these worlds in resistance and the voice of this book is engaged with the hundred others. This book is our attempt to convey their music, transmit their atmospheres, emotions, the human warmth and astonishment, the anger and hope. These are not small goals, and the task is so ambitious that one book alone cannot suffice. But this book seeks in its own way to convey the trajectory and fate of these struggles, because their success is largely dependent on their capacity to spread the new certainties and hypotheses they've generated, and that they might be shared and debated.

The book is organized around several questions that are not ours alone, but are those the struggles themselves gave rise to and try to keep alive. 'Our era is stingy when it comes to struggles', a TAV opponent told us, and these two spaces – Notre-Dame-des-Landes and the Susa Valley – indeed represent a radical rupture with the fastidious course taken by two societies at peace. Over and above what they have in common – from their massive oppositions to infrastructural projects to their obstinacy in embodying revolt and resistance now, in the present – what unites them here is the way that the two movements, via a thousand different ways of telling their stories, speak to each other and interrogate each other at the same time. On the one hand, a popular struggle has defined the life of an Italian valley of 70,000 inhabitants for over twenty years. On the other, the zad: a 1,650 hectare bocage that, having freed itself from all signs of control of the French State, has become the outline of an autonomous territory, the beginnings of a free commune.

Peoples

Eyebrows contract, faces take on a questioning look. In the midst of a discussion, one of those harsh, explosive words that command everybody's attention has been spoken. In French, the term 'the people' can barely be pronounced, burdened as it is with associations from the past, vices that have accompanied its political use: nationalism, Stalinism, and so on.

At the zad, we are timidly beginning to use the adjective 'popular', by dint of finding ourselves regularly filling up the roadways with crowds of demonstrators and hundreds of tractors. We don't go so far as to put it on banners or use it in pamphlet titles, but more and more the idea is floating around. Like a slow, minute re-appropriation, an inspiration. In the Susa Valley, they say: 'The NoTAV struggle is a popular struggle.' There, it is obvious, no one would say otherwise. There are popular committees, popular meals, and popular marches. We were present at the last one: tens of thousands of demonstrators from Bussoleno to Susa, one more time. So many giant processions have snaked their way through the valley that they couldn't be counted. On those marches were retired people, school children, unemployed, and firemen. Flags hung in windows, people marched according to their trade, their village committee, their political affinity, all in the ambiance of a village fair. Giacu, the totemic puppet, laced through the crowd and ridiculed a group of mayors, looking a bit awkward in their tricolour scarves. All this speaks to us directly, since it is a dimension of things we are not familiar with. It is perhaps here, somewhere between a territory and a politics, that the NoTAV people has come into being, rich with a common culture and fundamentally open to others.

Out of this popular dimension the power of the movement is generated. On the village billboard, a whole palimpsest of events can be uncovered: breakfast by the work-yard gates, an evening of support for prisoners, a discussion about mountain agriculture, a concert by a Turin rap group ... this isn't the monthly schedule but rather the weekly one. NoTAV is social life, each day there is something to do, a place to meet up. The valley is peopled with a force and a soul in combat.

Territories

Living in the zad is not the same as lodging. 'Zone d'Aménagement Différé', or Zone of Deferred Management, is a management acronym – it says nothing about what is lived here, no more than do terms like 'wetlands', or 'lawless zone'. To distinguish ourselves from this programmed, formatted language, we go in search of animals and plants with fabulous names: great crested newt, grand Capricorn, ribbon-leaved water plantain. We pass through the doorways of cabins made of sheet iron and palettes, or of a solid wood frame, each made out of determination and dreams. There are dozens of these living spaces, cohabiting with conventional farmhouses and buildings, those of the inhabitants and farmers who ceded nothing. There is no airport here because the place is taken. And by being occupied it engenders a world. A world where we get our bread every Friday at the 'non-market', where we meet up Thursday evenings at the Wardine, and where assemblies decide to barricade all the roadways in the area to prevent a judge from coming in. Everyday life here is intricately merged with struggle. Some 200 people, maybe more, maybe less, live here – what does it matter? Population surveys have evaporated in the kind of life being designed here day after day. Thousands of others join us depending on what is going on. New arrivals have to first put on their boots, to walk paths where your feet sink into the mud. Walking through the bocage, it transmits to us a little of the magic of something that persists. It is not immediately noticeable, but little by little, a difference with the rest of the surrounding region can be detected: the fields and the meadows here are smaller, bordered by hedges and paths while elsewhere agriculture management and redistricting has triumphed. Something persists, too, in the words of a retired farmer: he mischievously tells us that the suppression of the communal lands was not accomplished without resistance, and that by an accident of history, the commune of Notre-Dame-des-Landes was founded in the course of the illustrious year of 1871. He evokes a past that links together easily with present subversions. He continues, enlarging the geography: in a radius of 30 kilometres from here, we can find the sites of the ex-projects for nuclear stations at Pellerin and Carnet – 'ex', because the struggles there were victorious. Next, he ticks off the highpoints in the history of peasant struggles of the last century: Vigne Marou, Couëron, Cheix-en-Retz, and so forth. The territory of the zad, ardently defended against all incursions from the forces of order or bulldozers, remains open to the four winds of struggle: past, present, and those to come.

When, having climbed up the Montgenevre pass, you enter the Susa Valley, no boundary marks the transition. From Salbertrand to Avigliana a subterranean valley extends that is invisible on any Italian survey map: the NoTAV valley. A territory, that while maintaining a fusion with the mountain land, has managed to exceed any set of physical boundaries. Those who come to meet it with sincerity are welcomed, and, well outside of Turin, NoTAV insinuates itself inside the best guarded prisons in Italy. A territory both real and imagined, it exceeds the limits of political conflict: 'NoTAVs came to help me when the wind tore my roof off', 'we are going to the funerals with flags when the families ask us to'. There is a community that lives in the space and that gives to the term territory a vertiginous fullness.

Composition

Exploring the extent and scale of these movements cannot be done in a day. We ran into semi-punk naturalists and former railway workers, tenacious farmers and ski instructors, young runaway-squatters and radical women militants from the neighbouring city. We shared a little of the lives of those who are not waiting for a better tomorrow, but who throw themselves, with no railings or safety nets, into the boiling alchemy of the struggle. This is the place where that which comes together is everything that elsewhere is kept carefully apart. How can it seem to hold together? By what magic? NoTAVs like meetings, hundreds of them can be found in the Bussoleno festivals or on an occupied motorway. An old white-haired woman takes the microphone, she climbs up on the central platform so that she can be seen and heard. She is the owner of a chalet who has just been evicted, she begins at the beginning: why they built it there where the construction was supposed to begin, what their aims were, how it all got underway. Everyone listens, even those who are most on top of the situation. She is not trying to inform, she is telling a story, once again, the very real epic saga they are all pursuing together. She takes time for anecdotes and details, even though in this crowd, there is not anyone who has not heard them before. She traces the contours of a common narrative that, patiently, opens a pathway to understanding and to decisions made together. Listening and sharing are vital for keeping together the imperative mandates of political organizations and the azimuth spontaneity of affinity groups that blend into the movement. Something is being invented here on a patch of asphalt, something like a capacity to decide, at the level of gestures and practices, that is the opposite of representation and delegation. A few days later, on the same motorway, now reopened to traffic at 80 miles an hour, a friend unfolds for us, mile after mile, the escapades of NoTAV: 'There, in front of the tunnel, we made a blockade of burning tires . . . the fire lit up the whole mountainside'. Farther along: 'We made a blockade here, and when the police forced us to move and chased us into the village, the villagers opened their doors to hide us.' The sad concrete of the motorway is transformed into intoxicating décor, the overpass pilings become the crucible for shared gestures and acts.

At Notre-Dame-des-Landes, there is, as of now, no motorway. And yet the motorway-plan designed to serve the future airport is of very high priority on the schedule of construction, this winter of 2016. The motorway is supposed to join up the national roads that, from Nantes, extend to Saint-Nazaire and Rennes: eleven kilometres of road, one going through the zone. Opening up arteries in a hostile territory is as much about getting construction underway as it is a military operation, and the different groups in the movement make no mistake about it. These last months, they have thrown themselves into battle together, breathlessly: pursuing legal judgments, demonstrations, information dissemination, occupations, blockades to assure that none of the announced machinery shows even the tip of its hood in the area. At the same time, all of the anti-airport forces unite behind the so-called 'historic' inhabitants threatened with eviction, just as they united in the autumn of 2012 behind squatters who had come to defend the zone. The greater the battle stakes, the greater the solidarity and collective intelligence. The forms, presences and modes of action of the different sensibilities and political lines of the struggle learn to act together, and, in so doing, are themselves transformed. All this is a sketch in what we might call an art of composition.

To Make a Movement

Out of edifying victories in demonstrating strength, came a general desire to make a bit of these struggles come to life elsewhere. A little of these struggles – that is, especially the practices, tactics, and a frank and direct manner of taking on the task of the conflict, making it last, living it. This is also a political leaning, that of seeing in the opposition to infrastructures a space for thwarting the inexorable expansion of a nightmarish world. For this we certainly need more than a slogan like 'zads everywhere' or 'fermarci è impossibile' ('we cannot be stopped'). If the myth and the media images sometimes speed up our progress and bring about promising encounters, it is always perilous to try and copy elsewhere a method or a recipe that was elaborated in a specific context. What does it mean to spread combats whose particularity lies precisely in their being anchored somewhere specific? In the Tarn, the Ligure, in l'Isère, in Sicily, the Morvan, Trentin or in Aveyron, some people have not waited to formulate a clear response to that question to seize opportunities. This has led to striking successes and to severe disappointments. There again, the need to understand the long histories of the zad and of NoTAV made itself felt. Not in order to imitate them more scrupulously, but to sharpen our analyses and to understand the powers at work, to learn to ward off foreseeable blows and to make our gestures more certain.

Before we can elaborate these four structuring themes of the book, we need to introduce the two infrastructural projects and devote the first chapter to a narrative of the two epic struggles against them. It will then be easier to find our way and understand the befores and afters that mark the two movements. There are points of transition and of rupture, merry-making and long tranquil years, twenty-five days of battle on one side, forty on the other. Certain accelerations made us lose our breath, others gave us inspiration:

> The first day, the old lady brought coffee and cakes to the policemen. She said: 'Poor souls, they must be freezing, they are so young . . .' After the night raid against the cabin with its dozens of wounded, no one in the valley ever again had the idea of feeding the police. Never again!

There is the tempo brought on by modifications in the projects or by political deadlines, there is the rhythm which, despite all that, each movement manages to make for itself, and there are strategies and dreams: 'We are already together in the post-project', says someone who lives near Notre-Dame-des-Landes. Nothing is finished and yet we had to stop writing. The adventure continues beyond the final period.

The Two Projects

At first glance, what is striking is the absurdity of the projects: why in hell pour tons of cement and asphalt on a wetland in order to move a perfectly functional airport? Why insist on building a high-speed train line between Turin and Lyon when the two cities are separated by mountain summits over 4,000 metres high and when a railway line already links them? And why these huge projects, when we are bombarded every day with the news that our world is in a state of aggravated crisis – ecological and economic, among others? How can we not notice the blaring contradiction between promoting the construction of a new airport while at the same time bragging about hosting the world-wide climate summit, or between pouring millions of euros into a destructive infrastructure all the while preaching the need to reduce public expenditures?

One need only ask who profits from the crime. And who will be made richer by the destroyed lives of the people living nearby, or by the annihilation of the flora and fauna. It is certainly neither in the 'public utility' that is supposed to legitimate these projects, nor in the 'inutility' with which they can be accused, that the answer lies. It lies in a certain logic which, however absurd it is, nevertheless reigns over most of the globe. Capitalism quite openly depends on the fantasy of infinite economic growth. Yet, the limits of the resources on which that growth is based having well been reached, a critical phase presents itself – one that torments the managers of the world economy. Never mind! As worthy inheritors of western modernity, rather than working with the world, they will work against it: as long as our environment is a resource, it must be exploited, and if it becomes an obstacle, it need only disappear. And that is the real meaning of large transportation infrastructures: abolishing space.

Ignore the rivers, the dwelling places, the hills, the forests that slow down the circulation of human and non-human merchandise. Thus, the swamps, hedges, fields and those who cultivate them at Notre-Dame-des-Landes, the mountains, valleys and those who live in the Susa Valley are so many obstacles, seen from the very particular perspective of a territory-management plan. Exactly in the same way that salaried workers are one burden among others from the point of view of an economic restructuring plan. The logic is implacable, and can assure its own renewal even after the mere 'crisis' has become a veritable catastrophe. The more the economy and governmental planning prove destructive of the world that they claim to care for, the more the recipes provided by the economy and planning are mobilized to carve out habitable enclaves. Those who claim to act upon reality free from all its constraints are in fact working to sacrifice the largest part of it, and are always standing by to put a price tag on the non-ravaged areas for the benefit of tourists and the wealthy.

The Airport

Big businessmen from Brittany announced the reasons for 'displacing' the Nantes airport in the summer of 2014, at a moment when the construction at Notre-Dame seemed more and more imminent.

> Today, it is airplanes that are the vectors of economic development . . . In today's economy, we can't let ourselves slow down. We must always take the lead. I'm not asking for lines that go to the four corners of the earth, but which at least open the doors to all of Europe and connect us easily with all the big hubs.
>
> – Louis Le Duff, founder of Le Duff group
> (*Ouest-France,* April 3, 2014)

> We are certain of territorial development and we are working for our children and grandchildren. We need this supra-regional equipment that will allow us to take roundtrips to all the big European cities for our business affairs.
>
> – Patrick Gruau, director of Gruau group
> (*Ouest-France,* April 4, 2014)

So, clearly there are people in this world who are awaiting impatiently a new airport that would respond to their 'need' to regularly traverse the continent both ways in a single day. The project has the support of local leaders, on the left as well as the right, who share the same vision of progress, as grey and unbreathable as it may be for lowly mortals. The 'citizen's association', 'Wings for the West', in charge of propaganda for the 'yes', has its offices in the regional chamber of commerce and industry. At its head reigns an opulent automobile dealership and a band of real estate developers avid to construct their glass and steel towers on the lots close to the old Nantes Atlantique airport, finally opened up to urbanization. The future Airport of the Greater West, a crossroads of the traffic between Saint-Nazaire, Nantes and Rennes, will offer an additional new captive territory favourable to the construction of future zones of 'competitive' activity.

These entrepreneurs, certain of their rights, have seen the project stumble in the past few years. But there are others for whom it has proved a trampoline: Mr Notebaert, in charge of the mission to the Ministry of Transportation in 2000 at the time when the project was revived, became director of the Vinci group, the company tasked with building the airport through their affiliated company, AGO, and a multinational at the head of the worldwide market in public construction works. Or Mr Hagelsteen, former prefect of Loire-Atlantique, and then Pays de la Loire from 2007 to 2009, who, after having gotten through the Declaration of Public Utility for the airport, found himself occupying the position, the following year, of counsellor to the President of . . . Vinci motorways.

By undertaking the construction with the financial aid of local collectivities, within the framework of what is called a 'public–private partnership', Vinci was also awarded the exclusive concession and use benefits, first of the Nantes Atlantique airport, and then of its presumed successor at Notre-Dame-des-Landes, for the next fifty years. Not without forgetting to add a clause requiring payment of a sum equivalent to the total of the projected benefits in the instance of the abandonment of the project.

This whole little world, in the AGO offices or in the business centre of the Brittany Tower, is counting on maximizing the returns on its investments. To this end, it can count on the active help of its sponsoring partners, the state and the region, who have not been stingy in finding ways to justify the pertinence of the 'displacement' of the airport, in the face of growing opposition. Even if it meant falsifying documents, they had to show that the existing infrastructure was too small and too close to a nature reserve, even though the opinion of their own technical services – kept secret at the time – showed the displacement to be much more prejudicial to the nature reserve. They had to convince people of the urgency to destroy, beneath the tarmac, lands placed at the confluence of two watersheds considered a veritable water-tower for the region. The ultimate argument, at a moment of crisis, is always that of jobs: the public utility of any project can be defended so long as it employs a few dozen interim workers.

Nevertheless, it becomes more difficult to defend the need to augment airport traffic when it becomes clearer each day that human activity in the industrial era and its release of CO_2 are irremediably devastating the planet. But since it is always possible to put a good face on things in the era of 'durable development', the airport at Notre-Dame-des-Landes has thus become a project of 'High Environmental Quality', with trees to adorn the parking lots, gardens to cover over the smell of kerosene, and terrains purchased in the surrounding areas to compensate for the losses and recreate the swamps and the hedges elsewhere.

> The conception of the airport targets an optimal integration with the landscape by proposing an airport built in a single floor, very horizontal and covered with a 'vegetalized' (plant-covered) roof. Thus, at a human height, the terminal will appear like a section of the bocage that rises up.
>
> – Presentation of airport project on AGO-Vinci website

The prose wielded by the propagandists of concrete is caught in its own trap, for the bocage has, in fact, risen up. The project has become the very symbol of the harmful and imposed character of market development of the territory – and soon its Achilles' heel.

The TAV

The Susa Valley has always constituted a privileged route for crossing the Alps, as testifies the Domitienne Way used at the time by the

Romans to reach Gaul. A border and a passageway, the valley has always enjoyed this double role, making of its confines not a cul-de-sac, but a space of exchanges. This was true at the time when distances counted and the borders of motorways were places full of life. The concept of transportation having been modified, the valley was not the same. The hills lost their importance to the Fréjus Tunnel built in the 1980s and from which emerged a bewildering motorway which, from the galleries to the viaduct, absolutely negates the mountainous geography. Truck engines are heard in it at all hours, leaving the two national motorways that snake their way through the bottom of the valley a little freer. The idea of adding a TAV line to all of that, a supplementary projection from the embankment, not surprisingly, gave rise to opposition from the outset.

In the 1990s, the Susa Valley became for Europe a link in the chain of 'Strategic Corridor Number 5'. This corridor was supposed to link Lisbon to Kiev at great speed, passing through Lyon and Turin. Only one problem: between the two cities can be found the highest mountain range in the continent. No matter, the tunnel entries were pierced: five on the French side of 86 cumulative kilometres, three in Italy of 68 kilometres, and the longest, along the border section, of 57 kilometres. Finally, of the 221 kilometres separating the two cities, 154 would be underground. No matter, either, that a TGV already runs through the valley, on a track that somewhat limits its speed, it is true. And no matter, either, that the trains travelling today between Turin and Lyon are half empty.

The construction work began with opening up descent tunnels perpendicular to the principal gallery, which would serve as access ways from that point on. In France, three of these digs have already been completed, but in Italy, the unique work zone has hardly advanced at all. It is located at the Maddalena, beneath the little village of Chiomonte, in the upper Susa Valley, near an important archaeological site. In an area that has been cleared of trees and leveled, behind imposing barbed-wire fences, an immense militarized zone surrounds the hole, from which thick spouts of dust escape depending on the mountain winds, that climb or descend the valley following the sun's path. It's a dust that causes coughing and teeth-gritting when you are aware that the mountains contain asbestos and uranium. The valley is even the principal source of uranium in Italy, and the mines lie a few hundred yards from the construction site in Maddalena. Geiger counters go off crazily at the site and at football games on the Gaglione terrain, made out of fill taken from the mountain – fill, by the way, that has attracted the attention of the 'Ndrangheta, the Calabrian mafia, which has made its transportation their specialty. 'TAV = mafia' is written in huge white letters on one of the slopes of the valley, recalling the scandals that came to light inside the companies working the construction. Because there is money to be made there: the digging of the tunnel alone is estimated to cost 13 billion euros, a sum that balloons bigger every year. The European financing plan is so extravagant that a number of Valsusians predict that the construction work will go on eternally, advancing slowly at the rhythm of the waves of subventions, and will be abandoned once these have all dried up. Unless the NoTAVs bring an end to it all sooner . . .

> We are already winning. It would be wonderful to wake up in the morning and read in the newspaper: NoTAV screwed with them so completely by slowing them down that they won. But we'll never read that! We'll write it ourselves, on our sites, in our books . . . and maybe in yours!
>
> – Luca, Bussoleno committee of popular struggle

Epics

History of a Bocage in Struggle

The 1960s: Farmers Versus the Politics of a Void

One day at school, my friends told me: 'There's going to be an airport over at your place.' That hit me, because it meant that the farm, the cows, it was all over. When you learn something like that at twelve years old and you're already a bit of a rebel, you say 'Well, no, not possible!' My parents weren't really revolutionaries, but they were asking some questions. Asking first whether it would serve anything. And then '68 happened, even in Notre-Dame-des-Landes, with a lot of farmers supporting the workers . . . and from there we began to think about it and see everything that was wrong about the airport project.

– Dominique, spokesperson for ACIPA,
native of Notre-Dame-des-Landes

If we refuse the airport project, it's because we refuse society as it is. Development consists in expanding the units of production, as much in agriculture as in industry. Personally, I can't conceive of fighting against the airport if we let the agricultural world evolve toward bigger and bigger cultivations.

– Julien, ACIPA spokesperson, retired farmer,
zad neighbour, interview 1976

You are living somewhere and learn one day that others, somewhere else, have decided it's no longer possible, that other interests come first. That is how, with the stroke of a pen, 1,650 hectares (4,077 acres) of countryside, 20 kilometres from Nantes, were destined to disappear from the map. The justifications for the airport project at Notre-Dame-des-Landes would change over the years: the Atlantic coast landing place for the prestigious Concorde in the 1960s; to allow the growth of air freight and regional demography in the 1970s; the accompaniment to the development of the Nantes-Saint-Nazaire metropolis in the 2000s. Somewhere between political megalomania and a lockstep march toward 'progress', the management of the territory ended up generally being imposed. But in the bocage of Notre-Dame-des-Landes, from the outset, the concerned residents and farmers, supported by other farmers in the region, organized themselves to avoid eviction.

L'ADECA, Farmers in struggle and action committees

The Association to Defend the Farms Threatened by the Airport (ADECA) was created in 1972, born of the rupture between local farm unions and the Chamber of Agriculture that was promoting the airport, hand in hand with the local government. ADECA brought together the farmers working the land that became, in 1974, the Zone of Deferred Management (ZAD) which was to be entirely subsumed by the project. That summer, during the corn harvest, a first march was organized on the ZAD, posters were hung along the roads and slogans painted on the town hall walls. In the following years, ADECA, bolstered by the action committees that sprang up in neighbouring towns, began a long labour of counterinvestigation in order to refute the arguments of the developers:

> At that time we had no information, so we went fishing around trying to find out. The local media had presented the airport project as happening on what they called fallow land where there was practically nobody. That created an intellectual revolt among us, the feeling that they considered us to be pathetic rubes. We spent the winter in meetings. There was a split with artisans and shop-keepers who hoped to make a profit from the fall-out of the airport. The hardest was with the café/tobacconist: he really believed it, we didn't. But we realized we didn't know much of

anything, so we decided to spend three or four days at Roissy (Charles de Gaulle Airport). We recorded the airplane noise, interviewed the folks in the neighbourhood. And then all winter, with the action committee, we made presentations in the farms, and woke everyone up as to the harmfulness of the airport. We were able to show that the corner café had closed because passengers went to the airport café and the village was dead. We said: 'You think you'll have Eldorado but you are dreaming—with the airport, Notre-Dame-des-Landes will be an empty hole.' We succeeded in spreading doubt even among the population in the bigger towns. And ADECA made a minute study evaluating the impact of the airport on the farms and that study was very useful afterwards.

– Julien

The region was at that time one of the bastions of the Farmer/ Worker movement that was shaking up rural conservatism in a revolutionary way. Heir to the alliance between workers and farmers in the Loire-Atlantique during the '68 years, the movement was largely inspired by Bernard Lambert's book, *Les Paysans dans la lutte des classes*. Later, it would give rise to the *Confédération paysanne.* In a world of sharecroppers and agricultural workers without land, the access to land and the priority given to working the land over private property were fiercely disputed. Methods of action were at the level of

---

* Translator's note: The Loire-Atlantique region can lay claim to being the birthplace in France of a new agrarian left that had its origins in the Paysans/ Travailleurs movement of the 1960s and 1970s, cofounded by autodidact farmer, Bernard Lambert. His 1970 book, written in response to the influx of industrial and finance capital into French agriculture after 1965, was the first to place farmers and urban workers in the same situation vis-à-vis capitalist modernity. Lambert was also active in the protracted struggle in the Larzac, a plateau in southwestern France where mass protests succeeded in blocking the extension of a military base in the 1970s. Addressing hundreds of thousands of people in 1973 who had come to support the farmers, Lambert proclaimed 'Never again will farmers be Versaillais'. Larzac activists (such as José Bové) in turn played a role in the 1987 founding of the Confédération paysanne, an anti-productivist union of agricultural workers that is active today in the support of the zad at Notre-Dame-des-Landes.

ambitions: occupations of fields and farms, blockading roads or railway lines. These underlying frictions and impulses could be found everywhere in the region, nourishing that phase of the resistance to the airport whose aim was to make sure that the lands of the ZAD remained cultivated.

At the time, many of us still went to mass, so pamphlets were distributed on the church steps, not in the supermarket parking lot. In other words, there were shouting matches leaving church that continued on into the café. At the peak of these fights about land access, there were two rooms in the café, one for owners and the other for renter farmers. When the airport happened, it was a little different – given that everyone had a knife at their throat and risked losing the tools of the trade, we all felt attacked. ADECA was born at that moment, trying to get beyond those tensions. That said, our idea nevertheless was about defending the tools of the trade and not private property as such. That's why at that time we didn't create an association of property owners against the airport.

The general counsel had pre-emptive right to buy properties on the ZAD, even when the project went into abeyance during the 1980s. And it was a period of rural exodus, when farmers reached retirement age and their children tended to not take up the work and were willing to sell. That's how the general counsel little by little acquired 850 hectares (2,100 acres). We were fighting to keep the zone going and have it not become a desert.

– Julien

With the help of the oil crisis, the airport project was put on the back burner throughout the 1980s and 1990s. This gave local and national authorities the opportunity to spare themselves a potential new battle at a moment when the Larzac struggle had consumed the whole decade of the 1970s and the region was enflamed by several other battles: the movement against the management of the riverbanks of the Erdre or against the nuclear centres of Plogoff and Pellerin.

Yet the General Counsel continued to buy up land and houses, using his pre-emptive right for each sale, in the wake of deaths and departures. In the buildings he acquired he installed people whom he hoped would not make waves when told they would have to move.

In that suspended space, where no one any longer was supposed to make a future, the course of progress in which the rest of the world was engulfed slowed for a time, before the moment came for it, too, to make the great leap forward. This is the paradox of territory management – what was meant to destroy the bocage in fact stabilized it throughout several decades, preventing redistricting and in that way preserving the hedges, swamps, paths and forests from the imprint of a more and more industrialized agriculture. Thus, the riches that the zone still possesses are the secondary gains from the illness of the airport planning.

The Beginning of the 2000s: Neither Here Nor Anywhere!

In 2000, the government officially relaunched the project: the first airplane would take off in 2010. Nothing had changed in forty years: a new infrastructure is always a synonym for the future and economic development. A new argument was added that resounded pleasurably in the ears of the local leaders: competition between territories. Nantes must affirm its domination over the 'Great Western' region and welcome a 'central' airport. But a new protagonist had arisen to throw a wrench into these ambitious plans.

L'ACIPA

When the project started up again, I realized that it was only opposed by ADECA, which represented the agricultural world alone. In November 2000, nine ordinary people called a meeting to found the Intercommunal Citizen's Association of People concerned by the airport project at Notre-Dame-des-Landes. There were 500 people in a room that held 200! And everyone wanted to join. Two years later there were 1,500 people, and we were launched. We wanted to both group people together into a citizen's association that was distinct from political parties, and to bring together the various communes.

– Dominique

For ACIPA, the thrust of the struggle first took the form of a detailed labour of investigation and counterinformation. Many of its members spent most of their time buried in dry dossiers belonging to those promoting the airport, trying to extract errors, contradictions and lies. The Association in this way amassed a set of technical data that enabled them to take the project apart, piece by piece. At the same time, using public meetings and information circulars, its members turned themselves into vulgarizers of the stakes involved and became capable of taking on any of the airport promoters. In the surrounding villages, and then farther and farther away, a profane knowledge spread out, and with it, the unpopularity of the project.

> We went to all the different associations that would have us in France, at every election we interrogated the candidates. We learned everything along the way: it's the struggle that formed us. At first, when we tried to dismantle the airport project, there were many around us who smiled. Then they began to ask us questions to see if our arguments held water. And today, we are feared or respected. But not ignored.
>
> – Dominique

When you go up against the choices made by deciders, being right is not enough. As soon as 2001, ACIPA began to establish the groundwork of a political relation to power. They began to oppose the legitimacy of elected officials with that of citizens, using the classical means of political expression: demonstrations (on the zone and in Nantes) and gatherings during the annual summer picnics that became a veritable tradition and were more and more frequented in the course of the decade. The yellow and red sticker with an airplane underlined with a big 'NO' became a fixture in the region, showing up on mailboxes, vehicles or on big banners in the fields as a rallying sign.

But the Association also made the choice of playing the game of "participating," in 2002, in the "public debate," the consultation that accompanied the Declaration of Public Utility. Hoping both to use the occasion as a means to get their argument heard and to benefit from an impartial government hearing, it was quickly disabused when it came to the latter goal:

I remember a big disorderly place where you couldn't find your way. You came out with a strong sense of manipulation, a kind of big machine that you tell yourself will finish in the end by crushing you, whatever you say and whatever the strength of your arguments. It was tiring, a bit nauseating.

> – Marcel, farmer on the ZAD, member of ADECA, joins ACIPA

ACIPA, what is more, chose clearly to articulate a political line that went beyond the pure interest of concerned inhabitants – something that is unfortunately not the rule in all the movements of opposition to development projects, sometimes incapable of getting beyond the famous NIMBY syndrome. The choice of 'Neither here nor anywhere' was not made without tension in the heart of the Association. Nevertheless, by affirming it loudly and strongly, the struggle began to move beyond its localized character and to ally itself more intensively with others.

In 2004 ACIPA participated in the creation of the Coordination of the Opponents to the Airport – a group of over fifty associations and unions, with openings to political parties. The Coordination supports ACIPA's work and engages in, among other things, the systematic court procedures brought to bear as the project advanced. These juridical appeals slow the adversary down and force him to keep his guard up; the least legal error can and will be used. This work of undermining allowed precious time to be gained and gave the movement the possibility to become deeply anchored. But soon, the airport project managed to bypass a number of procedures designed to overturn it, and entered into an operational phase with the first construction work beginning on the zone.

2007–08: At the Time of Validation

In April 2007, the commission in charge of the investigation into public utility gave a favourable nod to the project, which was made official with the Declaration of Public Utility in February 2008. Any pretence to democratic participation ended there. During this time, the General Counsel continued to empty out the zone and decided to leave the houses he bought unoccupied. ACIPA threatened in the media to find new inhabitants itself. An old dissident farmer from Couëron proposed to a few squatters in Nantes he had met at demonstrations and in soup kitchens that they come live on the zone. The squatters were interested in putting down roots for their struggle and they moved into the Rosiers farm in August. This was the beginning of the movement of occupation. The Coordination for its part inaugurated an organizational space in the centre of the ZAD: the Vacherit barn.

In April 2008, 3,000 people demonstrated against the Declaration of Public Utility and the Coordination launched a new onslaught of legal procedures. A few months later, a citizen's vigil was initiated in front of the General Counsel In Nantes. Every day of the week for several years, in sleet or rain, anti-airport militants, a pile of pamphlets in their hands, called out to passers-by and elected officials.

The 'inhabitants who resist'

Renters living on the zone or nearby, whether members of ACIPA or not, shared their disappointment vis-à-vis the strategic choices made by the 'official' opponents, who could not imagine physical opposition on the terrain where the construction was beginning. They began to get together informally and became friends with the squatters at Rosiers. Not drawn to militant discipline, those who called themselves the 'inhabitants who resist' preferred organizing big banquets and getting into trouble. They punctuated their various feats with sensible diatribes against the airport, but also against the logic governing its construction. Conscious 'that a territory emptied of its population is easy to conquer', they had the intuition that in order to win, a new generation had to come 'from all over Europe' onto the zone.

> On 1 May 2008, we organized a thing ourselves, it was a feast with concerts in a barn at Liminbout, we cooked, made crêpes. A party of support against the airport . . . I had done a photo exhibition on the Susa Valley, with translated texts, and quite a few people reacted. It was the

first time that the 'inhabitants who resist' began to speak up and call for people to come live there. What came out of our reunions was 'salvation will come from beyond', it won't come from ACIPA, with whom the rupture was complete, it won't come from the inhabitants of Notre-Dame-des-Landes, that silent majority that doesn't budge and that one day may or may not wake up. When we said, 'salvation will come from beyond', we didn't have an example or an experience of a movement of occupation that might have inspired us. The struggles that spoke to us, that we talked about, were Plogoff, Pellerin, Carnet, the anti-nuclear battles that had been victorious in the area. When we said that salvation would come from beyond, we were thinking at first of Nantes, of the region in a broader sense.

– Jean, former occupant of Rosiers

2009–10: The Call to Occupy, Against the Airport and its World

The year 2009 began with a big skirmish in a field. Opponents had broken into a truck and taken soil samples that had been gathered for preliminary studies. Two opponents were indicted for 'theft of soil', but, from that moment on, the construction machinery never came back without police reinforcement.

In the summer, several thousands of people assembled on the ZAD with a double program: 'Climate Action Camp' and 'Week of Resistances'. The first marked the arrival in force into the movement of radical, anti-capitalist ecological currents, who were intent on putting into place a temporary experiment in *autogestion* with 'a weak ecological footprint', and in promoting direct action. The 'Week of Resistances', on the other hand, welcomed the more institutional wing of the movement and some professional politicians. The two spaces rubbed elbows without really merging. The intrusion of one hundred masked people into a nearby supermarket, who filled their sacks, escaped through the woods, and then redistributed the fruits of the pillage, either made people happy or stirred up polemics, in one camp or another. The last day of 'Camp Climate Action', the 'inhabitants who resist' relaunched their call to come live on the zone – a call appreciated differently by some farmers and by local militants afraid of stormy installations.

In the next months, new people moved in, occupying abandoned farms or building their own cabins on certain of the fallow fields. Squatters from Nantes and elsewhere arrived, anti-growth people who launched a bakery project or yet a heteroclite and polyglot band of tree-dwellers, accustomed to occupations of threatened forests, who built the first aerial houses in what was becoming the Zone to Defend (zone à defendre). They had in common the will to fight not only the airport but also 'the world that goes along with it', and wanted to build here and now a life in rupture with the capitalist economy and relations of domination.

The occupation movement was haphazard at first but rapidly became structured, with the building of a 'cabin of the resistance' at the place called the Planchettes, the installation of a dance space and of a free 'supermarket' stocked through scavenging in the bins of the big supermarket or, soon, the arrival of a collective canteen and a library van. An unscheduled bulletin, *Concrete Harms* began to show up in the mailboxes of the villages in an attempt to connect with neighbours, all the while avoiding touchy subjects: elections, work, or sabotage as a usable practice.

The movement in Nantes and the Nantes Collective Against the Airport (CNCA)

The airport was at first protested by people in the places it threatened. But its planning and development was taking place in the heart of the Nantes metropolis. At the end of the 2000s, militant networks began to organize informally, then regrouped as the CNCA, designed to support the movement from within the city.

> At the beginning of the occupation movement we went regularly to the ZAD with friends. There were only really a dozen people actually living there, but there was lots of circulation with nearby cities. Everyone was asking themselves whether to move there. Among us, there was a group

that moved there, one that went back and forth, and another that stayed in Nantes. At Nantes, we quickly thought of a collective. We wanted to bring the struggle to the city, because that's where power is concentrated and decisions are made. The question of the loss of agricultural land is not necessarily relevant to city people, but these were the people we wanted to reach. We wanted to get them to understand that the logic of the airport didn't come out of nowhere. It's connected to a whole process of the extension of the urban fabric and the concentration of powers – 'metropolitization' that touches our neighbourhoods as well as our daily life. The airport seemed to us to be the cornerstone of a Nantes-Saint-Nazaire metropolis, with an "attracting" pole of almost 600,000 people. It's crazy, hallucinating, the speed with which Nantes is getting paved over and redeveloped: neighbourhoods are savaged, and the connections that existed before between inhabitants disappear. Construction is turning a whole part of the population into outcasts. We also wanted to question the relation to power and the local elites, the complicities between elected officials and entrepreneurs, and then the whole idea of participative democracy with which they want to make you think you have your say about what's actually a project that's already locked up. So we created CNCA.

– Arnaud, member of CNCA

2011–12: Vinci Get Out, Resistance and Sabotage

In winter 2010–11, the occupiers of the zad toured a string of collectives, urban squats and other self-managed spaces to disseminate information in view of building strength. The encounter with the members of the network *Reclaim the Fields* was fruitful: some of them were in the midst of launching a campaign to occupy land with future farmers and were seduced by the potentiality of the zad. On their side, the occupiers now wanted to collectively assume responsibility for squatting as a strength in the struggle and were trying to build bridges with local farmers. A group was formed that invited people to demonstrate 'pitchfork in hand' to inaugurate the project of a garden market in Sabot. In May 2011, one thousand people responded to the call, marched through the zone, and prepared a one-hectare parcel of land for cultivation. Sabot invited the inhabitants of the zad and the neighbourhood to come by twice a week to get bread and vegetables and meet for a drink.

The following winter, anti-globalization activists, attempting to go beyond their spectacular and non-rooted mode of action, decided to not go to Deauville for the G8, nor to Nice for the G20, but rather to reinforce a local struggle by having a 'No-G' camp on the zad. A few dozen participants chose to remain on site after the event and allied themselves permanently with the movement.

On 1 January 2011, the airport undertaking was awarded to the Vinci corporation via its subsidiary, Aéroport du Grand Ouest (AGO). Along with the contract came the permanent presence of occupiers, sabotage, and physical oppositions that proliferated in response to the preliminary construction and the companies handling it. A campaign of action against Vinci and its subcontractors was initiated outside the zone. The occupiers and their friends, an opaque and mobile threat always ready to emerge from the woods, adopted the habit of refusing to give their identities during the inspections and arrests by local police. With some losses and a lot of noise, they also performed actions in metropolitan Nantes – attacking an information van belonging to the Socialist Party in the midst of an electoral campaign, and occupying the Nantes Atlantique airport and the trees in Mercœur Park in the middle of the city. The strategy of open confrontation with elected officials, initiated by the 'inhabitants who resist', was in relative contradiction with that of ACIPA, which was betting rather on the possibility, with the support of the Green Party, of a return of a left majority in Nantes and the regional council. A Collective of Elected Officials Doubting the Pertinence of the Airport at Notre-Dame-des-Landes (CéDpa), established in 2009, went about trying to make heard the voices of a few dissident officials in institutional politics, when the major party apparatuses, whether on the left or right, had made a common front in favour of the project.

During this whole period, archaeological digs, drilling, public investigations, and visits by judges regarding expropriations were systematically disrupted and sometimes blocked by the militants of

ACIPA, farmers and squatters. The methods used, more or less viru-
lent, were not always the same, but little by little complementarities
were being sought out.

The occupation movement in action: in the forest with Biotope

Among the prophets of doom and gloom who began to show up on
the zad and attempt to move the airport project along were a new
type: environmental experts, like those from the Biotope Company,
mercenaries of greenwashing, hired by Vinci.

> In the beginning of 2011 we saw the Biotope experts arrive, they came
> serenely in a little company car, dressed like you or me: running pants,
> hiking shoes and jacket, a little kerchief around the neck, a walkie-talkie
> in their pocket, a notebook, some sample-collecting equipment: little
> nature lovers! Once I ran into Inga and Oscar in the Rohanne forest
> leading one of these guys out. I got there not knowing the situation, I
> give Oscar a kiss, then Inga and then the guy, I thought he was one of
> us . . . Inga gives me a dire look and whispers: 'He's Biotope.' 'What? He's
> a dope?' 'NO, HE'S BIOTOPE!'
>
> That time, we let him leave in his car. We knew they'd be back. We
> began to research Biotope and its ecological engineering companies that
> are supposed to 'protect and work for the environment', and that are in
> the service of the giant corporations and their rotten projects. We ran
> into them more than once in the following weeks and we talked with
> them. And we still don't know if it was bad faith or complete candour,
> but they refused to acknowledge that they were there to help build an
> airport. They believed they were there just to observe the newts and the
> frogs. And, what is more, they found their jobs pretty cool: being
> outdoors, hiking . . . We decided to organize and make them under-
> stand that they were not welcome. For that, it wasn't enough to just
> follow them everywhere. From that moment on, when we ran into them,
> we were wearing masks and we blew up their cars.
>
> So, after several amusing incidents, the experts' cars came back but
> now accompanied by a car belonging to a security firm, Securitas. So we
> would show up, 10 or 15 of us around the car. The rent-a-cop didn't have
> time to understand what was happening when he saw 15 masked people

who said: 'If I were you, I'd do nothing.' And he sits in his car while the Biotope car blows up in front of his eyes. And a little later the expert's documents are stolen out from under him. After that, they came with the Biotope car, a car full of police, and more police to escort the Biotope guy, along with a Securitas car with a guard to protect the two cars . . . That was when they first began sending helicopters overhead too. It was pretty panicky – we weren't used to it. At that time, too, we discovered the best tool to blow up tires. Piercing a tire with a knife is pretty dangerous, but with a metal tube ripping off the tire valve, you twist it and it pops off directly. So, we had that great thing, everyone had one in their backpack along with a headlamp: The Tube! . . . The cops were powerless, we could see them arriving from far away. I remember an action where we were talking with a guard who had been left behind to watch over the cars. We saw the cops coming back with the Biotope guy, but they couldn't see us, they didn't realize there were a lot of us. The Securitas guy was panicked, he told us he wouldn't do anything, and we told him he'd have to do without his car, and then he told us it was his own car! He told us about his shitty work contract, the lousy schedule, the measly pay, and on top of all that they made him use his own car! So, at that point, someone said, 'OK, let's calm down, put the tubes away.' Because his story sounded true. On the other hand, the cop's car was blown up, and everyone dispersed into the countryside, with the background noise of the helicopters and our hearts beating.

– Shoyu, occupier since 2010, member of a vegan cooking collective

In the spring of 2012, trials against the occupiers and their habitats occurred one after the other. The state was preparing to intervene, and media campaigns about the 'ultras' and the 'riff-raff' on the zad intensified their attempt to divide opinion, sometimes with the help of spokespersons from the Green Party, despite its being officially engaged in the anti-airport movement. At the same time, pressures, financial offers, and expropriation measures multiplied vis-à-vis the property owners, renters and farmers. Some of them cracked under pressure and accepted expropriation – others held firm and refused the AGO check.

In response, for the first time, a demonstration was organized in common between the occupiers and the associations. On 24 March

2012, more than 10,000 people accompanied by 200 tractors marched through Nantes, bringing with them a bit of the bocage and gallons of paint to decorate the walls. A few weeks later, the opponents, farmers from the zad, ACIPA militants and elected officials began a hunger strike that lasted 28 days, up until the presidential election. They extracted from the new government the promise not to evict the legal inhabitants and farmers before a certain number of legal appeals had been tried.

As for the squatters, they were expecting for several months to be evicted, without knowing what they could do to prevent it. Training and tools nevertheless began to be put into place in preparation for D-Day: pirate radio, a network of walkie-talkies, medical equipment, canteen, resting places . . . And then, pretty much everywhere, posters and pamphlets already began to announce a meeting to be held on an as-yet-unknown date: whatever happens, four weeks after evictions begin, reoccupations in great number of the Zone to be Defended would ensue. The movement was trying to get a head start.

Autumn–Winter 2012: Facing Eviction

On 16 October 2012, the Loire-Atlantique prefecture took up the offensive and launched what it officially called 'Operation Caesar', in a brilliant excess of arrogance in the country of Asterix. The forces of order were to expel the occupiers from the zone and destroy the houses that could legally be destroyed, in order to permit construction to begin. The operation was supposed to remain secret right up until it began and last just a few days. Certain of its outcome, the subprefect even declared that 'when there are 150 of them hiding in a barn, they won't last long'. This strategy had been envisioned by the occupiers for some time, and various ideas and tactics had been imagined in order to resist as long as possible.

Additionally, in the previous week, a concordance of convincing leaks and hints made it certain that an important operation was being prepared: for one group of inhabitants, occupiers, and collectives fighting the airport, this was an undreamed-of godsend: there was time to alert the networks of supporters to prepare for police invasion.

'So Caesar, caught in the mire?'

Even though expected, the attack was confusing because of its size and rapidity. 1,200 police mobilized, so that 600 were there permanently during the day, while the number of occupiers was estimated to be less than a hundred. In the first two days, a dozen living spaces were emptied of occupants and destroyed; vegetable gardens were ravaged. But the military had not yet gotten as far as the Rohanne forest to dislodge the cabins perched in the trees. Other habitations targeted by the operation were still standing, like the Sabot and the Cent Chênes. The barricades, the harassment of the forces of order, but also the daily departure of the police at the end of the work day, allowed the resistance on the terrain to manifestly disrupt operations. Every evening at 6 p.m., the police convoys would leave to the sound of electric saws preparing new barricades and pickaxes digging new trenches into the roads. The nights were awake with a thousand gestures, large and tiny, designed to throw a wrench in the works the next day.

It was also the first confrontations with the cops here, where we had shields and where we could move through fields and stick low to the ground. 'Over here!' we would call out to each one, to provoke them, it became almost a ritual. One time there were four barricades in the Sabot field where most of the conflict took place, where there was a tent with coffee-making equipment. You could rest for a moment there, eat a sandwich, drink a coffee while everything was blowing up 50 yards away. At the beginning, I wondered: 'Where are the tractors? Where are the folks who were supposed to show up?' Little by little I saw them coming, taking up the cops' time along the roads, then the Vacherit was opened up continuously and became a logistical centre for injuries, it was surreal. I remember saying to myself: 'At last. It's good, we aren't alone.'

– Ludo, in his 30s, occupier since 2011

And so, Operation Caesar did not end on 16 October at 10 a.m., unlike what was announced on the media by a somewhat harried prefect. The operation was bemired to such a point that the resistance continued for several weeks, in a common impetus uniting all the groups and their numerous supporters. Farmers' agricultural machinery from around the region reinforced barricades made of heavy telegraph poles and imposing bales of hay, when they didn't themselves serve as obstacles to the police convoys.

> I remember one General Assembly where there were quite a few people from outside along with people from the zad. It was chaotic, but we began to put together the structure for a long-term resistance to the evictions. With Julien, for example, the ACIPA office in Notre-Dame-des-Landes was used, so that food supplies could be taken there before being moved to the zad, finding ways to not be blocked by the police barriers. I was getting around in my van in which I could carry everything I could to the inhabitants of the zad – there they loaded things onto tractors and drove them across the fields to make deliveries. We were able to get through the police lines.
>
> – Cyril, in his 30s, farmer, joined struggle at time of the
> tractor–bicycle march organized by ACIPA in 2011

The houses and buildings that could not be cleared out, of which most belonged to inhabitants opposed to the project, became so many spaces of welcome, places to sleep and regather strength. Radio Klaxon was going full force, on airwaves pirated from Radio Vinci Autoroutes, its news bulletins enabling the coordination of actions and copious insulting of the police, who were listening. At the same time, the 'external committee' group put into place its newsflashes on the website *zad.nadir.org*, which made it possible for thousands of people outside the zone to keep abreast of events almost in real time.

If the resistance on the ground could not prevent the early destructions, its tenacity managed to arouse considerable sympathy. While the prefecture looked ridiculous trying to check the movement with a series of arrests, the supporters from outside the zad came in great number, populating the muddy fields with tents and caravans, or bringing dry clothes and food. Those circles close to the occupiers had begun to arrive with the first alert, soon to be joined by farmers and members of the opposition collectives, who made their way, more and more, onto the terrain. Dozens of people outside of any militant network arrived to take part in the battle.

The police checkpoints set up at the principle crossroads of the zone to keep control of the territory while waiting for the end of the legal pause accorded by the justice before the Rosiers could be evacuated (sometime in November) were harassed by some and bypassed by others. Galvanized by its own determination, the common resistance became organized for the long run. Soon the cabin at Vrais Rouges was draped with an amusing banner: 'And so, Caesar, stuck in the mire?'

During the physical confrontations, the antagonisms internal to the movement were momentarily overcome and the relation to what was considered legitimate, possible, or violent was shaken up. Everyone, each in his or her way was taken up, body and soul, with the effort to defeat the enemy: in the media, logistically, legally, physically. An insolent hope rose up, the idea that we were not destined to be crushed by the backhoes of territorial development.

That hope took on a real shape on 17 November, when, on the date set by the preventative call of the occupiers, the demonstration of reoccupation attracted more than 40,000 people onto the zad and resulted in the collective construction all day long of a new hamlet: the Châtaigne. All those who were fighting against the airport, whether it was for a few months or for decades, knew that a decisive moment had been reached. But the prefecture believed that it was still possible to destroy the symbol and rid itself of the 'cyst'.

On 23 and 24 November, hundreds of police tried to retake the Chat-Teigne* and to evacuate the newly reconstructed tree cabins. In response to this offensive, farmers and committees blocked the major axes and bridges of the region. Demonstrations, blockades and occupations took place as well throughout France. Thousands of people joined the skirmishes in the Rohanne forest where the Nantes

---

* Translator's note: The spelling of names of places on the zad is not standardized and sometimes several different spellings exist.

prefecture was converging. The police wounded a hundred or so demonstrators, but in vain: they lost the battle.

The evening of 24 November, the government announced the end of the operation and the creation of a 'Dialogue Commission' whose explicit purpose was not to question the validity of the project, but rather to explain it better to the crowd of troublemakers who certainly didn't seem to understand it. That very evening, a permanent police occupation of the crossroads of the zad began that would last five months. The next day, 40 tractors came and encircled the Châtaigne to defend it. Dozens of new occupiers moved to the zone and a great period of reconstruction began.

The local committees

If some local committees were created in preceding years, largely within a radius of a few dozen miles around the zad, 200 new committees were born during Operation Caesar, everywhere in France and outside the country too. In these committees could be found the same heterogeneity that characterizes the movement: card-carrying members of left political parties, anarchists and a number of people without any precise affiliation – all carried away by the reverberations of the movement. The committees relayed what was happening on the zone and joined up with local combats.

> When I went there for the first time, things were heating up in the Rohanne forest and I was super shocked. What I saw going on, the police violence, it frankly put me over the top. And it hasn't stopped enraging me. I couldn't imagine that it could be so violent in France just to impose on you what they want, it really shocked me, such a thing was inconceivable. This is a so-called democracy . . . That's when I said to myself: 'Have to do something'. But I didn't know too much what, I didn't know many people, and the people I knew didn't share my ideas. I was a bit isolated, I had to find people, especially since my husband isn't at all militant. So when I saw in the paper a committee was starting up in my town, I went. Because it isn't easy when you are alone to find people who you don't know and tell them that you want to do something.
>
> – Anne-Claude, member of the Blain support committee

The 'Naturalists in Struggle'

The 'Naturalists in Struggle Against the Airport at Notre-Dame-des-Landes', supported by certain associations to protect the environment, was created after the evacuations. By conducting inventories of the terrain, organized walks, and denunciations of the environmental good intentions of the pro-airport people, they gave material and weight to the ecological preoccupations that animate many of the opponents to the project.

When I came to the zad, I was more of a naturalist than a militant . . . I couldn't help getting involved in an inventory of what could be found on the zad and making a map of it. I was by myself and didn't talk to anyone. I tried to once during one meeting but someone yelled at me and said, 'Why not spend your time looking for Merovingian vases!' Then came the moment of the evictions when, because of the media attention, other better-known naturalists started to get interested in the subject . . . We wanted to make it known that in addition to the people who lived there, the houses, the farmers, all that, there were also beautiful plants, rare animals, with the idea that that might help out legally too. But we didn't talk much about the legal side, we wanted to keep the surprise factor and also because we weren't sure what we would find. And just like me when I made my first inventory, the naturalists who came found the richness of what they found incredible when they looked at it closely. In the end, we located new protected species among the plants and amphibians and showed that some of those species could endure only thanks to being on the zad . . . And just a few weeks after the creation of the 'Naturalists in Struggle', there we were, 200 of us, on a horribly foggy and frosty day, when there was absolutely nothing to be seen in the nature. But it didn't matter, there were folks who had come from Alsace or Provence, and all the local zealots. This network has lasted, because there is an historic anchoring of naturalists in Brittany, they have some lively associations. It was just super moving for me to go from my solitary inventories to be part of that community, which came regularly on weekends bringing all the material for specimen collection, but also to be able to eat and drink together. It was all the more moving in that, before, I never dared say that I was conducting inventories, and now everyone was praising the role of the naturalists. We were 'in', even if we didn't have hoods and masks . . . I think that for most of us, it was the first time that we were exercising our passion in the framework of a struggle, which is to say that people were coming together who elsewhere had lives and political visions that were very different.

We were very interested in the question of environmental compensation, which for us was a big issue. First, the term compensation isn't correct: there are milieux that will be destroyed that are impossible to recreate. What is at stake with the experimental model at work in Notre-Dame-des-Landes is obtaining the rights to destroy in order to carry out their project, but it's also just the conversion of biodiversity into a monetary value, to prepare the creation of a new world. There are all those traders who have been salivating for years about the emergence of new territories where it was forbidden up to this point to conduct the economy in that way. They will be allowed to speculate on biodiversity, to sell it or buy it, to augment the surplus value underlying it. For them it's win-win. It's not nothing to fight against all that. They talk around here about scientific experimentation. But to me it's clear it isn't about scientific experimentation – it's social experimentation, experimenting with acceptability, with the idea that if it gets through here, it will get through elsewhere and the opposite: if we succeed in blocking them here, we can maybe neutralize them in other places as well.

In the end, what we share in the 'naturalists in struggle' collective is a joyous wonder at diversity and a rejection of everything that tends to make the world uniform. For me that translates politically into feeling myself ready to fight for diversity in all its forms: I can rise up against the disappearance of an animal species, a vegetal one, a culture, a people, a landscape, and even a type of architecture . . . It's only capitalism that thinks making the world uniform is useful and necessary – for the rest of us, it is simply frightening.

– Jasmin, occupier from 2010–12, organizer
of botanical walks on the zad

2013: Free Zone

Winter hardened into a territory divided up by police barriers. The detours, altercations and insults, when we passed through the cross-roads, punctuated daily life. Departmental Road 281 still contains the obstructions and barricades that were set up, and some of the barri-cades were transformed into dwelling places. Everywhere could be heard the noise of hammers: cabins were multiplying.

In early April, the 'Dialogue Commission' supplied its report and announced, unsurprisingly, that the airport should be built, after some minor formal changes. It was nevertheless clear that a respite period had begun and the government, smarting, would let some time go by before trying anew to evacuate the zone. On 13 April 2013, the police occupation drew to an end and several thousand people came to the aid of initiating a dozen new agricultural projects with an operation called 'Sow your zad'. Other mass events – festizad, human chain, and summer picnic – succeeded each other on the zone the rest of the year, with sometimes tens of thousands of participants. The zad, as a form reuniting struggle and life, began to spread: in the Morvan and in Avignon, on a vegetable market threatened by the construction of a motorway.

In a few months, the number of zad inhabitants had tripled and the transformation was permanent. Life on the terrain and its links to the neighbourhood were reconfigured, with their moments of incomprehension, but also of beautiful encounters. In the seething, political laboratory of 1,650 hectares that had opened up, every-thing could be questioned and everything, too, could turn into a violent conflict: agriculture and the use of machines, the concep-tion of nature, reunions and forms of organization, gender rela-tions or differences in economic and social baggage, the opening up of roads and maintaining of barricades, drug usage, the welcome extended to people habitually rejected by the rest of society. After having defeated Caesar, the zad was threatened for a time with imploding under the weight of its own internal contradictions. All the more so in that the pro-airporters did everything they could to support division and to push surrounding communities to reject the so-called 'zadists'. In vain! The movement took on the challenge and little by little built the possibility of shared lives lived in a partially liberated zone.

The powerlessness of the prefecture and of Vinci on the zone was patently obvious: legal decisions were systematically being transgressed and construction attempts sabotaged. The police now stayed out of an area that those in power had begun to call a 'lawless zone'. In autumn, ignoring a prefectural ban of any sowing or planting on that day, the 'Sow your zad' assembly, along with COPAIN and ADECA, organized a collective sowing of a 24-hectare area that Vinci had designated as the place where work crews would begin.

The COPAIN farmers

The Collective of Professional Agricultural Organizations Indignant about the Airport Project (COPAIN) started up in June 2011. With this collective, farmers outside the zad took on a role in the struggle, especially during the period of the evictions and afterwards. In January 2013, COPAIN took a new step by occupying the farm at Bellevue and its lands.

> Taking Bellevue, we were talking especially about seizing buildings. For a month, we asked ourselves if they were going to throw us out one week or the next . . . then finally we said, 'Shit, there's land there. We have to do something with that land.' It made us start thinking about land redistribution, taking care of land collectively. And all that was tied in directly to the agricultural projects of the occupiers.
>
> – Marcel

The question of food production and land usage was taking on a bigger place in the movement. 'Sow your zad' in 2013, which COPAIN participated in, took up the task of discussing and collectively organizing the agricultural problematics of the zone. In the following months, land was taken from farmers who had collaborated with Vinci and numerous collective cultivations were started. What was happening on the zad in turn breathed new life into the region, the farm networks shaking up the corporatism and the classical union demands.

2014–16: Future Zad and Zads Everywhere!

In 2013, the developers began to rebound and announced 'the removal of protected species' from the bocage, as a preliminary to construction getting underway. In January 2014, on the occasion of a meeting of the local committees, the movement decided to block the region in case of an intervention in the zone, to prevent any preliminary work beginning and then to return to demonstrate in Nantes.

A wager that succeeded: on 22 February more than 60,000 people and 500 tractors submerged the city. If the forbidding of any demonstration in the centre of the city gave rise to intense confrontations with the police, the demonstration did not break down and the crowd stuck together. Despite media hysteria, the condemnations by political leaders, and the internal tensions exacerbated by the demonstration, the movement did not give way under attempts to divide it. The government retreated once again and postponed the beginning of construction until 'all legal appeals underway have been exhausted'.

Nevertheless, new areas of repression sprung up in the course of the year with a wave of arrests based on matching police and intelligence service files with fine-combed examinations of videos of the 22 February demonstration. People began to gather regularly outside the Nantes courthouse. Several people spent several months behind bars, supported by the movement's solidarity funds.

On 25 October 2014, the murder of Rémi Fraisse by the police during confrontations on the Testet zad led to a wave of demonstrations, heavily repressed and largely ignored by left organizations. Marches against police violence proliferated for several weeks, notably in Nantes and Toulouse. The 'zadists' were now on everybody's lips, all over the newspapers, to the point of entering the dictionary. Two days after the inauguration of the Roybon zad (Isère), the construction on the amusement park there was halted.

The developers could not allow this intolerable revolt against the market capture of territory and existences to spread. The state got to work curbing the epidemic by delimiting and extracting the sources of the plague, duly named and given folkloric dimensions: 'zadists', 'black bloc', or 'violent youth'. So many summary categories that threatened to paralyze the movements who set out to go beyond them. In the security context of the post-terrorist attack of January 2015, the intelligence law made use of the terrorist threat to gag opposition, and the Macron law freed entrepreneurs from a host of legal constraints susceptible of slowing down development projects.* At Testet, the productivist farmers of the FNSEA organized to encircle the zad and enable the police to evacuate it.

At Notre-Dame-des-Landes, about sixty dwelling places, cabins, farms and hamlets were spread out across the bocage, housing art studios, bakeries, radios, infirmaries, garages, sports halls, concert hall, carpentry workshops, computer spaces, bars, and conservatories. Hundreds of hectares taken back from Vinci were now collectively cultivated, generating provisions for inhabitants and friends nearby, as well as migrant squats and popular canteens in Nantes and Rennes. Without diminishing the lines of tension, life in common there has not ceased to be elaborated, and improbable friendships spring up in assemblies, festivals and work zones, in the everyday and in shared risks.

After each failure of the legal appeals mounted by the opponents, the government repeats that it has not renounced the project, and that 'soon', the construction and the evacuations will begin. As for the movement, it has gotten a taste for victory and is betting that the airport won't happen. It is engaged, rather, in creating the mutual

---

*   Translator's note: The attack against *Charlie Hebdo* in January 2015 accelerated the implementation of anti-terrorist measures including the 'intelligence law', passed in July of that year, which strengthened intelligence gathering at the national level and included controversial measures impinging on the right to privacy. The Macron law, passed in August 2015, claimed to stimulate economic growth through a host of various measures, from opening up capital for airports in Nice and Lyon to making it easier for employers to demand work on Sundays.

bases for the zad to remain a zone outside of the norm, made up of all those who have shared the struggle, imagining the way to make the legal and illegal forms of occupation of the territory coexist, and to keep in its own hands the fate of the liberated lands. The associative components, farmers and occupiers have agreed on a manifesto along these lines, and are thus at least one step ahead of all those who, if the airport project is abandoned, want to re-establish the republican order, along with the avid property-owners waiting to add to their lands to increase the size of their cultivations.

On the roads

At the end of summer 2015, procedures were initiated to accelerate the eviction of the renters and farmers remaining on the zad. On 22 September, barricades were erected once again along all the points of entry into the zone for one day, in order to prevent the expropriation judge, accompanied by the police, from entering. The prefecture launched a call for companies wishing to assure the start-up of the construction of the access roads to the future airport. In November, a convoy of tractors and bicycles left Notre-Dame-des-Landes and arrived in Versailles on the eve of the COP21, despite interdictions against circulation under the state of emergency.* A banquet was held, during which a call issued forth that the zads, as 'so many new free communes', not allow themselves to be evacuated.

The farmers and 'historic inhabitants' of the zad of Notre-Dame-des-Landes were summoned to the courthouse on 31 December. Vinci was demanding an immediate eviction, plus drastic daily penalties in the case of refusal, as well as the right to seize goods and livestock. Since the government no longer dared go back into the zone, it was trying in this way to isolate a few key people that it hoped to push to the point of renouncing their opposition by asphyxiating them financially. In the face of this new threat, a demonstration was organized in ten days. On 9 January 2016, 20,000 people, hundreds of

---

* Translator's note: COP21 is the 2015 United Nations Climate Change Conference held in Paris that winter.

bicyclists and 400 tractors converged on the ring road outside Nantes and occupied the Cheviré Bridge. Under COPAIN's initiative, 60 tractors remained parked together at the foot of the bridge at the conclusion of the demonstration to obtain the abandonment of the trial. A camp was established in the middle of the motorway with tents, hay for sleeping, a pizza oven, and a mobile radio. It was encircled, and then attacked in the night by the police. Then came several days of tractor blockades and slow-downs on the regional roads. Dozens of demonstrations, actions, and sabotages took place again throughout France. On 25 January, the judge pronounced the inhabitants and farmers of the zad 'open to eviction', but without any financial penalty. A few days later, one thousand people responded to the 'call for bids' launched by the 'Committee to Pilot a Future Without an Airport'. Multiple work-yards got underway simultaneously to reinforce the collective structures of the zad, to assemble an inn, a meeting hall, a sheep pen, and to open up new pathways. At the same time that the government, under pressure, announced in the voice of its prime minister that the onset of construction would be delayed one more time until the autumn, the Minister of the Environment declared that there could be no evacuation of the zad without a 'civil war'. As for the new president of the region, he flew into almost daily rages against the 'ultra-violent types' on the zad, whom he compared to 'Mosul' or 'Damascus'. He had the regional counsel purchase advertising inserts to put in newspapers launching a petition demanding the evacuation of the zone.

On 11 February, on the occasion of a ministerial shake-up, President Hollande bought entry into the government of some old-time ecologists and tried to find his way out of the swamp by announcing a referendum on the airport project. But the wool could not be pulled over the eyes of more than 60,000 opponents, who occupied the motorways close to the zad two weeks later, held a concert on the asphalt, and helped begin the construction of a steel watch tower, ten metres tall, in the very spot where the first construction was supposed to break ground.

The history goes on, seething, uncertain, and continues to be written beyond these pages.

The History of a Valley that Resists
The Beginnings of the NoTAV Struggle

In the Susa Valley, the epic tale of NoTAV is being told at night, under the roof of an impromptu cabin tucked away at the edge of the forest, across from the blinding lights of the Maddalena construction site. While bottles are poured, that long tale of a generation unfolds, interrupted by shouts directed at the police shivering on the other side of the railing. This is when each person, everyone, is transformed into a fantastic character, the hero of a battle, or a ridiculous clown when the story turns to funny anecdotes. There's a lot of laughter in the Susa Valley. And a lot of learning: tenacity and patience are learned, along with the understanding that time is the principal ally of victory, if you can figure out how to get it on your side. In its wake, the great shared story of the struggle takes form, making it an unfinished history, and, for us, a source of inspiration.

At first there is the surprise, almost the exoticism, of these tales, as when a child of eight years old explains to you how to protect yourself from tear gas, or when an old gentleman talks about that life, the life they created, that he personally feels to be an antidote to death. And then the emotion brought on by the thickness of the friendships that surround us, which lights up their faces, as when Chiara and Claudia talk about their nighttime adventures, unknown to their husbands, during which, hooded, they went to hang tree stumps in front of the town halls, so much the deforestation had angered them. And finally, the depth of the history of the valley makes itself felt – a place where Vaudois, resisters, heretics and now NoTAVs, rub shoulders with each other. To follow all the turns and digressions of the story, we need to tell it ourselves, and put it into a chronology. Perhaps then, who knows, we might spark in readers the desire go to hear it on the edge of the forest, told in its maternal tongue.

The 1980s: bridges and lines

The 'NoTAV generation' did not emerge spontaneously. It learned past struggles, drawing lessons from the defeats and successes that the

Susa Valley people experienced in the 1980s. At that time opposition arose against the construction of a motorway connecting Turin to the Fréjus tunnel, which twists along the length of the valley, from the viaducts to the tunnels. Major ecological associations had negotiated with the entrepreneurs in order to minimize the damages, without putting into question the construction itself. That's why that portion of the motorway is called 'the ecological motorway of the Susa Valley' – a sign of the compromise and the icy irony of its developers. For the concrete standings, drained streams, and ugliness of this ribbon of asphalt escapes nobody. The inhabitants now know what came of all the promises of employment that amounted to nothing, and even the money that was supposed to buy up parcels of land and that they are still awaiting. This failure and its analysis gave rise, when it came to the TAV, to a decisive and definitive 'No'. And the idea of a real resistance began to slowly grow.

In 1987, it was a victory that this time taught a lesson to the valley residents. Their determination definitively blocked the construction of a 400,000-volt electrical line joining the French Superphénix nuclear reactor to Italy via the Susa Valley.

> For the first time in the valley, autonomous committees sprang up . . . We got the mayors involved. They were with us, and the Montagne community as well. They weren't leading, but they were with us. That's pretty much the model we reproduced later on with NoTAV: it was the first fight without delegation. We delegated nothing to the political system – the institution was free to come with us, but we had direct control. It was the right way to go about things and in the end we won. They abandoned the project in 1989, and that victory helped everybody because they buried electrical lines throughout Italy, and above all they built less of them.
>
> – Nicoletta, 69, member of Bussoleno committee of popular struggle

By the 1990s, the principal elements of what would constitute the backbone of the NoTAV movement were already in place. The mechanism of delegation was strongly discounted, at least in so far as it involved institutions and political parties. This no doubt explains the unity of the story that unfolds, since collective decision-making on the part of the entire movement implies the enunciation and invention of common speech.

1991–96: expertise and sharing knowledge, from the Habitat committee to the 'Indians of the Valley'

In the early years, the opposition to the TAV was quiet. No media presence, just a meticulous labour to disassemble the project, point by point, and to spread as widely as possible that information. The Habitat committee, created in 1991, was the first to be opposed to the TAV. The group came out of a nonviolent anti-military group in Condove, which denounced the arms factory established in the village. This group organized all the meetings, the information evenings, where people learned of the environmental consequences of building the line, the feasibility problems and the irregularities. Just like the opponents to the airport at Notre-Dame-des-Landes, they taped the noise of a high-speed train that they disseminated in the valley. The committee produced documents, worked on publicity; today, the majority of the people in the valley know more about the TAV than do governmental experts. The members of the Habitat committee, even though it no longer exists today, had and still have a considerable importance in the NoTAV struggle.

The Habitat Committee was not born with the fight against the TAV, it was born because the Susa Valley is not a picturesque Alpine valley. Since the modern era, it's been a place where huge amounts of public money have been spent on what we've begun to call 'big, useless, and imposed projects' . . . Thus, whether from the point of view of the environment or from the point of view of organized crime, we were already vigilant before anyone started talking about the TAV.

We founded Habitat because we wanted attention to be at a high enough level to take on these problems. From the outset, we were able to take advantage of professional and university skills, since we are near the biggest Alpine city, Turin – this creates problems, but there are advantages too . . . Today, Habitat is just a name, because it melted into the movement.

– Claudio, in his 60s, one of the founders of Habitat

The sharing of information that continued for five years was not, for all that, an end in itself. On 2 March 1996, at Sant'Ambrogio, the first demonstration of consequence took place against the TAV. Several thousand people took to the streets, along with tractors. On a roll of paper twelve metres long, the NoTAVs unveiled the precise route the railway line would take and the destruction it would cause. A tepee was erected in the middle of the crowd of those who called themselves for the occasion the 'Indians of the Valley', signifying in this way that the project represented the extinguishing of their way of life, and that the tomahawk of war had been unsheathed.

1996–98: The 'Sole and Baleno' affair, sabotages and antiterrorism

The history of the movement is not one of a slow and regular development into a popular, massive and radical movement. It is made up of jolts, ruptures, surprises and short circuits. Thus, a few months after the Indian demonstration and for more than a year, a couple dozen nocturnal sabotages took place in the valley: the burning of drills accompanied by NoTAV graffiti, but also explosions targeting telephone and television poles, and the burning of motorway infrastructure.

> In the middle of the 1990s, at the same time as the early legal and ecological opposition to the TAV, there were a series of attacks viewed by the ecological movement as provocations or as strange, obscure events . . . The demands [associated with the attacks] denounced capitalism, the mafia, the church, and Albanians, in a mix of antifascism and racism. It was very confusing and contradictory. But in the midst of all these sabotages, there were explicit NoTAV actions.
>
> – Pepe, committee of the upper valley

On 5 March 1998, anarchist militants Maria Soledad Rosas, called 'Sole', and Edoardo Massari, called 'Baleno', and Silvano Pelissero were arrested in the occupied house in Turin where they lived. All three were placed in solitary confinement, accused of certain of the 1996–97 attacks, and accused of 'subversive association with terrorist aims'.

The NoTAV movement wasn't as strong as it is today. There was little reaction in the Susa Valley to the arrests . . . On the other hand, at Turin, when they were arrested, there were many demonstrations, including a big one on 4 April 1998.

– Luchino, 42, runs Radio NoTAV

On 28 March 1998, Baleno was found dead in his cell. On 11 July, Sole committed suicide in her halfway house. In 2001, the terrorism accusation against Silvano was dropped, but he ultimately served three years and ten months in prison and was freed in March 2002.

1999–2001: The links between Turin and the valley and the birth of the Committee of Popular Struggle

It is difficult to say exactly where Turin begins and the Susa Valley ends. The agglomeration of 1,700,000 inhabitants is the historic home to the Fiat corporation, which gave the city a strong workers' history. It houses a large 'antagonistic' milieu, which became more and more involved in the NoTAV movement after 2000. After the deaths of Sole and Baleno, the alliances intensified: the valley demonstrated in the city and the summer campgrounds allowed the youth of metropolitan Italy to become familiar with the valley. At this time, the Bussoleno committee of popular struggle began to take form. Principally made up of people with a militant experience dating to before NoTAV, it breathed a more political dynamic into the struggle and became an inspiring example as well to the committees that emerged later in the villages throughout the valley.

The links with the antagonistic milieu in Turin that helped politicize the movement shouldn't detract from the fact that the Susa Valley has its own subversive history. A radical militant component was present in the valley since the 1970s, when more than a dozen people from Prima Linea were arrested. Nevertheless, the major force behind the movement was not ideological discourse, but rather a position-taking on the basis of what was happening in the surroundings, the wound inflicted by the TAV on the soul of the inhabitants, whether or not they were politicized.

As for me, I was a political militant, I spent 8 years in prison. But I'm from here, I love nature, I became very . . . ecologist is not the right word, but, yes, I'm connected with nature. Thanks to the struggle but also thanks to my own trajectory. The TAV is not an excuse to fight, it bothers me, it bothers me personally, not for political reasons but because it means construction sites, it means fucking up the whole valley where I live. I don't want the TAV. It's a concrete refusal, absolutely not ideological, it's not because it represents capital and because I'm a communist I'm against it. No. It's a shitty project because it devastates the valley for me, it surrounds me with asbestos, it's disgusting, and I'm fighting it for those reasons and that's why I'm trying to get others to agree. If we had fought saying the TAV is bad because it's the incarnation of capitalism – which is perfectly true – that would have pissed people off. So we said, it's because they are opening up a site, it's a public health issue, water, noise, the occupation of the territory . . . in our pamphlets we used these kind of down-to-earth arguments, you'd never guess that a political collective wrote them.

– Stefano, 57, Bussaleno committee of popular struggle

2003–05: The arrival of the drills – first popular battles

In 2003, the first concrete incarnations of the TAV appeared in the valley: drilling equipment. Theoretically, this was to be used to unearth samples to analyse the soil and the rocks in the places where the construction was to occur. But core sampling was above all the occasion, for Italian companies, of gaining control of a considerable sum of money. The stakes were really much more about being able to promote the advancement of the project than in furnishing any real geological information. But this drilling met up immediately with opposition from the population and the elected officials. These latter played a central role in the opposition, bringing a certain energy and legitimacy. They participated in the gatherings, draped in their tricolour scarves, often on the front line, alternately stoking and moderating the will to resistance. Their presence was all the more remarkable in that opposition to the soundings couldn't happen without infringing somewhat on legality. At Pianezza in 2003, then Chianocco in 2004, the movement broke into the sampling sites and occupied them in such a way as to prevent the machines from working. At the same time, the first big popular march between Bourgogne and Bussoleno, a march of 20,000 people, took place. The banners of all the local communes decorated a municipal truck, and were present from then on in all the big demonstrations of the movement. From then on, each of the big demonstrations brought together tens of thousands of people. On 20 June 2005, the blockade of a new drilling in Bourgogne gave birth to the first permanent encampment, the first *presidio*, as they were called, in a long series.

At Bourgogne there was a field up high, with the road just below, and between the two a ditch. We were in the field and the police started to arrive, then the chief of police. The village Catholics carried stakes with pictures of the black Madonna of Rocciamelone (our highest mountain) on the top, with below the image the words 'Protect us'. The police chief was going back and forth between us and the police, trying to figure out whether they should attack us, because we were completely normal people, not squatters or antagonists.

The first morning we had just a few seats and a picnic table. The next day we had an umbrella and two tents to store food in, and a week later, little by little, there was a small house. The following week, in Bruzolo, the same thing happened, then Venaus was the third presidio. At each of the places where they wanted to drill, we made a presidio: little popular houses, houses of the people.

– Patrizia, 57, vegetarian chef at Avigliana

October 2005: The battle of Seghino

On 25 October 2005, a rumour spread that three drillings were under preparation above the village of Mompantero, on the abrupt and rocky slopes of the Rocciamelone, the mythic mountain long believed to be the highest of the Alps, and that towers over Susa with its 3,538 metres. Among the vines and orchards, a little road winds its way up, deep into the woods. On this road, near the Seghino Bridge, one of the most famous battles of NoTAV took place. Today, near the waterfall, carved into a rock, this inscription can be read: '31 October 2005, the battle of Seghino, never forget'.

Up until then we hadn't had any big confrontations with the forces of order. They would say 'we are coming to take over the area', and we would say 'no', and they would leave. On 31 October, the mayors had called a meeting of everybody for 7 a.m. near the Mompantero cemetery. But we got there ahead of time, during the night, because we knew what was going to happen. There were oldsters, people from the popular struggle committee, but there were also many young people who had started to come from elsewhere, because they found here a way to satisfy a need for opposition they couldn't find anywhere else. So we climbed up high, and in the morning we saw the blue beacons on the autoroute, and they came up, at first in cars and then on foot, in anti-riot gear. We were on a bridge that has since become famous, and at a certain moment, we were face-to-face with them. With no mayors to serve as buffers. Just a hundred of us and there were lots of them . . . We made the choice to continue to resist. They advanced, they started to push us, and we pushed back. Can you imagine? I'm thin, and I thought my ribs were going to snap. We oldsters were out in front and we were sandwiched. The police had taken down the railings of the bridge and the waterfall was a few meters below us. They could have killed us. But a miracle happened and we began to see lights arriving from all sides of the mountain. From 7 to 8 a.m., the hundred of us stood our ground alone, and then the people below started to come up . . . the whole mountain came alive, with people coming to join us. In an instant there was a thousand of us and things looked a little bit different! Finally, the mayors joined us.

– Nicoletta

At 11.30 a.m., a small group of *carabinieri* attempted to dismantle the demonstrators' blockade, but above them they found 200 NoTAVs awaiting them on a steep slope with rocks in their hands. After a few negotiations, they turned tail. At 7 p.m., an agreement was finally reached between the elected officials and the authorities, everyone promising to leave. But during the night, despite their promise, the police returned and manned the drilling sites. At daybreak the feeling of betrayal led immediately to a strike and blockades on the crossroads and railway lines of the valley. It was the first full-force demonstration in the valley and the proof of the movement's capacity to respond spontaneously to an aggression. In response to this show of strength, the police reinforced their checkpoint at Urbiano, completely isolating Mompantero from the rest of the valley.

Liberate Venaus!

Two weeks after the Seghino episode, on 16 November, a valley-wide hunger strike was declared, and followed by such a great number that 'there was not one café open in the whole valley'. Some 80,000 people demonstrated from Bussoleno to Susa. Two days later, in that effervescent atmosphere, the valley inhabitants learned that exploratory tunnel work would begin 30 November near the village of Venaus. The change in scale was significant: no longer was it just about samples and preliminary studies – now it was the beginning of real construction. Danger was imminent and the movement decided to set up a permanent *presidio* on the threatened territory starting on 28 November. The *carabinieri* arrived, took up quarters for a time near the NoTAVs, until the latter's harassment forced them to leave the area. Behind them the roads were already barricaded and the valley people in great number came onto the tiny strip of land, which became at that point 'The Free Republic of Venaus'. For some days, the situation was frozen. It was snowing. The Valsusians were masters of their territory. Firewood and clothing arrived non-stop.

Two days later, in the middle of a winter night, a mass of helmets advanced toward the cabin and its fifty occupants. The eviction began, and its savage nature is well remembered. Taken by surprise, the occupants watched clubs rain down without being able to react. Many NoTAVS were wounded, without distinction of age, and the cabin encampment was destroyed. But popular reaction didn't delay: at dawn, the village priest rang the church bells, the firemen sounded their sirens, and the municipal police drove through the village streets, loudspeaker on the roof: 'Come lend a hand to the NoTAVs of Venaus attacked during the night!' Immediately, barricades were erected everywhere, from the autoroute down to the smallest village streets. A spontaneous general strike pushed schoolchildren as much as shopkeepers into the streets. Finally, a few days later, 8 December, a demonstration of 70,000 people marched on the *carabinieries* and chased them from the site designated for construction.

To calm this quasi-insurrectional climate, the Venaus terrains were placed under close watch. Given the tensions, the company chosen to do the work decided to remove its machines. On 23 December, the police lifted the Urbiano checkpoint. The imminence of the Olympic Games in Turin, 80 percent of which would occur in the valley, pushed the government into an 'Olympic break', which in fact came down to suspending the project indefinitely.

> Before, we were the NoTAV people, the NoTAV committees, the NoTAV Valsusians. It wasn't until after Venaus, that we started talking about the NoTAV movement. It happened because we realized we had exceeded the boundaries of the valley, people from outside had begun to be interested in the struggle and were coming here: we had become a point of reference for many. That's a movement.
>
> – Stefano

Seghino and Venaus became the founding victories of the movement. They brought an end to the first phase of the struggle and their memory allowed a relaunching of oppositional activity, without equivocation, five years later. Commemorations were held each year. On 31 October, NoTAVs climb the slopes above Mompantero and touch up the inscriptions worn away during the year: 'Today and always: resistance'. And each 8 December, via a demonstration at a work area or in a village, the movement recalls its past victories and summons them up to create energy for today's battles. Ten years later the Venaus *presidio*, even if it is no longer responding to any direct threat, remains a central gathering place for the movement. It welcomes summer camps and numerous evenings of information; people meet up there before going to a construction site or to eat a warm, delicious pizza. It is a reminder each day that if the Susa Valley today has not taken on the appearance of an immense construction site, it is because of the determination and the victories of the movement.

2006–10: Intermission

The Venaus victory bore fruit: the 'Olympic break' in fact lasted over four years. The movement made use of the victory to strengthen its organization. Beginning with Susa, numerous committees were created throughout the valley, but also in the surroundings and in all of Italy. Among other initiatives, a 'march at human speed' was organized in 2006, from Venaus to Rome, stopping at all the areas devastated by big projects or threatened by them.

The state, for its part, moved into the institutional terrain and tried to break the mayors' opposition. The year 2006 brought a new change: the Berlusconi government announced that a new route for the TAV was under study along the right bank of the Dora Riparia. In May, the arrival into power of the Democratic Party, in the person of Romano Prodi, induced a change in governmental strategy. From that point on, the government opted for negotiation and created for that purpose the 'Observatory', presided over by the architect Virano. 'The Observatory' was supposed to bring together elected officials around a table, under the declared optic of rallying people for the project. This procedure resembled identically the 'Dialogue Commission' that would try in vain, a few years later, to convince people that a negotiation was possible concerning the airport at Notre-Dame-des-Landes. In the valley, several NoTAV mayors accepted to go to Rome to participate in these discussions. This decision estranged them from the movement, which denounced an organism that took as a given the construction of the TAV, and allowed barely any discussion that went beyond the means to realize it.

With the Observatory, the president of our community of Montagne, Ferentino, changed his ideas completely. He's now a regional counsel, well-placed in the Democratic Party. And yet, he had done incredible things for NoTAV: in 2005, he was the most adept of all the political figures. But, little by little, he withdrew from the movement; he marginalized himself and finally left completely in 2009. Maybe if we had kept up relations with him we might have prevented him from going completely over to the other side, but that's the way it was. The problem was that up until 2005, Ferentino stood in for many of the other mayors, he was very decided, took a lot of initiative. Courageous mayors, there were only about one in ten. So when Ferentino withdrew from the front line, many were afraid to continue positioning themselves against the TAV. All this means that in 2005 there was a real presence on the part of the mayors against the police and in 2010, we still had their support but they were no longer there for the physical confrontations.

– Mario, 68 years old, Bussoleno

2010–11: Counter-attack by the Empire, New Sample Drilling and the Multiplication of the *Presidi*

Hostilities on the terrain were reopened in January 2010 with a new campaign of sample drilling. Virano had promised that these would be conducted 'in full transparency'. And yet, though each one was supposed to last several weeks, the drills remained in the valley only a few days, in spots that had been chosen more for their capacity to be defended than for any real interest they might contribute to preliminary studies. Adding to the provocation, machines were brought in during the night, guarded by massive escorts of *carabinieri*. An urgent call to come demonstrate went out; organizing took place in the snow and cold to try to take possession of these spots before the *carabinieri*. All the drills were tampered with and the police response was severe: at Colissimo, several NoTAVs were seriously wounded by police clubs. But in the end, out of 91 sample digs scheduled for January, only a tiny handful were conducted, and the movement came out of these skirmishes strengthened.

During this time, we witnessed a movement that was not succeeding in being completely popular, because it relied on moments of very rapid mobilization, people who were ready to move at any time, day or night. The hard-core centre of the movement was made up of people who mobilized in very little time. This was certainly the reflection of a very strong popular consensus, and yet already a part of the movement was becoming specialized in doing actions, while the others participated in the big marches.

– Maurizio, libertarian hotel manager in Turin

Along with this 'battle of the sample drillings', the movement spread to the villages touched by the new projected route for the tracks. New *presidi* emerged in Susa and Sant'Antonio on sites designated for drilling. Also, at this time, the most symbolic of these, the *baita* in Clarea was built. *Baita* means chalet, and this is what this *presidio* looked like, built of stone and wood, tucked into the mouth of the Clarea Valley, an enclosed, wild valley that meets up with the Susa Valley and traces the contours of the Maddalena site, which was to increasingly become the focus of NoTAV attention.

2011: The Free Republic of the Maddalena

It was at the bottom of the village of Chiomonte that the exploratory tunnel was now supposed to be dug. The Venaus site had been abandoned in the new plan and replaced with the Maddalena. This is a wooded area of old chestnut trees, which borders certain archaeological remains – among the most important in Europe. These few wild acres, barely visible and barely accessible, dominated by a huge motorway viaduct, would become the Free Republic of the Maddalena, with reference to the Free Republic of Venaus, but above all to the partisan Republics, those patches of territory liberated from the Nazi–Fascist occupation by Resistance fighters at the end of the Second World War. On 26 May, 10,000 torches descended in the direction of the Maddalena. These were the first signs of that Free Republic whose months of existence remain one of the most striking experiences in the whole history of the movement.

> The Free Republic of the Maddalena was not the result of planning or collective thought. We started to occupy the space on 22 May . . . the police were getting ready to move in. At 11 p.m. there were about 250 of us. The police arrived at 4:30 a.m., ten or twenty vans of anti-riot police who blocked the motorway. The police came out of the tunnel and it was the first time that we threw rocks at them, a lot of us did. The police withdrew. Newspaper articles, public debate: rocks, no rocks. But clearly many people were happy with the situation – even those who hadn't

thrown rocks were aware that it was the only way to stop them. So, the police were gone and that night many of us left as well. The Free Republic was born a couple days later. We said, 'No *carabinieri* allowed here.' We put a camping car across the road, let the vineyard workers through but not the cops. They said, 'But you can't do that. We are the Italian State!' And we responded, 'Here is where the Italian state ends and the Free Republic of the Maddalena begins.'

– Luca, 40, upper valley committee

On 27 June 2011, I was sleeping there. Since they could arrive at any minute, we had put barricades across all the roads – the biggest, we called 'Stalingrad'. We had had a meeting the day before and decided that the old people would man the barricades, so that they couldn't have free rein to attack the young. And I was one of the oldsters on the barricades. And then we saw them arrive, from all sides, and they were very numerous . . . and then the drama of seeing them there, the following days, when we could go back to our tents and they had urinated on them, broken everything, left filth behind . . . they took everything. We took away cartons of things they had destroyed . . . they thought it was over. But the fight continued.

– Nicoletta

The demonstration of 3 July and summer 2011

Immediately after the eviction of 27 June, the NoTAVs called for a big demonstration on 3 July, to encircle the work area. It was imagined on the model of when Venaus was taken back in 2005. Six years later, the notion of the inalienable force of great numbers remained the strategy of the movement. But the state had learned lessons from Venaus too, and this time the thousands of demonstrators found themselves butting up against an impenetrable fortress.

Four kids went up to the fence and were yelling slogans: 'Go home', 'Slaves of the State'. Even though they were in no physical danger, the police attacked with a water cannon. My wife is a strong woman but she's asthmatic . . . I had never seen gas before, it was the first time that I found myself in a cloud of gas, I breathed it . . . I thought I would die on

the spot . . . I was looking for my wife in the white cloud, and I found her
on the ground vomiting, and that enraged me to the point that if I had
had a bomb, I would have thrown it at them. From that point on, I threw
all the rocks that existed in Clarea.

– Emilio, 60, fishmonger in lower valley

Despite the violence of the confrontations that erupted in three different areas, the forces of order, present in huge numbers, never gave
way. From the morning to the end of the afternoon, more than 4,000
tear-gas grenades were thrown at the demonstrators. Projectiles
continued to rain down on the police for several hours leaving 200
wounded among them. Toward 5 a.m., as fatigue set in, a *carbinieri*,
during a daring raid, was left behind by his colleagues in the woods,
among the demonstrators. Captured by the NoTAV, he was immediately relieved of his gun and other accoutrements. After lots of discussion, the return of Vice Brigadier Luigi de Matteo and his revolver
marked the end of the day. The next day, the media castigated the
'black blocs' infiltration into the movement'; reading between the
lines, they were inviting good NoTAVs to dissociate themselves from
them.

The most important thing for me was what happened afterwards,
the press conference, where everybody, together, proclaimed: 'If
wanting to rid the valley of this military presence means being black
bloc, then we are all black bloc.' It wasn't certain that it would go in
that direction that day, that the movement would take responsibility
for that style of action. The pressure was enormous on people to
dissociate from those who had more seriously attacked the police.
And inside the movement there's all kinds, including citizens who
are afraid of radicalization. The day of the conference, all the
committees were there, and when we understood that everyone,
even the Catholics, were agreed to say: 'All of us acted that day', we
knew it was very important and that a decisive step had been taken
that day.

– Maurizio, in his 50s, union member, committee of the upper valley

After 3 July and its national, even international, media attention, harassing the police around the work area continued, and the NoTAV summer camp lasted into September. Campers, who came from all over Italy and neighbouring countries, occupied a terrain near the electricity centre where the first police checkpoint was set up, or at the *baita* in the Clarea Valley. The idea of taking back the work zone was still present in everyone's heads and frequent attacks erupted. Inside the work zone, military soldiers arrived to provide reinforcement to the police and the *carabinieri*.

2012–Today: The Arrests of January 2012

The state responded with a ferocious wave of repression to the radicalization of the form of action taken by the NoTAVs and by their refusal of any dissociation from it. Thus, on 26 January 2012 in the morning, dozens of arrests took place in the Susa Valley and everywhere in Italy: Turin, Milan, Rome, Genoa, Florence, Palermo . . . A total of 26 people were jailed. It was the first step in a judiciary procedure that became famous under the name of a 'maxi-trial': in the end, 53 NoTAVs were indicted for their presumed participation in the confrontations of 27 June and 3 July 2011. It was also the beginning of the systematization of the *fogli di via*, territorial interdictions placed on people getting out of prison, Italian or otherwise, who risk retrial if they are caught again on the forbidden territory. From that point on, any action, even the most banal, ran the risk of jail: more than 1,000 legal procedures were initiated against NoTAVs in the Turin courthouse.

I never went to prison. When I got there, they put me in a room for two hours, there were fifteen of us, seven NoTAVs and a few others. The detainees were very nice to us. In the newspaper, it was reported that among those arrested was a town councillor who had hit the police with his cane. Each time someone passed in front of my cell, he said: 'Are you the town councillor who caned the police? Bravo! Bravo!' The other detainees asked us if we needed anything. They knew that NoTAVS had been arrested, and they had a certain respect for those who, like us, had broken the law not for personal profit, but for an ideal. The next day I saw the judge and they let me out that evening. They assigned me to a residence and I had to sign in with the *carabinieri* for several months.

– Guido, retired, 70, retired town councillor of Villar Focchiardo

There was a fierce phase in the battle that began in 2010 and ended in 2012, because we didn't have the strength to stop the construction site. In January 2012, during the big wave of arrests throughout Italy, out of the 54 indicted, only one decided to have a separate trial. Thanks to how anchored the struggle was in the valley, we managed to maintain a unitary front, everyone else stayed together, despite difficulties, even if certain people risked a great deal by having a common trial. The comrades arrested came from different milieux: anarchists, autonomous . . . but there were also people who weren't, strictly speaking, militants at all, who participated in the struggle, but without a very clear political perspective. This created a pretty favourable situation for an immediate reaction to the arrests: people reacted immediately and there was almost a week of a general mobilization of solidarity throughout Italy . . . The Susa Valley had the possibility of generating slogans that could be embraced throughout Italy.

– Gillo, in his 40s, citizen living in the valley

2012: The expulsion of the baita and Luca's fall

On 25 February 2012, a popular march of support for those arrested brought together thousands of people between Bussoleno and Susa. The following Monday, the police attacked and evacuated the zone of the *baita*, contiguous with the fortress, to expand the latter and begin work operations.

The cops were already there, around the baita. Luca came afterwards, and he succeeded in entering the perimeter. Then there was confusion, the cops weren't sure that he wasn't one of them, a secret cop, and they didn't react in time. It all happened quickly, he climbed up the telegraph pole and called Radio Black-Out – he was recounting the situation live on the radio. Then the cops did something they have no right to do, there's a protocol involved, talk to the person, lay out mattresses. But with Luca they did none of that, they just climbed the pole, and Luca continued to tell them to stay off, all this live on the radio. Luca climbed a little higher, he didn't know that even without touching the wires an electrical charge could happen. And that's what happened, he took a charge and fell from a great height. Electricity passed through his body a dozen times, and he was lucky, he fell between the rocks. But everyone, including the cops, thought he was dead.

After that, Luca spent three months in the hospital. Now he's OK. Many people told me afterwards that they had never thought it was possible to die in the NoTAV struggle . . . We organized attacks everywhere, in the upper valley to block the carabinieri reinforcements, and on the railway lines. The guys who work in the yacht factory Azimut d'Avigliana went on strike. The second day, more and more people were on the motorway and there were blockades throughout Italy . . . In the end, Luca's health got better, which calmed things down.

– Maurizio, committee of the upper valley

At the same time that the valley had erupted, the 'motorway days' contributed to the national ramifications of the movement. The support throughout Italy for the struggle, already apparent with the solidarity shown toward the 53 arrested, grew into common action. The same day that Luca fell, spontaneous blockades took place in railway stations in Rome, Pisa, Bologna and Palermo. Then a call went out for similar initiatives on 1 March, to which 60 towns responded. The slogan 'bring the valley to the city' had a brief but substantial success. The struggle invited itself into football stadiums, NoTAV graffiti covered trains: the Susa Valley was everywhere, beyond the construction, beyond the valley itself.

We always dream of that perspective, whenever there is struggle, we say to ourselves: it will die if it stays like this, it has to be generalized. The problem was that those were only words, we went all over Italy, information tours, and nothing happened. It only happened when emotion took over, as when Luca fell.

– Maurizio, Turin

The camping that summer of 2012 united once again a large number of Italian and European militants in Chiomonte. It was now time to add new forms of action to tried and true methods: the target was no longer the work site but also the companies and partners collaborating in the project, including banks.

2013–15: sabotages and trials

This opening up of other targets and other modes of action, in a period when causing real damage in a large group was perilous, allowed the idea of sabotage, in thought and in practice, to make headway. Discreet attacks in small numbers that escaped more easily the attention of police surveillance, took on meaning and strength. The year 2013 saw nocturnal offensives targeting all the ramifications of the TAV construction sites. *'Quella notte c'eravamo tutti'* (that night we were all there): this was the response of the NoTAV movement to the burning of a generator on 13 May. During the popular assembly, Alberto Perino, one of the most popular figures in the movement, developed an argument to explain the choice to the pacifists in the movement, using writings by Gandhi, Mandela and Capitini, an Italian non-violent leader. Once again, the movement demonstrated its capacity to evolve according to situations and refuse the dissociation that the press and the political classes were urging them to do. And that is what allowed them not to fall into the trap of anti-terrorism on 9 December 2013, when Chiara, Claudio, Niccolo and Mattia were arrested for incidents on 13 May.

It was four anarchists accused of sabotage and terrorism! And yet there was an extremely broad solidarity and the level of public discussion was high, very interesting. You opened up a newspaper and you could read about how sabotage was not the same thing as terrorism. In Italy, there is not the same tradition of engaged intellectuals who speak up in support of struggle that there is in France. So the fact that Erri De Luca took a position, and said that the TAV had to be sabotaged, well, of course, that was a scandal . . . For us, members of the most antagonistic camp, it was very interesting to see that our reflections on anti-terrorism, the state, sabotage, were shared by many . . . We stayed very strong against the juridical offensive, the four of them received letters every day for months. And that gave us the illusion of being in a strong situation. But the strength that was expressed in solidarity masked the weakness that persisted on the real level of the struggle. All the initiatives were tied to solidarity for the four, but the struggle itself wasn't moving forward . . . we had lost sight of the plan for the struggle.

– Gillo

The autumn following the arrests, after eight months of imprisonment, the four decided to speak up during their trial. Surprising and courageous, their words built a bridge between their exceptional situation and their numerous supporters outside.

The night of 13 May 2013, I took part in the sabotage of the Maddalena workplace in Chiomonte. I understand the bewilderment of public opinion and its storytellers vis-à-vis the reappearance of that illustrious stranger, sabotage . . . The fight against the TAV has merited dusting off that old practice, knowing when and how to choose to employ it, we have managed to distinguish the just from the legal.

– Claudio, Turin courthouse, September 2014

As for us, we took a heartfelt step beyond resignation. We threw a grain of sand into the gears of a progress whose only effect is the unceasing destruction of the planet on which we live. I was present that night, and the female voice that was intercepted is mine. I lived part of my life with the men and women who, for more than twenty years, opposed an incontrovertible 'no' to an idea that is devastating the world. I'm proud and happy to have done so.

– Chiara, in her 30s, garden marketer, Turin
courthouse, September 2014

The terrorism accusation was finally dropped, and the seven arrested for the night of 13 May 2013 were sentenced to three and a half years in prison for the first four, and two years and ten months for the three others (commuted after a year in prison to house arrest). In

January 2015, 47 of the 53 indicted in the maxi-trial were sentenced to three years in prison as well as exorbitant damages and interest. Confronting these fines and condemnations became one of the principal preoccupations of the movement. The tunnel excavation was underway as well in the shape of a 15-metre drill that began work at the end of the summer 2013.

> The movement had become an experimental laboratory for the systems of repression. Fines are extremely practical for them, because then they don't have to worry about public opinion, there's no more bloody film footage. During this time they prevent you from acting. They're requiring you to pay damages to the police, to the police unions, to companies that have already been convicted of collusion with the mafia? No way! But then someone has to pay for all the others and the movement falls apart, because the philosophy of the movement is that no one gets left behind, for whatever reason. We really had our back against the wall. Especially since the number of people indicted for NoTAV was by now about a thousand. That meant, theoretically, that it was impossible to keep paying. First, because it wasn't just and secondly because it wasn't possible. Unless we held up a bank!
>
> – Fulvio, 63, frequenter of the container *presidio*, Bruzolo

The movement, for all that, did not stop harassing the work areas. Of course, the construction advanced, but at a snail's pace. At the dawning of the year 2016, less than half of the exploratory tunnel of the Maddalena had been dug. And, as a kind of Christmas present, the NoTAVs learned that on Christmas Eve the mountain had collapsed onto the drill, damaging it considerably. As for the rest of the infrastructure needed by the project, and above all the main tunnel that the high-speed train was supposed to use, their realization seemed difficult to envision. The Susa train station, for example, whose architect wanted it visible from the moon, and, as such, wanted it built entirely of aluminium, or the tracks, perched on embankments 35 meters high across several kilometres of the valley, or yet the designated displacing of the motorway – any initiation of these constructions would necessitate an intensive military presence and an engineering staff particularly sensitive to security measures. Pressure had borne fruit, which is why the pro-project people were examining other solutions, like digging the tunnel entirely from the French side. The game is not over. As the Piedmontese slogan of the NoTAVs goes: 'A sarà dūra!' (It's going to be hard!).

2

Peoples

'The NoTAV struggle is a popular struggle.' The statement is echoed on every mountain slope in the Susa Valley, in conversations and in writing, in an assured tone that conveys far more than just self-persuasion. And first encounters in the Susa Valley immediately confirm the statement: flags in windows, tales of demonstrations attended by 70,000 people (as many as there are inhabitants of the valley), meetings filling gymnasiums. But beyond the large number, what is striking is the nature of the crowd on the big days as well as during more ordinary activities: the spectrum is so large that describing the social composition of the movement would create jobs for a horde of sociologists. In the valley, people are more than a little proud of the improbable participation of the high society of the valley, elected officials, Catholic dignitaries, doctors, people living on the outskirts of society. At a banquet or a *presidio* one might run into a yogi wearing a plain white robe, a hermit living in a cave near Oulx, or a former convict just out of prison – not to mention all the 'ordinary people': the hairdressers, fishmongers, librarians whose omnipresence and importance in the struggle are also extraordinary.

The most banal activities and objects become affirmations against the high-speed TAV train: a football match, a cocktail party, Christmas Eve for children with Santa Claus wearing a bonnet that reads '*A sàra dùra*', the NoTAV calendars hanging in every hallway, the sweatshirts, bumper stickers, cakes.

'The NoTAV struggle is a popular struggle' can be taken as a definition. But because the goal of this book is not to find correct categories in which to place the histories it is trying instead to open up from the inside, it will be a reversed definition: it is not so much the qualifier 'popular' that defines the struggle, it is the substance of the struggle that illuminates what popular might come to mean. And since we must wade through the vast field of questions such a term gives rise to, let us begin by clearing the ground.

'Popular' is not a harmless term. At Notre-Dame-des-Landes it is rarely used, and the question: 'Is the fight against the airport a popular struggle?' would be answered doubtfully, with a touch of distrust by even those most enthusiastic about the strengths and hopes of the movement.

The adjective, and even more, the noun 'people', are not used easily in the political register. This is the fault, perhaps, of the failures and errors of revolutionary campaigns undertaken in the past under that name. Those on the margins of society and minorities made a place for themselves throughout the second half of the twentieth century at the forefront of the political stage, sometimes against those whose conception of the unity and cohesion of the 'people' depends on the negation of the so-called 'secondary struggles': feminist, anti-racist, homosexual. It is also the fault of 'populism', and the way this has of establishing people as a mass that can be manipulated by flattering the basest instincts and often using reactionary tricks – reactionary in the sense of playing on the simultaneous necessities of an increase in pride and submission to an authority.

But at a moment when the government is staking everything by playing the referendum card as the best way of opening up the bocage to bulldozers, it is certainly around terms like 'democratic' and 'republican' that one would be wise to be the most circumspect. Let us leave aside how grotesque the president's referendum decision was, pulled out of a hat in February 2016 after weeks of silence that was supposed to show firmness, rejected by the local authorities on the left and right, and undoubtedly lacking the least legal accountability. For despite the stumbles of the president, the manoeuvre is not lacking finesse: to call forth the people to legitimize the airport project is to try to deprive the opposition of a good part of its reason for being by disputing its legitimacy on the terrain of a certain type of direct democracy. But the movement does not believe we are witnessing a sudden access to democracy on the part of the state. Even without broadcasting it those people standing in opposition to the airport are those who cultivate, walk, work, love, travel, breathe – in a word, live – on the territory of the project. A territory with a geometry that varies according to whether we consider the airport from the angle of a concrete jungle, of sound pollution, global warming and climate change, or, why not, of the possibility of finding yourself on the other side of the world after a short trip over the ocean. For the government, what counts are the polls that will indicate the right perimeter in which to conduct the referendum: the one where the chances of a 'yes' vote for the airport are highest. The odd 'people' who are the object of the consultation will be reduced to a disembodied opinion, worked on for weeks by a massive push in pro-airport propaganda, by those who have already spent hundreds of thousands of euros on advertising campaigns in the last few years. People will vote 'yes' on the basis of statistics manipulated by the General Direction of Civil Aeronautics, of being hostage to employment, of lying anti-zad campaigns, and with a degree of personal conviction that will not go further than dropping a ballot in the box. The stakes of the battle over the referendum lie in its definition: on the one side, those who act, feel, think, and conduct themselves, for better or worse, in an attempt to create an everyday, and on the other, public opinion that is only taken into account, at best, from time to time.

The battle to impose the republican abstraction of the people extends well beyond the manoeuvre of popular consultation, notably, there where the 'war' declared in its name against 'terrorism' threatens to ceaselessly polarize the political field. We heard 'the people' invoked less to describe the 60,000 who marched through Nantes against the airport on 22 February 2014 than we did for the 75,000 who assembled in the same city on 10 January 2015 after the attacks on *Charlie Hebdo* and a Hyper-Cacher supermarket. The fable of popular unity as the foundation of the nation functions better in the post-*Charlie* anti-terrorist myth-making than in the case of a struggle undertaken against those who claim to represent us.

The republican people, who emerged from the mould of the French Revolution bearing as many political blemishes as potentialities, was quickly neutralized by the installation of the bourgeoisie into power, only to be later worked over, polished, stabilized and integrated into the vast system of democratic governance. Assigned the task of incarnating national sovereignty, in a paradoxical prolongation of the figure of the king, though by way of a more metaphorical body, the 'French people', in the name of whom every legal decision is rendered, can only be a homogenizing fiction, as are its cousins, 'the general interest', and 'society'. No contradiction, no ethical divergence, no internal relationship to power is supposed to fracture the unity of the people, lest the very principle of sovereignty be shattered. The 'unity of the people' is also a way to rationalize government acts: the fiction of shared belonging limits the deployment of costly techniques of controlling and containing internal battles. A sovereign body that self-mutilates would be in bad taste. And what could be more efficient than to declare 'citizens equal before the law' the farmer who has just been emancipated from semi-slavery and his landed proprietor, so that the former continues to pay a steep rent to the latter, instead of burning down his chateau and parading his head on the end of a stake? Thus, after having long been excluded from the domain of sovereignty, the proletariat – those who, possessing nothing, were deemed unqualified to vote – women, and the colonized all ended up integrated, but at the price of the negation of any relation of institutionalized domination. Any eruption of political conflict, in the Susa Valley, the Nantes bocage or elsewhere, is thus a radical putting into question of the paradigm of the republican people, which is based on the idea that one can only truly go to battle with exterior enemies, those 'of impure blood'.

We should clarify that this model presents some conceptual problems, and even at the time *La Marseillaise* was written it was not always easy to detect and denounce a foreigner's hand behind the internal troubles of the nation. The art of governing thus also included the capacity to designate and excommunicate 'internal enemies', thereby refining the management of the population while conserving the principle of unity. The notion of an interior enemy today is fast interfering with the French Constitution, with the possibility of officially excluding dual-nationality 'terrorists' from the national community. The threat by the current French government of activating 'deprivation of nationality', beyond this old far-right theme being useful for electoral purposes, has as its goal to remobilize the abstraction of a united (and pure) people, all the while giving itself the means of intervening against those who are part of it. And given the dozens of people who have been imprisoned for declaring that they were not Charlie, we can assume that the interventions will not be surgical.

In the autumn of 2015, the conjunction between the threats of evacuation of the zad and the terrorist attacks of 13 November made the tension surrounding the idea of 'the people' and 'the political' manifest in a crude fashion. The 'French people' were exhorted to identify entirely with the so-called 'Bataclan generation' – a generation that, as the governmental campaign portrayed it, was open, hedonistic, flexible, and whose principal political demand consisted of the right to go out on Friday nights.* First and foremost, it was crucial to make a common stand against the enemy, the barbarian, the terrorist, the Islamic State – an enemy that could, according to circumstances, interlocutors, and verbal slippages of various kinds, extend to include migrants and Muslims. What was abject about the methodical, cold acts of the murderers in Paris was presented as completely alien to peaceful western civilization. The declaration of the state of emergency made clear, as though it needed to, what was meant by 'a common front': no other split would be tolerated but the one dividing, according to context, 'France' or 'the west' from 'barbarians', and especially not one dividing world leaders from demonstrators during the COP21 climate summit. With disconcerting aplomb, prefectures of several regions in France decreed house arrests for militants on the basis of their political leanings (often fed by their participation in the anti-airport struggle) and their supposed will to participate in the climate counter-summit. These were procedures explicitly allowed within the framework of the state of emergency, and thus within the war against terrorism. The operation is crude but

---

* Translator's note: 'Bataclan generation' is a media expression used to designate what was targeted in the November 2015 attack on the Bataclan concert hall in Paris: a certain youthful, hedonist, urban lifestyle.

seems to work: you are either with the government or with the terrorists. In or out, and pity those who are out.

It was the zad that managed to break through the bewitchment that
had seized the country in November 2015, in the wake of the auto-
cratic reaction of the executive branch just as much as the eruption of
armed violence in the streets of Paris. Convoys of tractors and bicycles, departing from Notre-Dame-des-Landes and other places trying
to demonstrate at the COP21 defied the bans against assembling and
demonstrating and forced them to be retracted. They united for a
banquet – certainly an anti-absolutist one, but one that could not be
described as republican – in front of the chateau at Versailles, a triple
symbol of absolute royalty, the crushing of the Communards in 1871,
and the validation of the state of emergency by parliament that had
met there a few days earlier. Along the way, the welcome assured by
dozens of local groups, sometimes improvised in barns or local town
halls according to the whim of the prefecture, made it possible to see
the popular dimension of the struggle completely differently from the
patriotic unanimity in action. The zad had responded in the best of
ways to the order to get in line behind the authorities (whether to
exterminate terrorists or to limit climate catastrophe): if there is in
fact a people at work, it has infinitely much more to do with the insurgent working-class neighbourhoods during the Paris Commune than
it does with masses rendered and maintained in a docile state by the
threat of foreign aggression and being excommunicated from the
national community – as well as by the mystified narrative of
sovereignty.

The terms 'people' and 'popular' remain nervously used by those in
power, brandished parsimoniously, even when they are trying to
justify the regime of soft terror they are looking to instigate. The problem is, once stripped of their republican clothing, the terms carry a
subversive charge and a semantic weight sufficient to open paths to
understanding what the two struggles against the TAV and the airport
are really about. Their most intense episodes, during which adverse
offensives are completely overturned by the welling up of strength
unimaginable until that point, evoke the popular uprisings that adorn
the history of the nineteenth, twentieth and early twenty-first

centuries. This people, seeming to emerge suddenly from all pores of ordinary life, can be understood as the ephemeral juncture between the population, object of state sovereignty, and the plebes or common people, its ungovernable part. The first group is the mass of souls under the pastoral empire of a large system of government, which exceeds by far the executive cabinets and its network of administration to merge with all the mechanisms that make us adhere to our social status, gender and supposed economic interest. The second group resists openly and, in so doing, becomes the object of attention for those in power and their agents of repression. The situation becomes critical when the taste for insubordination and the irrepressible ardour of this group manages to electrify the numerical force of the first. In an instant, a few hours, a few weeks, power seems to evaporate. Not that it is absent, nor that its troops hold back from striking hard, but its sorcery no longer works. It acts, it has recourse to its most powerful magic – white and black – but none of its spells succeed in maintaining its command over the population, nor in isolating and freezing the common people into the inoffensive figure of a gargoyle.

Popular force that affirms itself is thus too explosive, too impetuous to maintain a stable form. After the great NoTAV victories or those of the zad, everyday life falls back into place again, but not without having been perceptibly transfigured. The eruptive manifestation of the people, which showed itself capable of sweeping everything up into its momentum, raises the question of the relation between numerically great struggles and 'popularity'. For we can also find in the notion of the people and what it implies about uniting or bringing together, not a homogenizing force, but something that can affect each and every person, beyond sociological or political characteristics. There is in the notion of the popular something meta-social, like a call to transcend the categories that habitually separate us while claiming to unite us in the greater social body. If it is particularly true in the valley, we can find in the bocage as well, though to a lesser extent, an unexpected mix of different life trajectories, professions, levels of education, political sensibilities and so forth. This does not mean every social determination has been transgressed or that many BTP entrepreneurs have become anti-airport, but it indicates a large front that offers hope we are seeing the end of several decades of defeat of sectoral social struggles. Hope of this kind was sparked recently by the Occupy and *Indignados* movements, which went so far as to extend the front to include the famous 99 percent of the population who suffer the domination of the remaining 1 percent. We can remain sceptical of such a simplistic division, which is not without recalling the fictive unity of the republican people, but their aspiration to a broadly based offensive and a possible victory resounds with the NoTAV movement as with the anti-airport movement that has turned itself into a zad.

If there is nevertheless a difference between the relationship to the popular in the Susa Valley and in Notre-Dame-des-Landes, it is born of the very motivations of the two struggles: in one, the movement directly concerns all inhabitants of the valley, affected by the construction of the railway line; in the other, the direct impact of the infrastructure is limited to a few towns on the immediate periphery of a metropolis of 600,000 people. This difference of scale is evidently determinant of the forms taken by struggles and their ability to claim popular support. The tens of thousands of demonstrators on the big days defending the zad are far from being concentrated in the outskirts of Nantes, and the popularity of the struggle lies primarily in its ability to incarnate and make common questions – the future of agricultural lands, climate, biodiversity, the ravages of economic logic, and so forth – that broadly exceed the mere reality of the bocage or of the Loire-Atlantique.

If the valley, too, allows such a larger focus, the basis of the movement is nevertheless taken up directly with the territory, to the point of structuring the social life of all of its inhabitants. As such, we can perhaps see in what is being built around NoTAV the first indications of what could become the foundation of a people in a way that is both different from the republican people and from that of an insurrectional uprising: something in the order of a culture. An ensemble of implicit codes by which the opponents to the high-speed train recognize themselves in a history and a story, as belonging to a shared destiny. The 'NoTAV people' they proclaim themselves to be takes on the dimensions of those peoples without a state that are so many points of struggle flickering across the planet, from the South American forests to the mountains of the Basque country or Kurdistan.

Upheaval
NoTAV – When the People Appear

In the history of the NoTAV movement what is most striking are those rare but precious moments of reaction shared by the entire valley. The battles of Seghino and Venaus in 2005, the Maddalena in 2011, Luca's fall in 2012: what happened at these moments was not simply on the order of a successful mobilization. As opposed to big demonstrations, foreseen and foreseeable, these episodes – high points of the struggle – are characterized by their explosive side, by a skin-deep emotion between joy and sadness, which sweeps through at enormous speed and gives the valley itself the air of rising up. In the Susa Valley, as in Cairo, Sidi Bouzid or Athens during the same years, the term 'people' was given to the force that rises up at the same time, that it is born of that uprising and that, in the midst of the twenty-first century, breaks open the habitual everyday indifference. A people appears, reacting to one of their own being struck down, or to the military occupation of its territory.

> When Luca fell, I had left work. My cousin called me and told me something terrible had happened. I got on a train and went to Chianocco since there was a meeting there. What got to me was not the fall, it was that while Luca was lying on the ground, the police decided to move the diggers and the workers forward. They put a red and white cover over Luca and they made the workers get back to work. And for me this was . . . inhuman. They didn't know if he was dead or alive.
>
> – Joe Panther, in his 50s, DJ at Radio Black-Out

> Everyone in the valley knew Luca. People still tell the story . . . The smell, the smell of Luca, burnt, and the cops who were clapping because there was a guy on the ground nearly dead. Every day you write arguments on the internet or in books, but when something like that happens they say

you are violent, when it's the cops who are applauding and blocking the ambulance that showed up forty-five minutes later.

– Alice, ski instructor, Bussoleno

Here in the Susa Valley, the movement operates above all on emotional dynamics far more than through political planning. The demonstrations are generated through planning – we get together, discuss, say 'let's do a demonstration', but with a general agreement throughout the valley. The blockades and barricades are never planned, they are emotional responses to an arrest or someone falling off a pole . . . And everyone is affected, we build barricades without having discussed anything. The NoTAV people sometimes need tragedy to awaken.

– Luca, Cels

Zad – The Victory over Caesar

Even if an 'anti-airport people' on the model of the NoTAV people does not feature in the history of Notre-Dame-des-Landes, the struggle has not been exempt from episodes of crowds seized by collective emotion, or massive battles. And it is clearly the resistance to the evictions in autumn 2012 that comes to mind when considering the popular support claimed by the zad.

During the first three weeks of combat, the movement drew in the people it was lacking. The resistance tenaciously transmitted its own potential for subversion. The images and stories of the destruction of houses and vegetable gardens, of armed police and faces swollen by gas or flash balls, and of tireless barricaders, touched hearts, giving rise to a thousand spontaneous gestures designed to reinforce the movement and stop the destruction of the zone. The inhabitants of neighbouring towns helped throughout the battle. They brought tractors, construction material, litres of milk, kilos of grains, and even oysters to eat on the barricades.

There are thousands of stories of improbable help, like the guy who arrived in a BMW and stopped in the middle of the barricades. You ask yourself: 'Who is this guy?', and then he gets his chainsaw out of the trunk and says: 'What tree should I cut down to block the road?'

– Inès

During the evictions, all the usual realities were overturned. I remember one morning at the bakery where I was with two town councillors who asked me to talk with them outside. They told me: 'We want to do something to help you. We are too scared to come to the zone, but we want to do something anyway.' I thought I was dreaming because up to then the town council was very hostile to the zadists.

– Julien

In a few weeks, the zad internet site was overloaded with announcements of the spontaneous creation of more than 200 support committees across France and their multiple actions. Throughout the country, the defence of the bocage became a central political question, the focus of militant initiatives, taking up a significant portion of police time and harassing the promoters of the airport, Vinci and the Socialist Party first and foremost. The committees thus constituted the skeleton of a formidable network of material aid that nourished the zad for several months. Several houses and living spaces had been destroyed, but the occupiers and opponents were now more numerous than ever, and united in adversity as they began to rebuild.

Thrown together: from the reoccupation demonstration of 17 November 2012 to Caesar's defeat

On 17 November, the demonstrators arrived by busload (seven buses from Spain!) and the parking lots overflowed. The 440 tractors driven by farmers were stuck for a long time in Notre-Dame, overwhelmed by the more than 40,000 demonstrators. Police that day were conspicuously absent after a month of almost continuous presence.

Arriving on the site, the number of buildings under construction exceeded available material. A whole new village was springing up out of the earth, as varied as the opponents building it: a communal kitchen and meeting hall, designed by a carpenters collective close to the zone and occupiers; a dormitory, 'la Barbotine', designed, despite their administration, by architecture students from Nantes; another dormitory, baptized 'Kulon Progo' in homage to the peasant struggle in the eponymous Indonesian province against the installation of an iron mine, built by the Dijon-NDDL collective; a workshop collective called 'the Manufacture', founded by supporters from Rennes; a bathroom collective, the 'Sanitary Black Bloc', by an association from the Morbihan region.

On the Friday following 17 November, the police again attacked different parts of the zone: the Chat-Teigne was evacuated in the early hours of the morning; tear gas was fired into the dormitories; the Rosiers house, recently deemed open to eviction, was razed to the ground despite a defence by farmers and occupiers; some tree houses in the Rohanne forest, destroyed and rebuilt several times, were demolished again, sometimes endangering the life of their inhabitants.

News travelled fast and as of Friday morning hundreds of people arrived in the zone to lock horns with armed police. Farmers blocked the regional routes across the Loire. The influx of supporters grew and exploded on Saturday, with more than a thousand encircling Caesar's troops in the Rohanne forest, while a demonstration of 10,000 people confronted CRS water cannons outside the prefecture in Nantes. A varied crowd gathered around the tree cutters and their police escorts. Groups equipped with gas masks managed to hit a machine with a Molotov cocktail, while several hundred yards away people sang and danced in front of the lines of police. The resistance did not allow itself to be broken by the ferocious violence with which the forces of order intervened. During the whole period of the eviction, the numerous wounds suffered in fact incited sympathy and a growing determination on the part of opponents. A significant number of the most determined found that police violence was the source of their engagement in the struggle.

Claude: The first time we came to the zad was during Operation Caesar. I didn't like the way people were being hit on the head, so we came to lend a hand at the demo to build the Chat-Teigne.

Christine: Before, I had a colleague who tried unsuccessfully to convince me the airport was an abomination. At the time, my first reaction was to tell myself it was an individual struggle by local farmers. I was not convinced at all! Especially since we live under the airplanes of Nantes Atlantique ... And then Operation Caesar happened and Daniel Mermet did a whole week on it on [the radio station] France Inter, and that's when I started to ask myself questions ... The more questions you ask the more you are against it!

> – Christine, works in administration, participates in
> cartography of zad; Claude, works in engineering office

For the state, the objective of evacuating the zad and keeping its occupiers from coming back became politically untenable: to do so they would have to deal with the stated opposition of a whole section of the country and take on the military occupation of the zone, further increasing the level of violence.

Most of the reins of governance were broken: 'public opinion' was now largely in favour of the occupiers, repression did not provoke the hoped-for lockjaw and the law no longer assured the legitimacy of the intervention by public powers. On Saturday 24 November, Operation Caesar was interrupted and the government created the 'Dialogue Commission'.

The manoeuvre decreased the level of tension, even if most of the opponent associations refused to participate in this staging of participatory democracy. But in the agitation of those months, the life trajectories of hundreds of people were disrupted. From the new occupiers to the members of support committees, to the farmers who had spent more time that autumn on the barricades than they had on their farms, many were those who would continue some aspect of the spirit of resistance to Caesar in their own existence as well as in the heart of the movement.

Existential Upheaval

Sometimes you would see a huge guy from the social centre in Turin, six feet tall, 250 pounds, and the first thing he asks you is how those two old gentlemen from Sant'Ambrogio, 78 and 87 years old, how they helped build the baita . . . The friendship between the young, who we think are just out for a good time, and the old, who we think believe only in work, I never saw it anywhere else . . . And that is our strength after 25 years of fighting. A young person who shows up here can spend hours talking with an older person. That's the NoTAV people, the true people, solidarity between people.

– Joe Panther

It might seem paradoxical that the moments when the movements that activate the valley or the bocage can claim to be the most popular, when they attain their most massive dimension, are indissociably linked to their capacity to stir up each person at the level of their individual, almost their intimate, trajectories. Maybe it is the same mechanism at work, but on different scales, when thousands of people drop everything to come and build an opposition to the evacuation of the Chat-Teigne, as it is when an administrator whispers some strategic information into the ear of a NoTAV. It is about transgressing certain norms (moral, legal, economic) and no longer staying in one's place in the social machinery. It is a question of dignity, the meeting of profound aspirations, being fed up, and the need to take a position in the struggle. What is popular about the fights against the TAV and the airport is thus the opposite of conforming to normality, to the middle ground, that is imputed to 'the masses' – it is rather the aptitude to provoke unlinking, untimeliness. It is that aptitude that fuels the big moments of upheaval, and which also manifests itself every day in the small gestures of support, and in the way in which it becomes difficult to live 'as before' after contact with the movements. Not that they exist in order to set a course for each and every individual, but what they mean by concrete engagement can transform one day's curiosity into an implacable militancy, and alter the security of simple 'support' into full participation. And what they provoke in the way of meetings and confrontations with other ways of life cannot help but shake up the existence of those who dive in.

The week defending Rosiers in November 2012 was the occasion for long discussions about agriculture, on the manner in which the people from the occupation movement saw it and how they saw us, the farmers. The group for raising legumes collectively that got going later was born then. These were women occupiers and a few farmers from COPAIN who wanted to figure out how to produce less animal protein in favour of more vegetal protein, grown directly for human consumption.

Four years ago, if you had told me that I would get so seriously involved in that so quickly, and that today I would be growing lentils, I would never have believed it. The evictions really created the effect of an acceleration of possibilities.

– Cyril

Participating in the zad struggle is one of the things that has meant I can no longer work as a teacher. I was teaching little ones, and nearly a third of the program was 'learning to live together, build things with one another', and you notice that it's a shameful lie, that more than anything they don't want students to learn that. I can no longer tell students, in the name of the state: 'We have to live together, we have to respect difference' knowing that it is absolutely not that at all that is applied.

– Madeleine, in her 40s, Rouen support committee

I got angry with my colleagues at work during the evictions, I even stopped eating with them during the break. I sat in my office because they pissed me off. I had to be aggressive, they wouldn't understand. And yet I work in social services, these are people who, a priori, are open, but they are in their own little formatted lives and they cannot admit that there are people who want to live, and are living, differently. And besides, I could never get them to understand . . . I went part-time, I'm sick of working.

– Anne-Claude, Blain support committee

What has the struggle upended in my life? My retirement, that's what! I don't know if you realize it, but there are dozens of retired people in the area who spend about 80 percent of their time on this goddamn airport. Whether it's at the juridical commissions level, or putting dossiers together, preparing documents, participating in actions . . . Among the retirees, a good number of their retirements are being eaten up by all that!

– Genevieve, retired, representative of ATTAC

The broad and diffuse sympathy for the opposition to the airport is expressed in countless, tiny, daily gestures, in an invisible and unpredictable tissue of potential complicity, mutual recognition, shared dignity and insubordination. As a subterranean world reminiscent of an older solidarity based on class, it is not surprising it is often expressed in the workspace and professional practices, thus reactivating gestures of the workers' movement. The *perruque* (repurposing the work tool) and sabotage feed the struggle, sometimes inside the very companies or administrations in charge of building the airport.

One day, during the evictions, we go by to have a drink at the 'inhabitants who resist', and there's a guy there drinking pastis after pastis . . . he tells the story of his day: he's the truck driver who carted away the debris from the house at Coin that had just been torn down! He works for a company, it was his day to work, he's against the airport. He was in his truck, listening to Radio Klaxon, disgusted to be doing what he's doing . . . So we told him we had spent the day trying to throw rocks at his truck but were prevented by the police. Surreal . . . He had come back because he knew the people there, needed to talk, that's why he was drinking like a fish . . . can you imagine listening to Radio Klaxon while you're tearing things down . . . it's crazy! After just two drinks he had given us his boss's address, the code to get into the building, he spilled the beans on everything. It was so great.

– Ulysse, occupier

Ronan: I'm remembering the guy we called 'Father Christmas', who walked into our kitchen one time with a cake shaped like a tree and dozens of giant candles. He had driven all night from Lourdes to give it to us. We thought we were hallucinating when he unpacked the candles. He told us: 'It said pay whatever you like.'

Basile: No, it said: 'Pay according to your conscience.' So he says to us: 'It was marked "pay according to your conscience" so I paid nothing!' He had taken away 200 candles, passing by each day with his backpack.

Ronan: He's an amazing character. He finds everything, because he works in a dump and has a ton of contacts he exchanges materials with . . . As he is super attentive he brings us whatever we need: bikes, a trailer. There are lots of things he repairs for us. It's some kind of central area for a network of recycling and the circulation of objects that have dropped out of commercial exchange.

> – Ronan, former forestry teacher, occupier since
> 2012; Basile, occupier between 2012 and 2014

Christine: At work, I know very few people who like what they are doing, at least where I work, in computing. First of all, we subcontract a lot, it's always an emergency . . . Here at the zad, it's different, I have an amazing memory of a meeting of the cartography workshop . . . I had been doing map-making for thirty years. At work, in order to make a map and create a database, you have to make a list of requirements, there's a project director, procedures, 36,000 different stages, validations – it's mad. It takes hours and hours before it's finished. Here, in four hours we had done the essential. The satisfaction I feel coming here is also from a pleasure in struggle that I don't find elsewhere. For example, I never had the chance to put into practice what I know about map-making for a non-professional use.

Claude: You can't imagine the fear you create in company directors who work on the airport project: when the president of my company's name was published on the zad website he shit in his pants. His office was the only one with a coloured door; out of 50 doors, his was the only pretty red one – it was repainted in a week! . . . They are afraid of the people outside but they don't realize there could be people inside who are a threat too. I'd talked about the airport at work, and people knew where I stood, so whenever it was in the news, people would come and get me to talk about it . . . I even heard opinions from middle-managers, who are a bit lost right now, like everyone else, they don't know what they want, once, one of them said to me: 'I try to follow what's happening there closely, because in my opinion it's a laboratory for another society.' Coming from a fairly traditionalist kind of guy, it's surprising!

Christine: I think there are more people against the airport at work than you might think. They don't dare talk about it, there's some kind of omertà.

Claude: There's a 'clandestine' side to it, even to showing that you are interested in the subject.

> – Christine, works in administration, participates in
> cartography of zad; Claude, works in engineering office

As in the Susa Valley, those who are embarked in the movement against the airport can only work within the constitution of a certain community of struggle. But where NoTAV brings that community into being across the expansive territory of the valley, all the way to Turin, the zad concentrates the daily life of the struggle in a few hundred acres. Not that the community comes to an end, geographically, at the borders of the zone, but the occupation of the land has offered a rare opportunity to be able to really inhabit the struggle, and to endure within it, especially after the victory over Caesar. An Eldorado for runaways, a new world in creation behind its barricades, the zad seems available and accessible to everyone, as witnessed by the many long-term occupiers who came there thinking they would only stay a few days in the zone. And it would undoubtedly not be what it is if it were not capable of offering that terrain of experimentation, a place to change one's life profoundly and durably. The phenomenon may be brutal, even caricatured, like when one aspiring zadist shows up early one morning on a blocked road, asking at which barricade it would be best for him to leave his car, since he has decided to live there and does not need it any longer.

Living on the zad is paradoxically as much about finding refuge, a destination, as it is about finding an escape route. There again, it is often a question of work and its refusal. But whether one was destined to a future of skilled labour, or the uncertainty of the service industry or architecture, it is the absurdity of a life based on the triptych of work (alienated), family (in crisis) and leisure ('after me the deluge'), that is at stake.

The testimonies below could be called 'landing on the zad', like a return to the Earth, a *terra incognita* as fantastical as it is real. But the metaphor can also be reversed, as in the case of the occupier who, upon discovering the zad, exclaimed: 'At last! The flying saucer has landed, they've come to get me!'

I sort of remember the phone call. My friend said: 'What would you say to going and living on the zad together?' and I said: 'Well, you're really something – like I'd quit my life from one day to the next!' But I tallied up my life, and in fact my life was a project for a mobile kitchen, and so whether I were living here or there, it didn't matter much. I ended up telling him I'd call him back in a couple days, the time to think it over. And in fact I called him back fifteen minutes later: 'OK, I'll meet you in two days on the zad.'

– Shoyu

I left the shared music studio where I was, and the group of musicians I had played with for eleven years, I left my girlfriend . . . In fact, I think what I realized was working part-time in the theatre like I imagined wasn't going to be possible because it was overwhelming what you had to do to land a job like that. Already, when I was younger, I didn't really like the idea of working for a salary, with five weeks holiday a year – I never thought I could be fulfilled through work. And the experience I had in the world of work, whether in business or the public sector, was never great.

– Ludo, in his thirties, occupier

For people my age, pretty young, the zad was the first alternative experience – many considered it both their home and their school. When I got here, there was that great word 'deconstruction' on the tip of everyone's tongue – it's incomprehensible but perceptible: you arrive, you're confronted with all sorts of new things but mostly you're confronted with yourself, and you necessarily go through phases where you deconstruct what you learned before and you question the norms of the people around you.

– Charline, in her twenties, occupier since 2013

NoTAV Culture

During meals in front of the construction site, during the evenings at the *presidio* or playing bocce, the NoTAVs invent and reinvent their codes and customs into something that can be recognized as NoTAV culture. This culture has become the crucible of ritual, common references that form a language, created and maintained by a shared history of victories and hard blows, a crucible, as well, of ways of living marked in their rhythm and their tone by the struggle. The whole valley is coloured by this culture, vehicled via objects and images. There are the scissors that the seamstress pulls out of her bag to cut the security ropes cordoning off the Venaus work site, or the roar of the chainsaws that cut the trees from Seghino to Maddalena that barricade the roads, the emblems of popular revolts and their names: 'Rising Sun', 'Stalingrad'. A famous T-shirt called 'NoTAV Clarea kit' features mountaineering shoes, a wrench, a lemon, a helmet and a gas mask, as so many objects that have become symbols of the movement, reinforced by as many anecdotes that are trans-formed bit by bit into myths. Like the two hitchhikers, informing their drivers they have gas masks (whose transportation is illegal) in their bags, who are answered nonchalantly by the elderly couple: 'OK, fine, put them with ours in the trunk.' More than just a minor tale, these objects reflect both a shared savoir-faire and a common belong-ing, they are the signs and the receptacles of a popular culture, one that cannot be mistaken with a simple group subculture, but that is diffused to the point of creating a visible, audible, complex world with its songs, places, legends, festivals and forms of sociability.

The village communities were often torn apart by rivalries, and sometimes made up of people who were not speaking to each other. It's important not to have too romantic an idea of things. I knew the old villages. Of course, they aren't going to let you die alone in the street like you can in Turin, but it's not idyllic either. Social control exists in any village, but here it's differ-ent because NoTAV created something different. For example, you are driving somewhere, and someone cuts you off, instinctively, you would say: 'Fuck you!' but then you see a NoTAV bumper sticker on the rear of the car and you say to yourself, 'It's OK, drop it'. The struggle is visible in small acts like that as well. There is fraternity, you don't have stupid quar-rels with another NoTAV.

– Alberto

As a Catholic group in the valley, we decided to build a prayer pillar to signify the earth belongs to us and to the Madonna, it isn't something that can be sold, only loaned, we have to save it for others and for future gener-ations. So to convey that, we built the prayer column in five or six days. It was beautiful. And when they enlarged the work area, they took it inside.

The pillar became a meeting point, for non-believers as well, because it didn't have just a religious meaning, it was about defending the territory too.

– Mira

When we say the 'NoTAV people' we are doing politics. We are representing things, constructing a discourse that doesn't necessarily represent reality but that forces it to move forward. There is no politics that corresponds to reality. The NoTAV people is a discursive construction. This people exists in given moments, in phases. Is it there? Yes, there is a part of the population that can be summed up by that term. And then there's also the return to normality. We helped forge the representation of the NoTAV people, it corresponded to something which the people of this territory could recognize. It's full of contradictions. In the valley there are different interests, conflicts, and that's the opposite of a people, isn't it? Even if the general position is very straightforward. The people, it's a little like a fantasy that has an impact on reality.

On the other hand, the 'SiTAV people' do not exist. They never succeeded in representing that position. The mayor of Turin wanted to have a summit meeting of people in favour of the project but there were only union or Democratic Party civil servants. No one came. One day a guy wanted to create a SiAV committee in Turin and comrades wanted to spy on it, but they were told: 'There's only five people in there, if you go in you'll swell their ranks'.

The idea of the people also has to do with the way the movement was able to construct its own culture, its imaginary, its battle songs like 'A sàra düra'. We don't know who made up that slogan first, it became a slogan, a signature and song for the movement . . . The movement has its own mythic patrimony that has been deposited in the collective imaginary. It's a myth for everyone, even for those who've never set foot in the valley.

– Gianluca, radio operator at Radio Black-Out, Turin

A people against the state?

A mythic people, a people in struggle, a people to be constructed, and a people with customs, a common language, legends – here, all mixed up, is what is meant by a NoTAV people. One thing is certain, it was constructed by and through confrontation with the Italian State, seconded by the mafia and the Big BTP companies. It is a people born of the struggle, not just reinforced by it. It is clearly much more of a composite than an 'originary people', its existence is all the more affirmed because it is fragile and those who make it up cannot be completely defined by their belonging to the NoTAV people. If the NoTAVs have sovereignty of any kind to conquer, it is not the pre-existing one of a nation that has undergone colonization. And the world this people creates does not subsume the other worlds that make up the valley, of farmers, Catholics, those in the mountains, and so on. This is undoubtedly its richness, its precious and fascinating character: the inscription of revolt and openness in its very roots, and its constitution against a state whose bosom it is progressively deserting.

The closeness it feels and manifests towards people without a state – or even against a state – Kurds, Basques, Palestinians, Amerindians – is thus not so surprising. Basque and Palestinian flags have become the patrimony of the movement, which is in turn frequently talked about in the Kurd Valley. Italians travel to the Rojava mountains and a group from the upper valley conducts exchanges with Latin America.

An empty category comes into view when the question of the revolutionary goals of the NoTAV movement is raised. This people has no golden age they are marching towards, and, for this reason, it escapes populism, its own objectivation (as a people to be governed) as much as its subjectivation (as a sovereign or revolutionary subject). 'The people don't make revolution. It is born of the revolution', wrote Blanqui. Perhaps the revolutionary aspect of the NoTAV struggle should be seen in this optic: its revolution is to have created a people, without a nation, without boundaries and without making itself into a society. It is an almost *imaginary* people, whose force is very often enunciative. If this apparition is mythical then it is the return of myth, its positive possibilities, that constitutes a part of the revolutionary charge of NoTAV in a disenchanted world.

3

Composition

There are seven of them in the photo, serious and smiling. One is wearing farmer's overalls, another the famous red and yellow badge, another a salamander's mask, and his neighbour's face is hidden behind an enormous hat and sunglasses. There's a farmer threatened by the airport, an elected official from CéDpa, a member of the Coordination, a spokesperson for COPAIN, a spokesperson for ACIPA, and a male and female occupier of the zad.* What we have become accustomed to calling the components of the struggle are all present. They stand arm in arm, after showing journalists at the Vacherit on 27 February 2014 their determination to remain united in the face of the threats of evacuation. But also not without making clear their divergent points of view on the events of 22 February: some disapprove of the 'excesses', others 'understand the rage' that was expressed on the streets of Nantes and refuse to be called 'pacifists'. The COPAIN farmer concludes: 'Divergences are normal in a movement that federates so broadly.'

With the end of the paradigm of the revolutionary party, that is to say, for some time now, political struggles have something openly fractal about them. Without (or despite) the historical agent that is supposed to arrive to ensure their cohesion, that directing organ

---

* Translator's note: CéDpa stands for the Collective of Elected Officials Doubting the Pertinence of the Airport. The Coordination refers to the umbrella organization that brings together the more than fifty associations and syndicates opposing the airport.

whose task it is to make all the sensibilities conform to the same model, the political dimension of a struggle is diffracted on two levels: in the open confrontation with the enemy, but also in the need to hold together its forces, impulses and disordered aspirations while at the same time not forcing them into alignment. It is true that at first sight the two operations – opposing a government and looking for the ways to function in common despite differences – do not seem to be the same. And yet, similar questions arise: first, in both cases, one must avoid the retreat into individualist and cynical comfort that justifies renouncements or that brings an end to any possibility of collective elaboration. Then, there is the problem of hegemony and the ways of escaping it. On the one hand, the well-ensconced hegemony of economic relations and other manifestations of structural power, against which there is hardly any option except open battle. On the other, the never-really-absent temptation of a false solution to the problem of the one and the multiple, which pushes a developing strength to crush or to expel that which it cannot assimilate.

No established political force or organization is capable, either in Italy or France, of overturning by itself the TAV Lyon–Turin project or the Airport of the Great West. Not Five Stars, not the Green Party, not the Confédération paysanne or any of the other tendencies or factions among radical groups. So, a sincere and effective opposition demands taking into account a multitude of different forces, and, it must be said, in this lies one of the most beautiful successes of the two movements.

If each had counted exclusively on its own strengths and preferred dogmatism to confrontation and alliance with others, the Susa Valley today would be one more industrial and touristic valley like any other, and the fantastic adventure of the zad would never have begun. What has allowed the writing of these two stories is the inventiveness, the overturnings and brewings that accompany a broad movement in struggle, and the confrontation of sensibilities it implies.

In Notre-Dame-des-Landes, we talk about the different 'components' of the struggle: farmer, citizen, occupier components to which is sometimes added the surrounding support committees and the autonomous and anti-authoritarian militant movement in nearby cities. The term conveys well the diversity at the heart of the movement and recognizes the difficulty of making the movement speak with one voice. The same event (a demonstration, a stage in the legal situation) will thus give rise to several communiqués, each one being introduced under a common umbrella whose task it is to express the maximum points of agreement. Each component is recognized to have a certain autonomy, and it is this autonomy that allows enough leeway for multiple initiatives to be taken without the risk of being blocked (when it is not about stakes that are too important and that engage the entire movement). Above all, recognizing the existence of different poles allows forces to be constructed according to their own logics, practices, their own aspirations, for themselves but also in relationship to the others. By being the result of the back-and-forth of each component between construction for self and confrontation with others, the movement goes beyond a simple juxtaposition of each of the poles. What *composes* the components is larger than the sum of their perimeters.

In the Susa Valley, it is harder to separate out the movement into a few large political sections. Certainly there are constituted groups who participate as such – Askatasuna, anarchists, the social centre of Avigliana Spinta dal Bass, Catholics – but these are far from capable of representing the substance of NoTAV all by themselves. Its base is popular and not polarized around political tendencies, whose partisan logics and duelling schools of thought are often considered to be parasites of the struggle.

> I always compare the NoTAV movement to a big bar of soap, or, if you prefer, to a crystal ball: very fragile, very beautiful, but which must be treated carefully. I always say: 'We are so strong that no one can destroy us but ourselves.' For we are capable of destroying the struggle from the inside in the space of twenty-four hours. All it would take would be two shitty positions, insisting on two stupid positions and it would all be over.
>
> – Alberto

Hence an affirmation of the unity of the movement that is much stronger than at the zad: whether it is in practices, objectives or modes of functioning, the Valsusians tend toward forms that must be collectively embraced and shouldered under the name of NoTAV. And thus the importance in the Susa Valley of the themes of the people, the narrative, myth: it is from the way in which the movement tells the story of itself that it draws its cohesion.

Nevertheless, the story is obviously not one big homogenous totality, and what it contains of multiplicity can always be traced back to the search for a shared enunciation. When a meeting endorses certain practices in its name, it is much more a way of putting into circulation something in common – a shared determination, solidarity, imaginary – than it is an attempt to generate a generic NoTAV entity based on a unique model. The movement's famous unanimous 'We are all black bloc' response to the attempt to divide pacifist demonstrators from violent outside agitators must certainly be understood in this way: all the Valsusians did not adopt black bloc tactics during the demonstrations, but that tactic was condoned as an integral part of the movement. 'We are all black bloc' should be understood as we are all (in our diversity) NoTAV (one movement).

In the same way, the rather crude image of three or four components to the Notre-Dame-des-Landes struggle should not hide the heterogeneity at the very heart of each of the supposed camps. None is a monolithic bloc and the cracks of internal division are sometimes more pronounced than those supposed to separate each component from the others. To cite a few: the question of direct action is sharply discussed among COPAIN members, that of recuperation by political parties divides ACIPA, and the occupiers have not reached agreement on the ways to go about reaching a collective decision.

Paradoxically, what we are calling 'composition', the play between the components, is rendered possible by the play at the heart of each component, thus by that which makes it such that there are not uniform components in a strict sense of elementary unities. In this way, the links holding the movement together are not a pure marriage of reason, calculation of interests, or the result of absolute necessity: there is a whole mesh of intermediaries, bridge-builders, fugitives and translators by way of which what is common comes into being and circulates.

What is being invented in the anti-airport composition or the narrative of the NoTAV movement is a certain kind of political intelligence. How do you produce a force using that which is available to be deployed, but which goes beyond that measure? There is no recipe, and it is only through lived situations that one can find a way. It can just as much be a case of moving forward head-on (supported, of course, by one's base), as it is of putting into question one's own positions. The motivations for engaging in struggle are as various as the kinds of action, and are sometimes just as incompatible. Overthrowing capitalism, defending a landscape and countryside dear to us, preservation of agricultural land, saving trees or concern about global warming – if it is not about giving up on what one believes, the articulation of aspirations calls for real finesse in order to make them reinforce rather than neutralize each other.

Errors and failures are many, but these serve as lessons. Nothing is a given, and decades of political stultification precede us. We must learn, develop our knowledge and our savoir-faire; become acquainted with the logic, functioning, and history of allies and enemies; listen, speak, show empathy, a critical sense, the ability to take oneself lightly, or to laugh at oneself. And this apprenticeship must be shared: politics is something too complex to be left to specialists.

There is a fight to be fought here as well. Cynicism, power struggles and the settling of accounts sap a little bit more of the possibility to re-appropriate politics every day. But the zad and NoTAV teach us that in the act of holding diverse elements together, it is more a question of tact than tactics, passion than sad necessities, opening up the field rather than carving up the terrain.

It is a long process marked by as many extraordinary accelerations as it is by phases of going backwards. And yesterday's truth may become today's impasse. The so-called 'diversity of tactics' doctrine, for example, can sometimes open up situations, and other times be helpless in pushing the movement a little further along. The heir to anti-globalization counter-summits, it is the common idiom by which huge citizen assemblies could co-inhabit the many-coloured stagings by clown activists and the masked offensives of the black bloc. Results vary, according to events, from the simple failure when people quit the movement after a demonstration, to the happy composition when different groups with different political cultures take on the same challenge with good coordination and, in between these two extremes, something like a reluctantly agreed-upon mutual tolerance. But in a long-term movement, if 'diversity of tactics' can open up a space for the expression of certain unconventional practices, its limits eventually make themselves felt. They are overcome when each group, rather than huddling together over its own repertoire of actions and practices, circulate between groups. Limits are reached when we realize everyone is allied with each other in the heart of the movement and the consequences of actions do not fall only on their authors.

But this feeling of all being in the same boat that some become aware of in the course of the struggle while others participate actively in making real, is not always experienced negatively – far from it. As a community in struggle has taken on consistency in the Susa Valley as in Notre-Dame-des-Landes, many find in it a way to hold at arm's length a malediction that, if we believe the dominant imaginary, is ubiquitous. For if we allow ourselves to be taken in by the vast Hollywood frescos that stage revolt, from *Hunger Games* to *The East* with *Star Wars* in between, when it comes to community, there are only small sectarian groups on the one hand, or, on the other, unformed masses more or less loyal to a leader who is single-handedly responsible for the future of the rebellion. And in real life, the contemporary figures do not deviate from the script: the Julian Assanges and Edward Snowdens show genuine courage but we wonder what would have become of them, and the causes they champion, if they had not accepted to play the dangerous game of personification. A handful of heroes will never be a match for the hydra of digital surveillance, and we would do well to imagine more collective forms of resistance. Among the pantheon of revolutionaries, there are luckily more figures like Anonymous, whose community we hope is not limited to virtual or coded exchanges, however much security might demand it.

On the zad, occupiers who have often thrown themselves into struggle after struggle up until this point, start to project themselves there, in the zone, for years to come, and the zad farmers respond that they will build a future there together. In the Susa Valley, the NoTAVs courageously confront the threat of years in prison knowing they will always be supported, and find in the struggle a second family. The communities that have been constituted in these places are built of blood and mud, anger and joy, and the feeling of founding together the possibility of a power and an intelligence that carry hopes well beyond the bocage or the valley.

Confrontation:
NoTAV – The Opposite of One

'Never give them an inch' – this could be the motto of the movement. Resistance occurs wherever the project tries to take shape, so that it cannot get a foothold, a reality, any hope of realization. The movement searches among the heterogeneity of practices for a path on which to move forward together, having as the only guide the question often so difficult to answer: is this good for the struggle? As long as the TAV existed only as a project, it was mostly about convincing and informing. Then, from the *presidii* to the free republics, when drills and forces of law and order turned tail amidst jeers, the certitude that the TAV would never manage to be built in the valley took hold. The cementing of the movement culminated with the battles of Seghino and Venaus. But, after the expulsion of the Free Republic of the Maddalena, a small fort haunts the Susa Valley. At first ironically named the 'non-work-yard', by locals, it has, in the end, finally become one. On an illuminated sign at the Maddalena, the NoTAVs read each day the progress, in number of yards, made by the 'mole' (drill) in its inexorable advance. At first this slow progress called into question the certainties held by the movement regarding its own capacity for opposition. But patience . . . the NoTAVs continue, week after week, to go to the work-yard to protest and maintain pressure, attacking, making noise, not giving up. The common enemy seems clearly identified. But where does the TAV actually stop? At the work-yard enclosure? The machines digging it up? The police guarding it? The hotel where the police are staying? The Susa Valley?

Every Friday for four years, I go with my friend Jani, we pick up Paolo who lives near the motorway and we have 'breakfast at Titonelle's'. We doctored the title of the Audrey Hepburn movie, *Breakfast at Tiffany's*, because Paolo's wife is called Titonelle. We have breakfast there with croissants, then we come here to Giaglione. At 9.30 a.m. we meet up with my cousin and a friend. The core is always the same six people, then reinforcements arrive in the afternoon. Relatives, but also people I've met in the movement.

– Joe Panther

I go to the work-yard at least once a week, to pray. We pray to the Lord to help us but also to keep an eye on the construction. It's very important to see how far along they are, to see if the 'mole' is at work. We see dust everywhere, and surely this is bad for our health. Ideally, it's best not to get to the point of real combat because once you're at that point everyone does pretty much what they can. When they fire freezing water at you in the middle of the winter or coat you with tear gas, it's normal to throw rocks at them. I've never done it, but when they do that, I want to hurl enormous boulders at them . . . it's logical, it's human. When someone tells us: 'Separate the violent ones from the non-violent ones, because they give a bad image to a movement that's non-violent, they are harming you', we don't agree . . . we feel united even with the ones who throw rocks, because before they arrived, the media said we were a handful of mountain people, while now, they take us a little more seriously. And if you read the Gospels, the Lord never chased anyone away, he ate with the fishermen and the prostitutes.

– Mira, 77, retired nurse, member of Catholics for life of valley

Not all excursions to the work-yard are so pious. Among the members of the group 'Women of the Movement' are some of the practitioners of the oldest forms of Valsusian witchcraft:

Each of us brought a long needle and we put a doll in the middle of the circle. Each of us struck the doll and said 'cursed policeman', or 'burn in hell, you who are ruining the earth!' Everything was very scripted and we invented a phrase to repeat, you know, one of those sentences that is meaningless but resembles a magic formula. One of us said the phrase then the rest of us repeated it like a chorus. And all the police touched their dicks to keep the evil spirits away! Here, almost all the police are from the south and they're very superstitious – I'm a southerner, I should know!

– Ermelinda, 53, Bussoleno committee

This kind of daily persistence is broken up periodically by large marches where thousands come to the work-yard. These are moments of cohesion, designed to show the struggle's immense area of influence. Other demonstrations, more overtly offensive and involving fewer people take place at night and are called *passeggiate,* which is a bucolic name that nevertheless indicates the will to attack and physically harm the fort and the machines inside it. This practice happens frequently in the summer, when camping draws young people from Italy and Europe to the area.

The movement is looking for new paths to take so as to not continue to hammer away at an impenetrable fort. In 2011 and 2012, road blocks were used, and this practice is repeated at moments of high tension. But in the valley, reticence subsists regarding blockading transportation routes. Especially in the high valley, whose economy is governed by tourism, media images of the Susa Valley with blazing barricades blocking motorway tunnels do not go down well. The fact that people whose adherence to the movement is desired are also disturbed by such images points to contradictions and hesitations arising in the movement.

The sense of legitimacy is something very rooted in the average Valsusian. Antagonistic comrades and anarchists have less of a problem with that. Because, as for me, if I think there has to be a blockade, I do it, I don't have many scruples, because my ideology says: we should attack, block, and so forth. The average Valsusian, NoTAV activist, who is an honest and respectful citizen says: 'What gives me the right to do it? If there's an arrest, or an attack by the police, then yes, I feel a blockade is legitimate, or throwing rocks, or a number of other things – but without that, no.' Another thing is the legitimacy of numbers. Anarchists especially, but not only

them, don't give a damn about numbers, they'll do an action with five
people, ten, two. Valsusians, in a popular movement with lots of people,
are used to being very numerous – thirty thousand, forty thousand for the
marches, so if there's a hundred they'll say: 'Something isn't right, where
are all the others? If they aren't here, it means they don't agree, why should
I do something if I don't have the support of the presence of thousands of
others?' This sense of legitimacy is hard to define in practice, it's a combination of a sense of justice, the emotion in the moment, and the number
of people, but it is what guides many of the practices of the Valsusian
struggle.

– Luca, from Cels

Zad – Conjugated Actions

Like a high-speed train, an airport is either built or it is not. It causes
the land on which you are living to be taken off the map – or it does
not. At Notre-Dame-des-Landes, the shared determination to prevent
the project, without any half-measure imaginable, progressively
pushed the opponents to think about what they could do together.
But the strength of the anti-airport movement does not derive so
much from defining a unitary political line – an impossible goal, in
fact – as it does from the deployment of an array of different ways to
block the project. This side-by-side combat has cemented into place a
community in struggle whose backbone is made up of the farmers,
inhabitants, occupiers and militants who persist year after year and
whom the others know will not give up. At the heart of the community lies a permanent tidal movement, a back-and-forth between each
component's promotion of its traditional forms of action (counter-
expertise, direct action, non-violence and so forth) and its capacity to
create complementarity between all the forms. This plurality has the
advantage of rendering the movement as difficult to circumscribe as
it is unpredictable. It thus complicates the authorities' job of finding
an appropriate response: should they exhaust the opponents by trap-
ping them in a trumped-up game of legal appeals – 'citizen participation' – or crush them by designating them as proto-terrorists?

This plurality also favours the inclusion of people of very different ages, physical abilities, technical competences, availability for or relationships to risk-taking.

Cohabitations

In the early days of the cohabitation, at the heart of the movement of the existing components, each did its own thing: sabotage, hunger strike, non-violent action.

In 2011, there was a box where we'd put notes about the actions that were happening, so we knew what was happening, something almost every day, but without knowing where it was coming from. After the sample drilling, for example, there was a message explaining a drill had been sabotaged during the night and an explanatory message had been left for the workers at the company, along with a six-pack of beer. Not long after, I remember an ACIPA guy coming to a meeting with a newspaper article and a smile on his face: the company had decided to stop work on the project.

– Jeanne, occupier

In the beginning of 2012, we were afraid of finding ourselves in the catastrophic situation of having them make us leave in six months, and we'd have to liquidate everything and start all over from the beginning. It created a lot of anxiety . . . We were counting on the presidential debates to raise doubts about the project. But no one was listening to us. So we said to ourselves: 'We can lose this battle, but we have to lose it having done everything we possibly could', so we don't spend the next ten years saying: 'It's fucked, we could have done this or that.' What we had in mind from our political culture, what's left of the Larzac, was one card still to be played: the hunger strike. So we created a group, a kind of collective. We discussed the idea and we calibrated it to the presidential election. Being pretty naïve, we thought that after fifteen days, the strikers wouldn't be able to stand up . . . But it didn't happen that way. We lasted 28 days . . . At the end, we were very worried about Michel because his gums were hurting, and that's a sign of weakness. He had really pushed himself to the limit of what he was capable of.

What we didn't imagine, was the motivation effect, the acceleration it had on all the militants who were interpolated by the action. What we didn't imagine either was that it wasn't until people become worried about your health that they get interested. The first fifteen days, only the regional press paid attention, it was only afterwards that there was a broader interest. In the end, you only negotiate effectively when politicians think the whole thing will blow up in their faces.

At the meeting, we quickly reached the formula that everyone could agree on. The idea was that all the inhabitants who owned or rented their property before 2008 were protected from evictions for as long as legal appeals were still in process. We started with the farms, added the houses, and after a couple phone calls it worked. Our analysis was that the people in the cabins were not asking for legal status, and in any case that wasn't negotiable within that framework.

Through the hunger strike, we made a lot of noise, popularized the struggle, which broke into the national level a little. We had established a forceful presence: to have as the first act the pro-project people stuck in place or even draw back – that suited us just fine.

– Marcel, farmer at Liminbout, on zad since
1990s, member of ADECA and COPAIN

During Operation Caesar, I told myself there were actions I didn't know how to do, that I hadn't yet tried, but I would soon understand. In any case, in the situation we were in of defending a territory against the police, I could understand throwing rocks at them. But, well, one time I tried to throw a rock in the middle of a cloud of tear gas and the next second, the cloud rose up, and so did my mask because it wasn't on right, and I found myself face-to-face with the police, frozen in place, with a rock still in my hand. And I told myself again that I really didn't know how to do this. So I went and climbed to the top of a tree in the Rohanne Forest, because I knew how to do that. I had learned how to climb trees in my life. I had also learned passive resistance techniques in a weekend class. I knew how to let myself be carried like a sack by police and to fuck with them as long as possible when I got arrested.

– Jasmin, naturalist

Opposition at work sites

Just like the NoTAV movement in the mid 2000s, the fight against the airport came to a turning point in 2009, at the moment of the first advancement of the project on the land: from then on, what was being opposed became concrete, physical, and the opposition had to become the same. The spectrum of actions compatible with democratic legality got smaller. The right to oppose is, in principle, guaranteed by the Constitution, but there is always an article in the Penal Code sanctioning resistance. A large part of the citizen opposition was reluctant to extend the struggle from the halls of justice and public opinion to the fields of the zad, for diverse and often complicated reasons as much to do with morals as with strategy, as much with the fear of being exposed to repression as with projecting a bad image. On the other hand, certain camps were more prepared than others: The 'inhabitants who resist', groups of farmers faithful to the spirit of the Farmers'/Workers' coalitions of the 1970s, the early occupiers who came from the squat movement, and militants from Nantes pushed for the physical blockading of machines used to carry out the preliminary soil tests.

Lines moved, and a growing part of the movement was implicated in practices that went beyond the legal limit: in reaction to the violence used by security forces who were soon systematically accompanying workers, and thanks to new friendships that tightened relations between the different components, sometimes even without realizing it. A convinced pacifist finds herself behind a barricade, because enough is enough, and she realizes she will never again make non-violence an unbreakable principle. A spokesperson for the citizen's association refuses to condemn an act of sabotage.

When you've lived this together, you know you are thinking the same thing, you know you're going to insult the police when before you would have been too afraid to do it. The more you carry out actions like that, the easier it is to organize. In the beginning, you feel you'll never be able to. And then there is so much frustration and anger against the police! Luckily there are people a little more inured than us, who are able to stay calm and who are there to tell us to carry on, and that we'll get there. If not you'd quickly fall back into the camp of those who say there's nothing to be done. But the first encounters with repression and violence are very hard.

– Bertrand, former inhabitant of Notre-Dame-des-Landes

With the feeling of progressively becoming a common front, a collective intelligence of the relations of strength develops, shaking up the certainties and habits of the radical camps as well. Despite the fundamental critique of the media spectacle, occupiers decided to form a press group to parry the crowd of journalists that arrived every day during the evictions. Some of the press group then decided to participate intensively in the combat being played out in this minefield, and experimented with ways of intervening incisively and collectively without being locked into the role of spokesperson. Others launched into the meticulous work, long left to the associations, of organizing meetings and information evenings with the support committees.

Occupy

Support for certain forms of actions remained largely dependent on the context. Thus, in March 2012, occupiers decided, without consultation, to open up an empty house at the crossroads of Ardillières, on the exterior boundary of the zad. Their enthusiasm was quickly dampened by members of ACIPA, who, once they got wind of it, categorically refused to condone the 'attack on private property'. In their opinion, since the house was not in the zone, it was outside the framework of the struggle. After a three-day siege, the police succeeded in evicting everyone and walling off the house.

In October 2012, several days before the start of Operation Caesar, a recently abandoned house at Liminbout was opened up, but this time in a coordinated way between occupiers who prepared a theatrical entry into the building and organized a vigil, the inhabitants of the hamlet, farmers who helped block access on the day, and the associations. Occupation became a major practice of the struggle and in early 2013 farmers themselves became squatters, taking over the Bellevue farm even while police were still in the zone.

Opening up Bellevue allowed me to cross a barrier. It's a strong action in that you find yourself in a squat. I had never lived as a squatter. And for many farmers, that's a big change: 'We won't always stay within the law.' And for us that meant from then on it was easier to defend all the others who had come as squatters or occupiers.

– Michel, farmer in farmers' collective, member of COPAIN

In 2009, like many, I liked the fact that people were moving in, but I wasn't at all of the opinion occupying the terrain could change anything . . . Not at all. It took time to perceive it; for me, it wasn't until Operation Caesar that I understood a power relationship had been put into place, because there were occupiers and a movement of solidarity with the occupiers, which was making the promoters of the project back off. It was unbelievable for me, but in the end I became conscious of the fact that without the occupation it would have been all over.

– Françoise, former mayor of Bouguenais, spokesperson for CéDpa

Reaching agreement

The habit of functioning together on the terrain continued to develop in the months that followed the evictions. It was thus no longer a question of the simple well-meaning juxtaposition of different registers but rather, in certain happy moments, of a higher level of common elaboration. So when the prefecture tried to relaunch construction for the first time after the police occupation of 2012–13, this offered everyone the chance to play a part in an epic orchestra, supporting one's neighbour's role, in harmony and without need of a conductor.

We had heard they were planning new sample drillings, but things had changed a lot since before the evictions: information circulated better and we felt there were plenty of people ready to do acts they would have condemned before. A guy from ACIPA whispered to us: 'Psst, psst, I have the drilling dossiers, I can pass them to you.' We went over to his place and looked at the different drilling maps together. Before it was always a disaster, because we had no information – now we knew what was happening a week before. So we said: 'How can we stop them?' Already, we could barricade the points of entry. This is classic. But then we read that a sample drilling is illegal if it takes place next to an animal sewage area. So we said: 'Let's get the farmers in on this!' We went around to all the farms and explained we had found a loophole in the dossier that could render the drilling illegal. And if it's illegal, ACIPA had recourse to appeal. To spread the cow shit, we took a tractor and a cart full of shit, eight of us, with shovels. It was the first time in my life I drove a tractor! The farmers also helped us with the barricades . . . In any case, on that occasion, all the components of the struggle took part in sabotage by every possible, imaginable manner – holes that had been drilled elsewhere were tarred over and stopped up, other points of entry were barricaded. Their drillings were ruined. They announced they were done trying and it was the last time they tried to perform any work on the zone.

– Ulysse, cow herder, occupier since 2011

Organizing:
NoTAV – An Autonomous Movement Without Delegation?

If leaders are thrown up, it's the end of everything, because people immediately begin to shirk their responsibilities. In the movement, no one has given the role of spokesperson to anyone else. Of course, there are some who speak more than others, and sometimes it's the media that creates such figures. They can be beneficial or deleterious, because all the responsibilities, including from the criminal justice point of view, fall on just one person, which lets the others off the hook. Each person should feel not just useful, but indispensable. It's certain that everyone can't do everything, but each person should do what they can on the basis of their possibilities.

– Nicoletta

Popular struggle and representation

'If there were elections every year, the movement would be dead!' said friends in the café after the last municipal elections, at the end of which several mayors had been lost to the NoTAVs. This is because the conflicts that are generated by elections penetrate the struggle, which gets lost in the ego games of party politics. Fundamentally, today's NoTAV movement counts above all on its own strengths. And yet, without being in their service it entertains relationships with parties, unions or institutions, in a subtle game between deep-seated distrust and the pragmatic desire to gain partial victories, for which the institutional fringe sometimes provides the ultimate and decisive push. Thus the Five Star movement, led by the former comic Beppe Grillo, openly NoTAV and assuredly populist, has conquered a certain audience in the valley. Its spokesperson shows up regularly to bring support to the movement and certain NoTAVs seek out its network regularly, whether on the occasion of finding financial help for those imprisoned, or to protest police abuse before parliament. Naturally, NoTAV votes in the valley tend toward this party. If the help it provides does not give rise to any alliance nor to any reciprocity on the part of the NoTAV movement, it nevertheless raises a number of questions. For the latest declarations made by the comic on immigration (refusal of birthright citizenship to children born in Italy to foreign parents) and other worrying remarks, are not appreciated by everyone in the valley – fortunately. Certainly, the TAV has become a social fact that anyone can make into his or her battle horse, but we suspect political help without hidden motives is rare. The question must be asked of how to know when an alliance or help engages a struggle.

The independence the movement insists on may be an antidote. In this way, its healthy mistrust of power is incarnated and affirmed regularly in its refusal to give itself one or several leaders. If it is true that no structure reinforces such a role, nevertheless, leaders do exist. In practice, certain spokespeople are definitely more recognized than others. The importance of Alberto Perino, for example, is impossible to ignore. He represents 'the voice of the movement' for the press, the media, and within the movement itself. This is, of course, not free of problems, whether at a practical level – what happens if he becomes ill? – or an ethical one.

Here, there's a lot of personalization, but that's an Italian problem in general. The emergence of a leader draws a limit, because that goes against the principle of self-management and the democracy of libertarian, revolutionary – and also popular – movements. Exaggerated personalization can create problems. But we are a little bit human and a little bit Italian. The Susa Valley is also imprinted with a culture that idealizes individuals in the person of guides. If you talk with Perino, he'll tell you he isn't a leader. On the one hand, he likes being the protagonist at the centre of a lot of things, and, on the other, he is very generous because he has the time, he's retired, and does this all day long: he reads, he writes, he speaks, he makes phone calls; he's a professional unpaid NoTAV. And others, like me, like everybody, have a job, a house, problems – I can't be as present as he is. And beyond the fact of his availability, lots of people expect him to give guidance, they lean on an image of him that makes them feel secure. It's a comforting solution to expect someone to take responsibility rather than taking it yourself.

After my fall, I found myself at the forefront of the movement. I hadn't sought out that situation. I realized what was happening in the hospital, little by little. On the internet I saw my name everywhere and people said: 'Look, something's happening for the first time. There has never been such a high level of conflict in the valley and it's thanks to you.' I lived all that gradually, because I had to spend four months in the hospital in a protected situation, so I had time to think about things. When I got out, it was gradual, but I realized for many NoTAVs I had become someone important. There was a lot of affection and solidarity . . . this moment of the NoTAV struggle was lived by everybody in a very emotional way. It wasn't easy to figure out what I should do. In a way, I wanted to disappear and act like nothing happened, and in another I wanted to get my version of the facts out and thank everyone, and then contribute more to the struggle. I had many interview requests; I did a couple, one with a local paper with someone who was pretty straight, and another with a NoTAV journalist for La Repubblica, who wanted the scoop . . . At certain moments, it was useful that I was the one who said things – in other words, if it was me saying things or someone else, the perception wasn't the same. So sometimes, in that dynamic of charismatic personalities I was talking about, you have to use it. At certain times, I did press conferences or made appeals with other people, but using my image, and afterwards, the journalists would say: 'Oh, Luca said this, Luca said that.' I didn't exacerbate the level of mediatization, I wasn't interested, but without wishing for it I found myself inside its mechanism, so I tried to turn it to our advantage and play with it a bit, by testing myself to understand the possibilities of a game that's a little dangerous, but which it wouldn't have made any sense to refuse.

– Luca, from Cels

Committees, coordination and assemblies: the official organization of the movement

A formal, official and visible structure of the organization of the NoTAV struggle exists. It derives from the committees that keep the struggle alive in the villages and towns. These committees are varied: some are simply made up of the NoTAVs who live in the vicinity, others have a more political hue and have a particular idea of the struggle. All these committees are united in a coordination that is also open to people who do not belong to a particular committee. There, an initial selection is made of the different propositions for the movement to be discussed. The coordination tries to find an agreement between the most active elements in the assembly. Finally, the propositions, of which many come out of the coordination, are taken to the popular assembly, debated, and validated or not by it. These open assemblies are addressed to the whole movement. They take place in Bussoleno, four or five times a year, sometimes more, if necessary, and attract around three hundred to five hundred people. The assembly represents the NoTAV people, deciding its destiny and determining the decisions to make. Should there be a demonstration? In Susa or Turin? Peaceful or more aggressive?

It is clear not everyone in the assembly has the same aura. Some come just as spectators. The reputation and popularity of others is very important. But the chain of decision-making is clear, readable, comprehensible to everyone, even if what happens in reality sometimes differs a great deal from what was decided. It allows everyone to be informed and to reconnect with the struggle. What is more, the assembly is the occasion for the common history of the movement to be told, for a shared perception of the struggle and its progress to be elaborated. The patience and attention of the participants, sometimes sorely tested by interminable debates, attests to the importance the inhabitants of the valley give to their participation in making choices in the struggle.

> It was after Venaus that committees like ours at Susa were born, because it's important to have a presence in the territory, to make our protest happen in the different cities and villages, and we formed sixty-four committees in the valley, and surrounding valleys. Each valley had a committee, which hung flags, wrote inscriptions on the walls . . . all the little things that indicate the popular presence of NoTAV and that, today, is done much less because certain committees no longer exist. The committees in the valley have diminished, unfortunately, compared to in 2011.
>
> – Marco, 56, Susa committee

> In the coordination, there are pressure groups, people pushing one thing or another, and the best get things through. There's also some dead wood, but that's normal. For years, there's been no need to formalize the mechanisms of the way it functions, it's possible for whoever has some good ideas and wants to air them to participate. From the outside, it might look like things are always proposed by the same people, but behind that, in reality, is always a process made up of a thousand discussions, tweaking here, tweaking there.
>
> – Maurizio, 37, runs libertarian hotel, Turin

> Decisions are made at the assembly. You can tell from the applause after the interventions which ideas are most liked – sometimes we vote by raising a hand . . . A lot depends on who makes the proposition. After twenty years, you learn to know people, who to trust. I'm not bragging, but when I make a proposition, there's always a lot of applause, even though I don't speak well, I don't know Italian grammar well, and people applaud because it's a matter of trust.
>
> – Mimmo, 69, retired railroad worker

> Assemblies are above all the moment when you feel humour, fear, rage, adhesion . . . it's a thermometer. And then, in moments when it's necessary, assemblies become decisive. For example: the police arrive the day after tomorrow, what are we doing? There were very effective moments of that sort. Another

very important thing is when people manage to express their feelings, when they say, for example: 'I'm afraid.' It's very strong, very deep, you don't have that in the city, where there is often a whole pile of theoretical justifications which, in the end, cover up a feeling like that. As soon as it is expressed, we can work on it. And the movement, by the way, has worked on it. Mimmo said: 'I'm starting a group for people my age who are afraid . . . We will get together and decide what we will do together.' This has always made it possible for the struggle to be supported at different levels by many people.

– Gianluca, 38, Askatasuna, Turin

Nevertheless, the clarity of the structures and the decisive character of the assemblies does not mean there is unity in action or a strategy is applied literally. 'Here, there are neither soldiers nor generals', say the NoTAVs.

We decide on a strategy, but then we don't respect it! We always think: 'Let's do this, let's do that', and afterwards everyone does what they like and we drop the idea we had at the beginning. It's great: we have an assembly, we discuss, we have a reunion of the committees, we discuss again, and afterwards everybody does what they like! It's not the big Organization here. The main lines, sure, they are there, but afterwards it's useless to say: 'From here, we do exactly this', because it will never happen like that.

– Marisa, 71, committee of high valley, Chiomonte

That dynamic I spoke about, the charismatic characters, comes from the fact that the movement is not organized like a political organization. There's a lot of informality, and in informality things move forward by experience. Whoever wants to do something does it, organizes, says things, then there are discussions, some decisions are made collectively, but without rules or study groups. Those who are there decide, if they understand the general will. If I want to send out a communication, for example, I talk to a few people, I ask them if they agree, and then the communication is signed 'NoTAV movement'. Our way of deciding is not as great as it seems. In brief, if I want something to pass, I talk about it with three important people, I convince them, and that's it for everyone. It's not perfect. That's why we are looking for other ways, not the structures of political parties, but forms that are more democratic in the noble sense of the term, more libertarian or collective. But those forms demand a lot of engagement, time, will, precision, rigor – they demand qualities not everyone has, or doesn't have all the time, or doesn't have together.

– Luca

Zad – Becoming Organized: Groups, Movement and Assemblies

If there is one lesson to be drawn from Notre-Dame-des-Landes, in terms of a trade union or political moral, it's the way that such different movements could coast along side by side and advance together over such a long period, even in a chaotic manner. If you want to imagine a strong social movement, you have to move in this direction. There's also the fact that there is no big charismatic leader here. We couldn't do that.

– Marcel, farmer on the zad

Spaces of organization at first separate, and the bridges between

Until 2012, each component of the movement functioned separately. ACIPA, the driving association, with its decision-making office and its spokes-people, supported the coordination of the representatives of more than fifty political, trade union, and social organizations opposed to the airport. The occupiers had their weekly meeting and the proclaimed intention of organizing by consensus and without hierarchy. Even if the inhabitants of the different cabins and occupied houses did not all participate assiduously, these reunions contributed at the time to creating a community in the heart of the occupation movement. Along with the formal spaces of organization, the reunions of the 'inhabitants who resist' were at that time a kind of outlet, at once joyously chaotic and capable of making decisions.

The period of the evictions forced the establishment of common spaces of organization. For several months, large assemblies took place to prepare for the demonstration of reoccupation in the early weeks and to continue to coordinate on the land afterwards. The thrust of the movement forced us at last to start thinking together as a movement. During the military occupation, 'historic' opponents and more recently arrived occupiers had experienced their solidarity as much as their interdependence and realized they could no longer go back to simply cohabiting. And thus was born the ritual of the hybrid and open assembly. Once or twice a month, dozens of people, or hundreds during the periods of acceleration, met in a circle after milking time, in the barn shed at the Vacherit. What persists in these General Assemblies, is an open space where information is transmitted, strategic visions are shared, or certain broad common actions are elaborated. Conflicts and possible convergences – as much ideological as practical – on the uses of the land and the relationships with neighbours, are also laid out. The General Assemblies are a means of interface, as well, with more irregular participants, who show up from a local committee or one on the other side of the country, who want to take the temperature of the movement or connect it to their own struggles. In the middle of winter, laughter or ranting warms people up and keeps them going. In the moments of crisis that periodically punctuate the struggle, the space is full and the air is charged with electricity.

I'm glad to see the movement assemblies the way they exist now, because I am aware of how hard it is to bring together all these people, with different cultural relations, to speak. It's a real success to reunite every month for two years the members of ACIPA, occupiers, farmers, people from the area, in a framework where everyone knows that they won't understand everything about the other people, that there's a risk of having one's convictions or usual ways of discussing shaken up, but that it's worth it to put yourself in that situation. I think it's mostly tied to the fact that people have gotten to know each other, and to the way the period of the evictions renewed the vision that each group had of the others. There is a real recognition these assemblies are indispensable moments for the construction of the movement . . . For me, what we've discovered is the capacity, in the same assembly, of moving from a more structured mode to more spontaneous expressions with a certain toler-ance on the part of people who, before, would have given up on the whole thing once it deviated from their habitual mode of proceeding.

– Jasmin

The question of meetings has a particular importance, both because they are crucial for being able to find common ground, but also because a major part of the occupation movement holds to the principle that each person find a place in the decision-making process. Disparities over who gets to speak, especially gendered ones, and the attitude to or level of language-use are viewed as so many indications of relations to power. Structures are thus proposed in certain assemblies to regulate speech: moderation (to watch for how long and how frequently some-one speaks, to ensure the rhythm of the discussion or that the decision made is clear to everyone), taking turns speaking, silent hand signals to show approval or disapproval. Such a process, which aims at facilitating the most horizontal functioning possible, obviously creates tension with the more vertical practices of the associations involved in fighting the airport which answer to decisions in their office or in court. But they also have to contend with the role played by the 'big mouths' who prevail in certain meetings of farmers and occupiers and also in the heat of action. This formal structure is also criticized, including by some of the occupiers, for being too neutralizing to allow the necessar-ily emotional and tense aspects of politics to emerge, and also for excluding those who can't master the codes. As time goes by, the sought-after equilibrium assures the ability to listen, which helps allow multi-ple and otherwise silent voices to be heard in the meetings, while at the same time allowing bursts of enthusiasm to be expressed.

The fact that there are many people on the zad who for a long time have been preoccupied by questions of hierarchy, including informal or hidden hierarchy, really struck me. What it did was make me feel, little by little, like I had a right to speak, and even to be pushy about it if necessary. I was able to get beyond the doubts I had about whether what I had to say was interesting, or about my capacity to express it. I know that even if my French isn't perfect, there are comrades here who will support me. Especially since for some people in the movement, it wasn't completely natural to stand up and say something.

– Tila, non-francophone occupier

In the zad assemblies I participated in, even if at times they could be tense, that's normal, I found there was a degree of attention one doesn't find in union meetings. And besides, the unions and syndicates are making a huge effort now to find inspiration in these kinds of assemblies. It sort of works, but I don't feel the same kind of listening. There's a habit that develops in hierarchical functions, that of being a consumer. And then I also think that on the zad, people know why they are meeting and that changes the tonality of the discussions. It's very concrete: cultivating, building – all this gives meaning.

– Christine

Despite the importance of the monthly assemblies at the Vacherit, one of the characteristic, most pronounced traits of the movement remains the absence – seemingly ineluctable – of a unique space for decision-making. Neither the democratic imaginary – which supposes the possibility of making all the decisions taken by the majority be accepted – nor that of the search for consensus as an ideal are suited to the task. The resolutions of the General Assembly are always susceptible to being questioned by those who do not recognize its legitimacy – which no morality or police guarantees – and the partisans of unanimity are forced to admit that hours of discussion, despite all the well-meaning attitudes and mutual listening possible, do not dissolve all kinds of differences.

Sometimes the General Assemblies exhaust me. The last one I went to, six months ago, I said to myself: 'Never again'. It was when we were talking about whether or not to keep the obstacles on the road. Until midnight! It's my . . . I guess it's my old-fashioned side, undoubtedly, but in the end I said to myself: 'We can't agree, we have to vote, so that there's a majority.' On the zad, the search for consensus makes me laugh, because it's a real question: Is it possible to regulate everything through consensus?

– Françoise

It's not that I thought the assemblies were meaningless, it's more that they were aggravating, ponderous, long. Some of us attended from time to time to organize, or to get a sense of the atmosphere, but some others I live with were frankly opposed to the whole thing. And besides, you could always ask the people who went for a report, or read the accounts in [the newspaper] *Zad News*. In any case, there are other ways besides the assemblies to take the temperature. Going to visit people, talking with them in their space. For example, at one point, around the evictions, the argument was over whether to continue to barricade certain roads and paths. There was real tension, but often, the thing that brought a solution wasn't the assembly but rather sitting around on the barricades talking and arguing . . . we got beyond it.

– Lucien, occupier who arrived during evictions

The organization dynamic on the zad relies on a set of information and exchange tools, in crisis moments and on a daily basis. *Zad News,* a newspaper internal to the zone, is distributed to the sixty living spaces. Radio Klaxon, a pirated broadcast, is brought back regularly at the moment of actions or events. External communication, with the administration of the website that emerged from the occupation movement, *zad.nadir.org,* takes care of diffusing information to the local committees and the tumultuous links with the official media. Internal communications take care of maintaining and distributing walkie-talkies and emergency telephones, and establish codes in case of attack. Meeting spaces are organized according to activities, like the 'sow your zad' assembly on agricultural issues, or by situation, like the weekly meeting of the inhabitants. These spaces develop their own strategic choices and make decisions concerning themselves that are not systematically taken up by the assemblies. Thematic discussions, such as the primordial problem of the land and how to prepare the after-airport, are developed as well in spaces parallel to the assemblies.

At the heart of COPAIN, there's a group of friends, a group of fifteen farmers, all guys, no women, which is a bit worrying. The struggle brought us together. The group is not really defined as such, but in fact it's really the gang who got together every Friday to have lunch with the occupiers at Bellevue, and who then organized a tractor brigade to the courthouse for the trial of people accused of sabotage against the agribusiness farm in Amiens, the group who also went by convoy to Brest to get the hangar despite the prefectural interdiction. These friendships were created, and it's this that makes the real strength of COPAIN today.

– Cyril

The movement assemblies and other meeting spaces are necessary, but they don't really allow ideas to take on any real substance. I really wanted a durable group with whom I could think the struggle in its globality and its continuity without having to reform the group for each new action. Because strategy can't be thought in an instant – it's thought over months, even years . . . In this group, we don't always have the same political visions, we live in different places and we don't hang around the same people from day to day, but we share the same excitement about thinking strategy and plotting over a drink late into the night. Unfortunately, I find that there are not enough such groups on the zad who have that sort of ambition, and that can be a source of tension as well. What I'd love to see is more and more of that type of group.

– Justin

The fact remains, if no one can claim to hold the reins of the movement, neither have its different entities really, for all that, merged into one. ACIPA and the collective of elected officials continue to organize on their side to do battle on the terrain of legal appeals and set up workshops of citizen expertise to derail the airport project. The occupiers maintain their Thursday meetings and intensify the occupation of the territories, the support committees gather according to geographic proximity to launch initiatives of their own, and the COPAIN farmers coordinate surprise blockade actions throughout the region according to their own decision-making spaces and networks. This multi-polarity is not without difficulties when a decision needs to be undone in the General Assembly, since each group has to take an account back and await validation from its structure.

Organization on a scale this big and lasting so long is, in any case, a fairly unknown experience in France these last years – even decades

– and can only find its agencies and ways of functioning along the way. Apprenticeship is key, and the movement looks for inspiration to more or less nearby realities: collective spaces of long duration like the Longo Mai cooperative, the self-managed Tanneries in Dijon, the Kabe in Spain, the plateau of the Larzac.* But it's important to remember a struggle like the one in the Larzac was based on a clear understanding: the farmers of the plateau were the group leading the movement. At Notre-Dame-des-Landes the absence of such a spearhead has undoubtedly contributed to dissolving boundaries between groups and identities by forcing everyone to move out of their little corner and into the process of composition.

---

* Translator's note: Longo Mai, founded in Switzerland in 1973, is a network of anti-capitalist agricultural cooperatives throughout Europe and Central America. The self-managed tanneries in Dijon are a political and cultural center that evolved out of a squat that began in 1998. The Kabe is an autonomous rural community in Spain.

4

Territories

Territorial Struggles

It is certainly no accident the Susa Valley and the zad are so close, geographically, to metropolises like Turin and Nantes, cities reconfigured to be used by the *smart people* of the young creative class. Perhaps the valley and the zad symbolize a remainder that cannot be integrated, a remainder relegated (voluntarily!) to insufficiently lucrative spaces, but which are now designated to be opened up to the traffic of the merchandise-bodies that haunt airplanes and high-speed trains. It is more likely the proximity can be explained by the infrastructural necessity of transportation on the outskirts of these reconverted cities. For these cities, too, are involved in a 'territorial struggle', that is to say, in the artificial competition between territories, between metropolises that are now all, more or less, boasting of a new high-tech capacity. Consider the sign at the entry to an old worker's city once dominated by a now-forgotten porcelain industry: 'Limoges-Metropolis, world capital of the Arts of Fire'. Or the ridiculous moment when Pau, Tarbes and Lourdes united to create 'Pyrénées-Metropolis', on the basis that these mid-sized localities might 'share their handicaps and unite to invest together'.

More than an empty brand, it is sometimes a real remaking of space that is being undertaken under the aegis of territorial marketing. In this context, the term 'metropolis' should not be mistaken to mean a big city; it designates, rather, a worldwide fabric in which one tries to integrate more and more parcels of territory (including the countryside). Its meaning is thus much closer to the one that is the opposite of 'the overseas territories', at the time when the metropolis referred to that part of the state at the origin of colonization; except that today, this does not so much refer to a real space, as it does to a diffuse will to assimilate the maximum of spaces into the flux of marketing and trade. In this way, Saint-Nazaire is supposed to become the western pole, with the estuary of 'Nantes-Metropolis', the airport and the network of roads feeding it, constituting the missing link to that very arty perspective inaugurated by Buren's *Les Anneaux*.[*] Developers in the Susa Valley harbour the same ambitions: the valley is pure emptiness, a pure axis, and its population has now been rendered a pure enemy. Because, guess what? It is in the way. And it is in the way, precisely, where all should flow freely. The flux of the well-connected, the networked, and the developers stumbles up against what it perceives to be the rear-guard of the *process* of civilization, those mules who 'refuse change'. And these latter oppose valourization through destruction by using a network, a mesh or fabric of an entirely different order than the one that links connected capitals together. Two warring trades are weaving their strands. For this could very well be a question of texture: spun wool versus Gore-Tex, linen versus 'technical' fibres. The proclaimed goal of the new synthetic cloth is to prevent perspiration, the importance being, finally, that we smell good inside it, that we become synthetic in our turn, that we lose that which makes of us something of an animal: our odour. Without taste, without smell, *clusters* find *cysts* in their path, cysts who understand 'smart' in its original sense: as 'the sting of a whip or an insult'.

---

* Translator's note: *Les Anneaux* is a sculpture by Daniel Buren and Patrick Bouchain on the Ile de Nantes. Eighteen iron circles, each of a diameter of four metres, are lit up at night to symbolize the irons that bound slaves. (Nantes was the center of the French slave trade.) From the perspective of the Mauvaise Troupe, such a work is above all the sign of a political will to replace or cover over the Nantian memory of its slaving history with the new lucrative market in contemporary art.

Getting Lost

To understand what is being experienced in these stubborn territories, one must accept to get lost. Losing one's bearings, throwing oneself into the unknown and throwing out all the maps is a luxury normally unavailable to us these days. The 'lost territories of the Republic' are not lost for everyone.* It takes time, one hesitates and looks around, breathlessly, for a sign, something reassuring, something recognizable.

> One thing that shocked me on the zad, was that people built their dwelling places often right next to the road. Fear of grass, they call it. The fear of leaving asphalt behind. As if it were reassuring.

The simple gesture of erasing the names on a sign tells us also of the refusal of the world of indication. To get your bearings here, you have to merge with a geography of the senses, a lived geography. The first time you look at a map of the zad, hesitating between two paths, with the projection of the runways and the skeleton of the airport, you understand better the expression 'operational or military map'. You are reminded of those African countries with their borders drawn in a straight line by a distant hand to engineer submission. And yet, inside those segments, something emerges, a group of cabins, a tangle of pathways offering unorthodox choices for travelling from one point to another.

> For several months, I no longer used the roads. I only walked through the fields or in the woods, so as to not run into the police. I had a particular itinerary for getting to other places, for visiting friends. And I continued to use it even when the risk was over, even if it takes longer. There are dozens of small improbable paths that snake their way through here.

---

* Translator's note: The phrase refers to the title of a collective volume published in 2002, much touted by right-wing political figures and pundits, that treated anti-semitism and sexism among young French of Arab origin. By embracing the status of a 'lost republic', the Mauvaise Troupe, among other things, signals solidarity with the banlieue and other zones on the margin of French Republicanism.

The design for the airport project remains, subverted, and today serves to outline a space of swarming activity that mocks the photomontages of an 'organic' airport. The sketch opens up and the zone becomes inhabitable. A crease is formed in the map. The destinations for the visitor here are much more bewildering and unfamiliar – in the full sense of the term – than the names of the capital cities illuminated on airport signs around the world. One travels as if underneath. 'My cabin is at the end of the runway', they told us.

> We went through the valley in 2010, not really accidentally, but a bit by chance anyway. We saw the NoTAV flags everywhere, but we were lost, we didn't know where to find someone who would talk to us about the struggle. I said: 'I'll go to the tourism office', a bit of bravado on my part. In bad Italian I asked the woman behind the counter for a map of the valley, then, finally, not holding back any longer: 'Can we meet with the NoTAV movement?' She smiled, complicit, and handed me a map on which she had added several points with a pen: the *presidii*.

In the NoTAV valley, everything has changed. For now, something other than economy determines its geography. The capitals of the struggle might be a café, a crossroads where a battle was won, a tree that designates a meeting place called 'The Scream', because of the way its bark has hardened, recalling the painting by Edvard Munch, or simply a container near a motorway. Susa, Avigliana and Sestriere no longer play any role in this. And to get your bearings, you need to know, or to have been told all this – a sign is not enough. It takes time to stop getting lost, for there is a whole history there that has formed its particular polarities, there is a whole world. We need something beneath or beyond the map, we need legends, stories, and people to tell them. With just what the map lays out, we can see nothing of the force that has emerged in these places – we need the others. Geography and history are indissociable, not in the way the French school system tried to tell us about geopolitics and borders, but because the one is imbricated in the other, they both participate in one and the same thing: the lived territory. So if we were uneasy looking around when we first got there, searching for signs we could not see, we were sad when leaving, to return to those of the 'exterior' who are silent when it comes to conveying our worlds.

It is thus because we found ourselves – together – that the need to lose ourselves as individuals presents itself. The force of these two territories resides in its capacity to enrapture – that is, to take us out of ourselves by throwing us into the world that has become manifest there. Maybe this is why it is customary at the zad to abandon one's old first name in favour of one chosen on arrival, as much to become more unreadable to police operations as because a new life has begun. Identities flap in the wind of the community that circulates in these places. So much so that one no longer knows very well how 'to adjust to normal life'. It has become too narrow. To create a world is thus not something to be done lightly, since it is a question of finding enormous strength in belonging to what surrounds you.

Naming, Shaping

One only fights for causes one shapes oneself and with which one identifies, aflame.

– René Char

There are two ways of naming: the first indicates domination, while the second inscribes in the space and discourse a part of what is living there. The state names the world the way we name a dog: and in so doing looks to become its master. Walking down the Avenue Adolphe Thiers, one feels the weight of the leash. That toponymy might be political is not news: the history it narrates is often one of victories, and thus of crushing defeats, in the image of those saints' names given to villages in order to wipe out any lurking paganism. And yet in our own time there has been a marked acceleration in this domain. Cities and villages are erased in favour of 'agglomerations' whose homonymy speaks volumes about the life they want to propagate there. Territories are obliged to find their brand and logo, in the midst of the vast semantic reworking transforming everything into an obscene shop window. A name belongs to everyone, while a brand belongs to an owner, and its use is regulated by a price. And it is certainly not the inhabitants who choose it or who have the right to use it. That portion of the discourse does not belong to them any longer, and this is how the redefinition of places transpires: you no longer live in this valley but in the 'Natura 2000' zone that contains a heavy density of biodiversity; you no longer live in a city with its particular history but in an 'employment basin of valourized human competence in a zone of high-level consumption', in short, 'a strategic economic territory'. Everything is homogenized, covered over by descriptions that seem meaningless in certain respects, but not at all in their aim. Like a repeated order, attractiveness is the new slogan in this nauseating *logos*. In the end, we are shamelessly beckoned to live in places the way corporations fish for clients. And the new names are repeated so often we end up saying them too, without meaning to: National Park, UNESCO Zone, Immaterial Patrimony of Humanity, Capital of Culture . . . 'Language creates a reality. The swamps, bogs, mountain streams and ponds exist, and all the plants and small animals that live there. A wetland does not exist.'* This is how our history and the particularity of our way of living in these places, erased from language, escapes us. No doubt then, as the Minister of the Interior (and not the Ecology Minister, who oversees development) states: 'the metropolis is a new tool of governance.'

On the other hand, in the zad we walk along the Field of Discord, then we spot The Tower, the Cunning Bison, the Angry llama, Black Ditches and the True Reds, 100 Names and No Name . . . Like a palimpsest, the new names cover over the former ones, but there is transparency and nothing is erased – there is even an echo: another history, rapid, effervescent, has been superimposed on top. It is thus the war between the interlacing of stories, experiences and alliances, and a simple name for today: the Airport of the Greater West.

See, over there, that cabin is Le Gourbi, 'The Shack', but not because it's disgusting or a wreck. Before the evictions, there was a house there, the cabin was built on its ruins if you can say that, because they even carried

---

*   Victoria Xardel, *Sivens sans retenue* (Paris: La lenteur, 2014), p. 84.

away everything that was left after the demolition. An empty lot was what was left, it was impossible to guess that there had once been a house there and that people had made a life there. It was erased. A man was there, looking at the emptiness that had been his home. Mr Gourbit.

In a time-honoured gesture, we give names to liberated territories, names that retell history in the present. As opposed to much of the habitual toponymy, which requires erudite books and extensive archives to determine the reference to a given name, here, the reference is still alive, spoken, changing according to those who say it.

Our barricade was called *L'Ultima spiaggia*, 'the last beach', it was the last rampart against the police in the row of barricades on the road to Venaus. It was a joke between us, it referred to an old apocalyptic movie where the last humans are on a beach and hoping they aren't the last people alive on earth. We were thinking about that final image: the world has become contaminated, there are no survivors and on the beach a rag washes up: 'There is still time . . . my brother.'

There are also two ways to 'manage' contained in that word's etymology: to administer and to take care of. The battle over the shaping of the world has not stopped provoking outrage. For some, it is homogenizing the world so as to allow troops and merchandise (whether human or objects) to circulate. For others, it is being anchored in a place, building it without knowing anymore where it ends and where you begin. 'The *presidio* is the sky, it's us, and the *presidi* will disappear if our desire to continue fighting disappears.' For some, it is about denying one's geography, piercing a gaping hole in the mountains, or leaping over the oceans 'to go faster'. For others, it is 'to make with', and not 'to build despite', but to gain in depth and thickness.

Because of a chance GPS screw-up, drivers sometimes get lost on the outskirts of Notre-Dame-des-Landes and find themselves facing the 'obstacle course'. What opens up before their eyes is a road crossed by semi-barricades, some of them inhabited, and plants taking over the asphalt with a rapidity that fills us with the future. An improbable tower stands, made of a cistern and wood, spanning between the asphalt and the ditch. Rare are the places one can shape according to one's pleasure. Imagination remains just that, you have 'dreams', looking at your environment. In that landscape, so many viaducts, but few real bridges.

To bring life back to its conditions, that is what is being built on these territories. And its conditions are both material and spiritual, like love and cool water. Only then is the separation between us and the world, between what we are doing there and its aspect exhausted, and we can at last become attached. To build a house in the image of the way you want to live in it has a speculative power: what we will live there will have a reflection of our house. Outside the norms, outside the mould, outside Mikit. Thus the *presidii* of the Susa Valley and the cabins of Notre-Dame are made of dreams, for our use.

To Inhabit

We live here, and that's not a small thing to say. To live somewhere is not to be a lodger. A lodging, in the end, is nothing but a casing, in which one 'lodges' someone willingly or by force after his workday ends and he awaits the next one. It's a cage whose walls are unfamiliar to us. To inhabit is something different. It's an interlacing of ties. It's belonging to places as much as they belong to us. It is not being indifferent to the things that surround us, but being attached to them: to the people, the ambiances, the fields, the hedges, the woods, the houses, the plant that sprouts again and again in the same spot, the animal that shows up in the same area. It's to be taken, powerfully, by our spaces. It's the opposite of the nightmares of the metropolis where one only passes through. To live here is to no longer be able to imagine that it could all disappear: because all that is what makes up our lives.

– Extract from collective text by zad inhabitants

To inhabit has thus become a political gesture, and one that finds itself confronting the diffuse offensive of a technological government. The latter coils up in infrastructures, which can be perceived as invaders designed to rid places of that which lives there, of those who live there. As the colonized knew well, 'a work zone merits a battle'.* In this regard, the Valsusians do not fear seeing the high-speed TAV train go by one day as much as they fear undergoing endless construction horrors for twenty years. These will be denied in any case – this has become a strategy that urbanists fully embrace: 'We have left behind the old formalist, modern ideas about space, for more operational ones, like that of constructing in a void.' The inhabitants threatened by these infrastructures are not mistaken: 'We can no longer live at home; the noise is unbearable. They put windmills up only five hundred yards from the houses, but they haven't told us where they are counting on putting the people', said a woman whose region could soon be completely invaded by wind turbines.

To vacate the place, a 'milieu prospective' must be produced first, which is the same as saying the perception we have of that space must be profoundly modified by breaking the ties that attach us to it and then recoding the space. And the recoding works perfectly with the whims of 'ecologists' and their management of the living:

> It's crazy how it can be crushing, terrifying, the vision of a green peaceful world. I heard Danny the Green [Daniel Cohn-Bendit] on the radio, and just when he was claiming to defend the zad, he missed the essential. He defended it as an empty space, like a pure piece of uninhabited nature, and he proposed to fill that emptiness, in buildings built according to code, with the immigrants from the 'jungle' at Calais. In a cybernetic dream, tear people away from their destinations, like they transport endangered species from one pond to another.

Biopolitics claims to pilot the whole of the living, by reducing it to measurable quantities. Thus, compensation payments to Notre-Dame-des-Landes established an equivalence between a frog and a bird, by weighing them on sordid scales where finally everything can *have value* because life itself has been exchanged for value.

---

* Phrase attributed to Maréchal Lyautey, 'pacifier' of Morocco.

Their nature is economic. Everything is interchangeable, exchange-able – as though a salamander had nothing to do with the territory in which it lives, as if it could be transported somewhere else with-out consequences. For attachment has not yet been given a value. That is why it must be broken. This is what the expression 'accept-ability of projects' means. It is certainly not about making them acceptable, it is working to get the inhabitants to the point when they will accept anything. To do this there are methods, some more vile than others, that all have in common their dependence on breaking. Between the past and the present, by museum-ifying the first in order to void the second, between the living and the world by separating objects from their usages, by separating people. By creating a milieu, a biotope, an environment, on the one hand, and a population (animal or human) on the other. But not everything can be extirpated, and the territories of the struggle have acquired a manner of inhabiting that is indissociable from defending the territory. Confronting the government of the living, they have become ungovernable.

> On the wooden planks, animals are lying, observing, awaiting their moment, their trip to the city on a certain 22 February. It's dark, but the birds and the amphibians can be seen distinctly. A man approaches, his hands stained with paint. He tells us he's here for a few days, in order to explain the technique for making masks. Since then, his fingers have given birth to a small army, he can no longer stop working. He's no longer planning on leaving. I ask him why there are so many salamanders among his creations. 'There are a lot of them around here, but that's not the reason. Salamanders are us. We bathe in fire and we die if it goes out.'

The zad and the Susa Valley experience each day that lack of distinction between inhabiting a territory and defending it. One thing does change over time, however: what one is defending. If, at the beginning, it might be an environment or a farmland, to the extent that one fights, one begins inhabiting it each day a little more and these initial terms break down. One also defends what one has created there, what one has lived through while defending it. The initial urge to preserve adorns everything that the defence of the places has caused to emerge, the new life that was sketched there, and that has taken on form and depth. To safeguard the living and to revolutionize ways of life are not two opposite axes; on the contrary, their reunion uncovers more ancient attachments in the spaces, no longer defended as frozen or unchanging, but as crucibles of a memory that is being reanimated, if it was ever faded. The *communaux* are being reborn within the hedges of the zad, inspiring all those who dream of the Commune. The stories of heretics and the Vaudois are recounted in the Susa Valley, as are those of the partisan republics who seceded from the Italian state in 1943. We were taught – because it is useful to them – to have contempt for tradition, to see it as a waxened headdress gathering dust, so as to distance us from its real symbolic charge.

> The Maddalena work zone is not only destroying today's resources, it's also destroying history, the past. And all for a future that doesn't exist. They live in an eternal present; they don't even have an image of the future. We want to defend and conserve those elements, but not by freezing them. "Tradition" comes from the Latin tradere, which means to carry, to transport. It isn't fixed for all time, it's a rediscovery, it's defending oneself with a vision of the future.

In one and the same movement, the state is preserved in the power of myths, legends and histories that are reactivated during the most intense situations. It folklorizes them, separates them from the present, from places, to enclose them in a language that knows nothing other than the past, *the has been*. Whether it is the folklore of battles, or that of the memory of our places, their power remains contained, suspended, provisional. For it is well known that destroying and keeping under wraps are one and the same gesture – natural parks taught us that – and these two 'territorial struggles' have reawakened the dead they refused to mourn. The movements have discovered what 'populate' means.

Seceding

The NoTAVs and the inhabitants of the zad have forged two different ways of inhabiting their territories. The latter have cut their ties with institutions, establishing a 'lawless zone' that gives them the leisure of experimenting with new existences. The former, on the other hand, have designed another form of secession, less dramatic to non-accustomed eyes. They have juxtaposed to the Susa Valley a valley in struggle, the one not excluding the other, but modifying it in such a profound manner that the Susa Valley will never be what it was before the NoTAV movement. Their revolution resembles a qualitative leap into the ethical element. Their war is diffuse and secret.

> We came to look at the work yard for the first time, we snuck through the woods and walked down the streets toward its famous iron gates. There were all the cops and army guys, hanging around off-duty at the end of an autumn afternoon. It's at that moment that the bus arrived. It had all sorts of trouble getting in because it's so narrow, and thirty people got out quickly. In front of the gate they began to shout insults at the carabinieri, they didn't stop. Where did these people come from in their tourist bus? 'They are Valsusians who are returning from an organized seaside voyage, and before getting back to their houses, they come by to scream their rage', Maria told us matter-of-factly.

Each in its own style, these spaces have given rise to the unpardonable idea of a secession, sometimes defended by barricades, as the zad is, or as the free Republics of Venaus and Maddalena were, sometimes by modifying daily life in a less ostentatious way. In both cases, a strength has been born that renders its inhabitants more and more uncompromising. And it is thus without compromise that they must be subdued. For the secession has not passed unnoticed by those who govern, who are determined to treat these spaces as they do the ghetto suburbs, or any other territory that has been 'lost', as one says of a girl that she has been lost – that is, that she has betrayed morals and authority. But power wanted so much to become material, to be one with the flows, to make itself *real* in that way that it became attackable through those very flows. The idea of 'blocking the flows' that movements beginning in the early 2000s came up with (especially the movement opposing retirement reforms in 2010), seems to have found a way to be fully lived inside these cysts that have broken through the smooth continuity of the present. To make oneself ungovernable is paradoxically to become engaged, and that engagement has been given to us by these very *real* infrastructural projects.

Whether by chance or not, in the past few years, it is in the hollow of the mountains or in a bocage that has never been rezoned and repurposed that the challenge was taken up most strongly. These spaces had the capacity to bring to life the idea of a livable secession whose imaginary, today, the cities seem to refuse, divided up as they are under regimes of control, surveillance and counter-insurrectional urbanism. Could the dark corners and secret zones of our era, more and more eradicated in the big city centres, be lying nestled instead in the thickets and the foliage? Here we find both a scale according to which we can think the common and the sign of a life lived closer to the means of subsistence from which we have been dispossessed. These places are also the symbolic crucible for a certain idea of nature, susceptible to arousing the desire – be it romantic – to defend it. At a time when 'ecological preoccupations' are being proclaimed by governments, that serve as a pretext for an increased control of the population, such a determination to 'save nature' from being paved over has the air of a goal that the system recognizes as subversive. For in the face of the disaster, some of us are acting in a different way than just waiting patiently for its governmental management at the umpteenth COP meeting. And, by this act, we are moving to reduce the distinction, inherited from modern thought, between nature and us. Inversely, those who only see in nature a landscape or a work tool discover little by little to what point they can, from that moment on, be part of it, by leaving behind the perch of the observer or the exploiter. And in so doing, in a paradox that is not only rhetorical, seceding becomes seceding from a world of separation.

The Commune was the greatest festival of the nineteenth century. One has the impression, in the end, of the insurgents becoming the masters of their own history, not so much at the level of 'governmental' political decision, as at the level of daily life in the spring of 1871. It's also in this way that Marx should be understood when he says: 'The greatest social measure of the Commune was its own working existence.'

The histories being written at the zad or in the Susa Valley are not only those of two territorial struggles similar to others that may or may not exist. They are a form of struggle and a form of life at once unheard of and irremediably linked to a past that has refound its strength. Their existence even makes the facetious real; this best-of-all-possible eternal presents constitutes our décor and our horizon which vacillate and waver. Resolutely at war with the actual state of things, they are the perspective and, above all, the realization of other worlds – something thus far lacking in the different movements that have adorned this young century.

Between Mountains and Metropolis: Defending the Territory

When one takes on the task of defending his territory, one's perception will become strategic: where can the police's arrival, or the path of the drills, be blocked? Where are the bridges, what are the paths that allow you to get to this place in secret, how do you avoid that police barracks? In which part of the forest should we hide and by what hedge? Where is the place with the best view to put lookouts? What are the most sensitive of the infrastructures? The angle could almost be called military, if it weren't for the fact that the army being deployed is not an invading army but one that already lives here and is counting on staying. And yet everything is transformed: the motorway, no longer the fast way to get to Turin, has become both an invasive entity and a strategic place to block such an invasion; such and such an embankment is no longer the place that is difficult to climb but the ideal place to make a *presidio*. Surveilling, blocking and building makes a place your own; little by little you begin to cherish it, and by those very acts, to live in it.

Presidios

It's difficult to translate *presidio,* a polysemic term if there ever was one: presence, gathering, station, picket line. In the NoTAV movement, the need to defend the terrains over the long term gave rise to the construction of solid *presidii,* small cabins, more or less luxurious, to have protection from the rain, to eat in, sleep in, so as to 'preside' over entire days and nights. Far from being abandoned once the conflicts are over, they remain places where the movement gathers and takes root, open and welcoming spaces soon invested with everything that nourishes the struggle. Those that are burned down by the enemy, like at Borgogne, Bruzolo, and Vaie, are immediately rebuilt. At once symbols of the opinionated resistance of the Valsusians and living spaces, the *presidii* transformed NoTAV daily life, becoming in each village a place for meeting, organization and conviviality.

> Every day we went to the *presidio* (at Bruzolo), because of the threat but also because we wanted to, we needed to meet up, talk to each other – lots of people turned off their TV (I didn't have one), but the ones who had one were glad to say 'before, back when I watched TV'. Every day there was something, and if there wasn't there was us. There was already a need to become conscious of a reality bigger than just the passage of the TAV through the valley: sure, we don't want the train, neither here nor elsewhere. We started to talk about the capitalist model and that brought a big desire for knowledge. So there were many propositions for instructive evenings devoted to lots of subjects . . . Someone who wanted to deepen his knowledge of a theme organized it, contacted people and made an evening around that subject, and everyone came, always.
>
> – Patrizia

The *presidio* is important, because it's an address, a place to meet up. When they burned down our third *presidio,* we were all unhappy, and I said: the *presidii* are a way to have a roof over our heads, but the true *presidii* are in our hearts, wherever we are is a *presidio.* A *presidio* is a woods, a chestnut tree, because the *presidii* are us . . . The *presidio* is the sky, it's us, and the *presidii* will disappear if our desire to continue to fight disappears. Because what use are *presidii* if you don't have a true heart that has the will to continue the struggle?

– Emilio, fishmonger in upper valley

The NoTAV Valley

The NoTAV Valley deploys its strength and the daily life it invents throughout the valley, in all aspects of life. The *presidii* are one of the localized manifestations, just as, though to a lesser extent, a restaurant can be or a hairdressers, a grocery store, an association, a statue, a doctor's surgery, and so forth. If you get sick in NoTAV country, you go to a doctor from the movement – so too if you want to buy food or have a coffee. 'SiTAV' pizzas taste of enmity, even if they are delicious. Existence is thus completely divided; places carry other symbolic and real charges, and it is in this way that the very representation of the valley has been transformed. A NoTAV Valley has taken shape, not as an oasis closed in upon itself, but as a reality both parallel to and imbricated in the Susa Valley, and that surreptitiously duplicates it.

An abyss has opened between the two versions of the valley: NoTAV/ SiTAV, the central cleavage. As the movement intensified, democratic neutrality was replaced by the need to choose sides, erasing little by little the illusion of being able to remain comfortably on the sidelines, away from the conflict. The consequences of this division can be hard, but the movement takes responsibility for it and has allowed the establishment of a clear and solid base from which to live and struggle. The division, which has papered over all the pre-existing ones, has its own geography made up of the paths taken by the new ethics.

Mario: In a village like Susa, seven thousand inhabitants, everyone knows each other, we went to school together, made our lives together. With the struggle, a lot of us changed our way of life, strong conflicts were created, a very clear division.

Doriana: It's an injury caused by the TAV, an irrecoverable social damage.

Mario: At Susa or elsewhere, there were a bunch of 'pseudo-No's', so we decided to create a dividing line: to completely sever with those people, and they broke with us. We had no more relationships. There's really an abyss, something impossible to repair. The first thing you think of if you're going out to buy a cabbage is, where will I go? I won't buy a newspaper from him anymore because he's SiTAV. I don't like it because I bought my paper there for thirty years, but instead I walk three hundred metres farther to buy it from someone I don't know but who I know is NoTAV. To be clear: we don't want to give any money to SiTAVs, and we've all pretty much made that choice.

Doriana: We've also lost friends, or people we thought were our friends.

Mario: But we found others, we found solidarity. We found people with whom we never thought we'd share nights at Clarea, or share moments of tension confronting the police. We NoTAVs have been attacked, complaints have been lodged against us. When you hear people with whom you've lived moments of everyday life call you a terrorist or say that you are dangerous to the community or things like that.

Doriana: I'm a teacher. They came to the school and said I was teaching violence and subversion; it's a very serious thing because it's a small town.

– Mario, 56; Doriana, 55, Susa Committee

Ermelinda: The number of SiTAVs is not so high, mostly they are families linked to the companies at work on the construction sites, and then all those who believe in progress. People who, socially, are individualists, they exist, but . . .

Stefano: They don't have much of a place, there's no social body, there's no SiTAV social group.

Ermelinda: At the very beginning of the struggle, at Chianocco, the lands where they had put a drill belonged to a guy, and we knew he had gotten five hundred euros for it so we all went in a parade from the drill to his house and said: 'We've made a collection, we're giving you the money!' It was ironic . . . 'You sold the land for five hundred euros, if you ask us for it we'll give it to you.' It was a dissuasive act for the future, because then if you want to sell your land for the TAV, you know that everyone will show up at your house. It was a little thing, but it made an important step. We never needed to do it again. And the guy broke his contract and no one else sold.

– Ermelinda, 53; Stefano, 57, Bussoleno committee

When people at the shop say to me: 'Haven't you lost clients?' I tell them: 'No, I haven't lost any, on the contrary, I've gotten more because I'm sincere, I talk, I defend my ideas, it's not because you're my client that I'm looking to disagree with you, no, I respect you, we talk. But you have your idea and I have mine.' For example, I have a bunch of SiTAV clients, and with them I have to talk, because if I only speak to NoTAVs, we say the same thing, and I want confrontation. The prosecuter said I was a professional of violence! Can you imagine? I tell everyone in my store: 'Watch out, I'm a professional of violence!' And yet, I always have more clients.

– Mario, 62, Bussoleno barber

The NoTAV Imaginary

This is a very open valley, culturally – I say it because I wasn't born here, and also because the other mountain valleys where I've gone don't have the life there is here, I'd really like to see another place like this! Usually, mountain valleys live in their own little corner, lights out in the evening, nothing happens, you always have to go to the city. Here, on the contrary, it's the city people who come to see us. When we moved here, I thought my life would change a lot in relation to my life in the city, but I don't feel like I'm in the country here, I feel I'm at the centre of the world, the world that I know, the world I'm fighting, here is where we're doing together what I wanted to do.

– Ermelinda

The Susa Valley has always been a strategic point that has seen a number of conquerors pass through: Hannibal and his elephants, Julius Caesar in his conquest of Gaul, Charlemagne, and many others. It seems even though the world has flattened, this break in the mountains still attracts today the desire of those who see in the Alps nothing but an obstacle to overcome, or to drill through. Its identity, as is the case with many natural boundaries, is fluid, moving, multiple. From 1343 to 1713, the upper valley was part of the Republic of the Escartons who benefited from a substantial autonomy vis-à-vis the Dauphiné. All the territories of the community – forests, mountain pasturelands – were managed collectively, with representatives changing every six months. These communal lands were not, as the current usage of the word leads one to think, properties managed by the municipality, but rather a subtle system in which the people-community was indistinguishable from the community of goods and resources: the community was just as much the person as the village, goods and lands. A form of primitive communism, which disappeared when the upper valley was then attached to the House of Savoy, then to the Italian state. The actual border line only dates from 1947. Today, still, several languages are spoken in the region, since it is one of the Occitan valleys of Italy, where a Piedmontese dialect is spoken, as in the NoTAV slogan: *A sarà düra!*

This singular history of a zone that has its own coherence despite constituting a major passageway is renewed and reinvented, from the pre-historic men of the Maddalena whose remnants are defended, to the memories of the heretics and the Vaudois who chose these mountains for shelter. The return of packs of wolves that can be heard howling in the winter on the slopes of the Quatre-Dents (an Alpine summit) reminds us that at certain times the past roars again, if in fact it was ever silent.

It's clear that there are many big and medium-sized projects that are threatening to attack the territories of the mountains, including the Alpine areas. Obviously, the TAV project was one of those mega-projects that reveal a whole series of questions that are not just about ecological disaster or pollution, but that also show the manner in which the mountain is being reconceived in capitalist society. This periphery to be crossed through at great speed, becomes a periphery depopulated from this point on. Between the genocide of wars and the rural exodus due to industrialization, we can really talk about a forced exodus from our valleys, which has completely reduced what could have been the possibility to create a community and also to defend one. To create corridors that unite metropolises from one end of the earth to another, with all the ramifications of an urbanism that grows out and extends from the cities, it's making it such that the metropolis is swallowing up the territory – it expands, too, through a whole series of centres for energy distribution, news distribution. On the territory, we've been trying to talk about how we think about a free mountain. With

the opening of the TAV construction site, we realize that all this displacement, this militarization, the fact that the forces of order are free to move
around, escorting their equipment with great ease, could never have been
possible if there weren't the autoroute. The autoroute brought other
noxious problems that we see today, like, for example, the ease with which
people get up to the winter sports regions like Sestriere and Bardonecchia.
These are ways of consuming the mountain that are extremely injurious in
terms of the theft of resources and the destruction of communities.

– Guido, 44, member of Alpi Libere

There's a commonplace about the NoTAV struggle: that it's a determined
fight because this valley shelters mountain people who are not corrupted
by the metropolis, etc. It's true, on the one hand, especially for a certain
kind of village, and false, on the other, if you mean that you are dealing
with village communities like in the old days. The valley is a territory
midway between the mountains and an extension of the Turin periphery, even from the point of view of work – it must be the most industrialized, ruined, polluted, ravaged-by-infrastructures Alpine village in all
of Italy.

Historically, the mobilization developed first in the lower valley, clos-
est to the city, where you have villages of two thousand to five thousand
inhabitants right next to each other. 80 percent of the Susa Valley is in
the lower valley. The 20 percent up high is the old Alpine economy that's
become based on winter sports. Lots of Turin people have a vacation
home there. Even at the electoral level it's different. And so, it's a valley
near a city, but not completely absorbed by it and its life rhythms.

– Gianluca

Inhabiting the Zad:
A Zone to be Defended?

I was born here. I became aware of the airport project when I was about
five or six years old. That was about the time that the project was
relaunched. I was very worried, because I didn't want to leave my home,
and then there were all the trees. I remember that at the time I was very
attached to the trees around my house because I used to climb them. I

said to myself: 'Shit, if I don't see those trees anymore, what will I do?' I was young.

– Elias, teenager, resister

Reworking or hijacking an acronym remains obligatory in French political struggles, even when doing so retains an ambiguous relation to the old bureaucratic newspeak that cannot avoid marking its semiological territory with all those little acronyms deposited on everything it wishes to appropriate. On the one hand, it is a way of disputing the very meaning of things with the authority that claims to administer them, beginning with making fun of that authority's normative garrulousness. On the other, it at times leads unfortunately into the same terrain of codification, of flattening out what is complex, of making it univocal, a label. The ambiguity of playing with acronyms is only ever an exacerbated form of the ambiguity of language which, when it *seizes* the real, does so as much in the sense of 'understanding' it as in 'freezing' it.

It was not possible to build an airport on the entanglement of plants, roads, human beings, humus, recollections, animals, houses and machines that made up the territory between the towns of Notre-Dame-des-Landes and Vigneux-de-Bretagne. Before it could be done, all of that had to be reduced to a ZAD. The words had been chosen with care by a highly placed functionary a dozen years earlier, to be inscribed in the Law 62-848 'relative to the right of pre-emption in priority zones to be urbanized and in the Zones of Deferred Development'. The great precision of these terms was meant to assure a better occultation of that which makes up the singularity of each of the 'zones' that would henceforth become part of the plan. The legislator had designated a period of fourteen years during which the development could be deferred, and the inhabitants could get used to the idea that they would have to get out of there. The delay, though, was renewable, and it was not until 2008 that the developers decided that their project and the fruits of their operation of imaginary urbanism were ripe for action.

The Zone d'Aménagement Différé became a Zone à Défendre [Zone to be Defended] shortly thereafter. And if the vision of the zone covered in tarmacs, air terminals, tourists and businessmen was from that point on held firmly at a distance, it was still necessary to look behind the counter-acronym to see what the territory really was, lest one miss the essential: the question of what it was that was being 'defended' in the 'zone'. In the same way that popular language has not relegated the term 'zone' to the urbanists, by giving it infinitely more meaning than the poor geographic neutrality of a ZUP [Zone à Urbaniser en Priorité] or a ZUS [Zone Urbain Sensible], so we had to invest the zad with being much more than the simple preservation of a territory against a development project. It is for that reason that we prefer zad, in small letters, like a common name, to Zone à Défendre. It is for that reason that the notion of territory is interesting.

There are those who were born here, those whose families have always lived and cultivated the land here, those who moved here thinking they had found a tranquil place to live. But it is perhaps the point of view of those who came here because it was a place of struggle that best illustrates the circular path that leads from defence, to attachment to the territory, to attachment to defending.

First, there is something like a sense of disappointment, whether one admits it or not, because at first sight the zad has nothing grandiose about it. It is flat, wet, a succession of fields and hedges, and even the forest of chestnut trees looks like a field of posts or stakes. Only people who have experienced it in the soft evening light could find in it a certain charm. And then there are some enchantments: a starry sky, a patch of mushrooms, a salamander, hidden paths.

But as the eventuality of a general evacuation became increasingly likely, the relation to the territory was more and more marked by considerations that were, first and foremost, strategic or tactical. The first squat dwelling places were strewn across the zone without any logical coherence, making a collective defence difficult to imagine. Around 2011, that question became more important, in the light of training on how to move across fields, testing various means of radio communication, mapping the terrain, tangling with the cops on the occasion of the expropriation judge's visit or the visit of a research group, and meetings on a scale of the entire occupation movement to establish a strategy in case of police intervention. The integration of the necessity of defence was thus inscribed in the most everyday of gestures.

> We planned the layout of the garden and the cabin in function of resisting eviction. Our hypotheses didn't really hold up, but let's say that it put us into a certain dynamic: we put barbed wire across the rear entry points, we tried to lay out the plantings so that the first things to be destroyed would not be the tomatoes!
>
> – Akim, occupier, organic vegetable market worker

All this did not happen without a shared suspicion – after several false alerts, regular helicopter surveillance or the visit of a police physiognomist – that any resistance risked being merely symbolic when the big day arrived.

The big day did arrive and a tectonic shock would have left less of an impact on the territory. Houses were razed to the ground, roads sectioned off by barricades or police blockades, the centres of gravity in the zad moved (what we called before the 'centre-zad' moved to the west). New ways of getting about appeared, mainly by foot, across the fields and hedges. Defending the zone was as much about preventing the advancement of Caesar's troops as about reoccupying. A village emerged in two days in a hollow in the chestnut forest. New cabins appeared each week in the trees after the others had been torn down. The barricades were – literally – inhabited. They were much more part of a movement than part of a rigidifying of positions.

> The barricade is a political edifice, not a military edifice. All the best moments of a barricade occur during its construction. The big moment is when everyone is together building it, feeling a force, waiting together. And that's a thousand times more important than the moment of attack. That's when there are all the discussions and displacements at work.
>
> – Ulysse, occupier

Many of the inhabitants lost their dwelling place during the eviction operation. Most because of bulldozers, but often, too, because of the post-Caesar geographic rearrangements: an occupier abandons the big cabin where she was living by herself to a group of friends to move farther along, and her cabin becomes a hamlet; others, whose collective members had become dispersed during the evictions, move closer to new focal points on the zad, Fosses Noires or Bellevue. Some even set fire to their place to prevent the cops from taking possession of it. The zone is scattered with small emotional charges that linger beneath the ghost of a pile of debris. Everywhere they could, the machines had tried their best to make even the debris of the razed houses disappear, to prevent it from being recycled into projectiles or construction material, but also to erase more completely any memory of the place. And beyond the dwelling places, each corner of the zad is the place of a living memory of its relentless defence: this shrub had offered refuge against the riot police, this pathway was the theatre for an epic battle or the site of a more or less effective booby trap, this ditch was where tires could be hidden, that barn sheltered dozens of evicted occupiers and those who wanted to sleep closer to the operations.

Through getting set up there, defending, living on site, it is clear that the territory, even in its most physical aspects, is a construction – and one can lend a hand to building it. Opening up a path, occupying a part of the entire road by building a series of obstacles and cabin barricades on it, sowing an uncultivated field or, on the other hand, allowing the most invasive plants to proliferate in a space that had once been mowed pastureland. Discovering and prolonging the botanical history as much as the political history of the bocage, with its struggles against the swamps and the enclosures, the communal pastureland and its agricultural techniques. To feel oneself at home living there. This attachment to the territory is never without risk of self-enclosure and identitarian demands; these are a permanent danger.

> Living here is not just eating, sleeping, shitting, it's being in a strong relation with this spot. It could be coming here to gather mushrooms, or to go hunting, it could be about the struggle, it's ten thousand things, in any case it's dangerous to limit it to just having a cabin here. Because what happens in this place, these meetings between worlds, this is what's

precious. The reason why I don't call myself a 'zadist' is that I'm not here to defend a territory that has boundaries around it, what I'm defending here are relations, social links, manners of organizing. That's what interests me, taking our lives in our hands.

– Jeanne, occupier since 2010, in her 30s, cabin builder, mechanic

Anchorings Arriving

Wanting to bring an end to the feeling of being nowhere was, for some, a conscious motivation to move to the zad. But for many others who responded on the fly to the call from the 'inhabitants who resist', 'being anchored somewhere' was more of a collateral effect made possible by renouncing, through that engagement, a form of existential lightness or activist flitting-about. Because of the unfortunate ambiguity it holds for those who lived through the Nazi occupation, the political choice of the term 'occupation', could seem alienating to a world one was seeking as much to win over as to mark with an imprint. Differences of political vision, ways of living, appearances . . . Between the people who already lived at the zad or in its surroundings and most of the new arrivals, it was not easy to overcome distrust, and to make this transition often seemed to involve a kind of voluntarism.

One day people from the Secherie whom I'd never seen came by and invited us over: 'We're having a meeting at 5 p.m. with tea.' 5 p.m., that's impossible for us, it's milking time. They were people who seemed out of touch with the reality here. At a certain point, the vegetables and bread at the Sabot or at 100 Oaks changed our relations with the world of the squatters, because these were activities that looked a little like ours, there were things to talk about regarding how to work, there was a material exchange that could take place.

– Marcel, in his 50s, farmer at zad since end of 1990s

In the beginning, I didn't know how at all to get things done when there are a lot of people, with networks, so when I saw people arrive who looked Parisian with their computers in front of the Resistance cabin at

Planchettes, who were saying: 'For the garden, we'll put it here, we'll do that . . .' I took them as birds! Because I couldn't see how you could come from Paris, dig in the earth a little bit to make a garden and imagine coming back later to do the harvesting. To my mind, you had to stay in one place.

– Bertrand, former inhabitant of Notre-Dame-des-Landes

Meeting, Making a Path Together

Through one-to-one encounters woven into daily life, occupiers ended up becoming connected to those already living in the zad: a farmer, a gang of teens or a professional cook with dreams of starting an inn in his threatened house. The contacts were sometimes born of a simple neighbourly proximity, a need for tools, help, or a shared taste in parties or meals. They were above all the fruit of a reciprocal aptitude for letting oneself be traversed by other forms of life, even to the point of becoming distanced from one's own point of reference. This permeability is proper neither to the world of militants nor that of farmers, and it is one of the many wonders of the zad that it offers visitors the spectacle of an improbable mix of farmers and feminists breaking bread together after the sowing.

As the project went forward, the perception of a common enemy became accompanied by attachments that, in the end, also became shared – cultivation, woods, neighbours and dwellings – and that it made sense to defend together. At the same time as the *squatters* ended up feeling they came from *here,* and that the legal proceedings were uprooting the status of the *historic inhabitants,* the categories blurred to the point that some began to call themselves *inhabitants who resist* as well, while others, threatened with the seizure of their houses or their herds, ended up calling themselves *occupiers,* without rights or deeds.

M. and A. had strong ties to the inhabitants of La Saulce. In 2010, they invited us for Christmas – it was the first time I ate oysters! We wanted to bring something so we made a pathetic cake, but we didn't have an oven so we made a frozen cake that we left outside because it was cold . . . So it was a little bit like a band of filthy people landing in the middle of a family's living room, and they were super happy that we were there. It was the same thing when I was living at the Gare, with neighbours in the house next door: we had started building in the trees, and below it was a swamp, we were living on pallets, everything was wet all the time, and they came by sometimes with cakes, hot coffee, in the middle of our world. And then we could always go and borrow a hammer from them, little tools we didn't have. They weren't very involved in the struggle, so it's not through that that we got together. I don't know whether they felt sorry for us or maybe they were sensitive to a kind of courage that they saw in us.

– Ines, cow herder, cheesemaker, revolutionary

Neighbouring Towns and the 'Zadists'

The many committees active in the wider region are a reflection of the local support for the battle against the airport and the enthusiasm for the ongoing experiment of the zad. Whenever a public call is made to come plant an orchard or share a Sunday banquet, it is met with energetic solidarity and hungry stomachs from a surrounding ring dozens of kilometres away. The relation with some villages directly neighbouring the zad, though, is more delicate, and the boundary line paradoxically more pronounced. The large majority of their inhabitants certainly don't want to see airplanes landing on their lawns, but the direct cohabitation with the 'zone of autonomy' has been, to say the least, divisive. Conflicts with hunters, over graffiti, departmental roads blocked by not particularly affable maniacs, or regular confrontations with the forces of order regularly awakens hostility in a portion of the nearby population, who seem to forget that without the occupiers, the present situation would undoubtedly look a lot more paved over. Some of the local residents active in the movement, or simply more curious than others, have become friends with some of the occupiers. But for many of the other inhabitants of Vigneux or Notre-Dame, these strange neighbours have remained unknown, silhouettes glimpsed along the roadside or on a TV news report. Providential heroes or outcasts, Robin Hoods or delinquents, 'zadists' feed the fantasies at the supermarket, the corner bar, the rec hall.

> I took it on myself to make connections between the townspeople and the squatters. And I'm still doing it. I had to undo a lot of lies that were being spread around Notre-Dame, like that the zad was nothing but a stinking mess, a hellhole. That had to be done in the mayor's office too. Since I knew the people who worked at the town hall well, I knew who was saying what, and it wasn't always rosy.
>
> – Julien, spokesperson for ACIPA

> The police were telling the people who live nearby that they shouldn't pass through here because we were savages, dangerous people. But on Sundays, people came. One time, a mother came and told us: 'The children were very well behaved all week because I told them that if they were good, we'd take them to see the people manning the barricades.'
>
> – Paola, in her 40s, occupier since 2011

Some reactions and anecdotes from elected officials that were rushed into print by the local press made it clear the prefecture wanted what are diffuse tensions to be transformed into overt hostility. Elected president of the region in December 2015, Bruno Retailleau launched an expensive petition drive advocating the evacuation of the zad, and paraded before the regional council and the local newspapers two false neighbours, the Lamisses, who had left the area ages ago, but whose house had been 'squatted'. The zad press group countered the verbal attacks one by one. On 5 February, Bruno Retailleau made a pronouncement about the 'zadists' for an article in *Le Point*: 'They remind me of *Daesh*. They have their banner, a rural caliphate, they terrorize the population.' A few days later, sickened by the 'almost daily propaganda of the warmongers' being made in their name, dozens of authentic local residents gathered in front of the church at Notre-Dame-des-Landes and read a common declaration aloud to journalists: 'Country walks punctuated by rewarding encounters, a little coffee offered or a simple hello, we feel at home and safe on the zad. For many of us, it's the chance to redis-cover our bocage and its riches, to renew our ties with a territory and its inhabitants. [. . .] Be aware that we will be at the side of all those who are threatened with eviction from the zad.' Shortly there-after, Mr Retailleau confided sheepishly to *Le Figaro*: 'We've lost the communication war.'

Circulation

For a territory that never closes in on itself

As with any living territory, the zad is traversed by breezes that prevent it from closing in on itself. The willingness, there, to embrace a certain instability or insecurity opens up the possibility for the unimagined to transpire. An agricultural hangar, built by activist farmers in the 1970s, renamed the Wardine, is finally transformed, thanks to new occupiers, into a concert space for experimental music. After 2013, the proliferation of zads creates a new geography in which two threatened forests separated by a few hundred kilome-tres could become, for a time, neighbours. The power of attraction of the place and the incessant passage of people in and out bears witness to the way in which its spaces and the people who live there are kept open, porous.

Between October and December 2012 I came almost every week from Rennes to the zad. We were sleeping in big tents where we could. The more time I spent surveying the place, which I didn't like at all at first because of the dampness, the more I got used to it. In fact, I could say that it was the zad that tamed me, because swamps and humidity are really not my thing. I don't have a good sense of direction, but I got my bearings, and I managed to stop getting lost if I didn't try too many new paths. And when we understood that the danger was lessening at the end of November, that there was less risk of a new evacuation attempt for a while, we quickly wanted to maintain a link with the place we'd gotten attached to, and no longer as a symbol of the resistance it represented, but for all the hopes and possibilities it contained. Logically enough, we thought that along with people from other cities, we should ensure the permanence of the committees at the Chateigne, a bit like the presidii in the Susa Valley. So we came one week, thirty of us, from Rennes, to keep the place open in the beginning of January. It was important for us to be able to contribute to the movement by being on site, even if it wasn't always easy to meet the people living there when we landed like that, a group from the outside. And there was tension – I'm not exaggerating! – when we came with the project of hooking the Chateigne up to the electrical line that passed through a few hundred metres from there . . . For us, it was a way of being more useful to the collective organization, but for some people living there, it was a contradiction with their ecological or anti-growth ethics. So our proposition wasn't very well received, and pissed off some people . . . I have to admit too that we began doing the hook up before the discussion about whether or not to do it was finished! But in the end, people were mostly happy to have light in the kitchen and the meeting space.

– Aélis, 'Maison de la grève' collective, Rennes

Since the beginning of the occupation movement, newly arrived people have always been experienced in an ambivalent manner. From the first squat at the Rosiers to the demonstration for reoccupation, a question has been repeatedly asked: will these new arrangements not endanger the existing precarious equilibrium? The irony of the situation – an occupation movement fearing that which has permitted its own existence – should not disguise the fact that the tension between forces drawn to equilibrium and those who ceaselessly put that equilibrium into question has never been resolved.

For the people occupying the zad, there's always a kind of dialectic between openness and closure: do we open up to many people and risk not being able to manage what we are collectively, or do we hunker down with a hard kernel of people who know each other, who trust each other and who are more able to do things together? It's interesting to see how the people who came the same time as me, and who in the beginning were a bit rejected in the name of the cohesion of the collectivity and who strongly criticized that perspective when they arrived, have now found themselves one year later having a hard time welcoming other people coming to the zad! The question of openness/closure is raised all the time, even if since the evictions, the answer was given by the facts: now it's a super open space, with all the problems that entails – notably, the fact that you can't talk about the zad as though it were one big collective that can easily make decisions in common.

– Mael, occupier since 2011

As with any love story, a territorial history that no longer did anything but refer to itself, that no longer sought to confront the world together, would quickly end up buried under its own weight. One is never nourished by oneself, but rather by one's surroundings. And in this regard, the zad is lucky to be a territory irremediably in struggle. Without the opposition to the airport, this territory would not exist such as it is, and inversely, the airport would perhaps have already been built if an inhabited territory had not sprung up in its path. To defend oneself against developers, finding alliances elsewhere, projecting ourselves on other areas (Bure, Valognes, the Mille Vaches farm, and so forth) are so many occasions for opening up and making the territory take leave of itself. This is how, thanks to connections with migrants in struggle, the bocage in Nantes has also become home to bits of Sudanese culture.

One day, during a discussion at the General Assembly, we went around the table giving reasons for our presence here. I came here, of course, because I was against the airport, but over time I've realized that it's really against the world of the airport that I want to fight, and that there are many other struggles around that could use some of our space. There was a cabin, Youpi Youpi, that was empty, and we decided to reorganize it with migrants from Calais so that it could become a place of welcome for others. We gave French, English, and Arabic lessons, cooked meals inviting others . . . right now, Sudanese asylum seekers are living there.

– Sammy, occupier since 2010, also active in Calais migrant aid

Living at the Zad

Collective life

The occupation movement, largely derived from the experience of squatting, has not merely transmitted a practice of resistance (the occupation of houses and land) to the struggle against the airport. Spaces opened haphazardly and withdrawn from the real estate market and the rules of urbanism are also places where often non-normative ways of life are invented, beginning with those that break the constraint of organizing daily life around the tight circle of the individual or the household. To live collectively is to open up, in one fell swoop, several essential political zones: the sharing of intimacy, the division of domestic tasks, games of love and friendship, placing material means in common against an economic logic. In 2015, the zad was strewn with dozens of collective living spaces that might hold from two to fifteen people: in the woods, the fields, on the roadside, in trees, and even atop a pond. Their male and female inhabitants came together because of emotional ties, political ones, lifestyle choices, or simply by chance. The collectives are more or less stable, some are in perpetual recomposition while others are held together by collective projects that go beyond a mere sharing of the everyday.

For three years I've lived in a collective cabin in the middle of the zad: The True Reds. What makes us different from quite a few collectives here is that we know how many people we live with! Seven. It's very clear who lives here and who doesn't. There are people who come through all the time, close friends, but they don't live here. I think we needed that stability. Before, in the forest, we were just a few, and I realized I wanted more people around me. I like being with people, not eating alone. I think it's cool that there's always someone home, it means you can leave for a two-month vacation without leaving just one person behind to take care of things—things work, because we are all motivated and participating in lots of projects.

We have a 'house meeting' once a week. Those evenings nothing else goes on and we spend the evening together. We are hardly ever, all seven of us, in the zone at the same time, but once a week, everyone who is there eats together and talks, sometimes about a pre-arranged subject.

I was asked recently if I consider 'the True Reds' an affinity group and I said yes. But that depends a little on what that word implies. I'm not always in agreement politically with my co-inhabitants, sometimes people here make decisions that don't suit me. But there's a political affinity anyway, and we manage to talk about problems. What really brought us together was feminism, an attention to relations of domination and power, to kindness. It's not by chance that five of us are women. That contributes a lot to the ambiance at home, how we live, and it's something that we truly chose. Even if I'm not certain that every one of us considers him or herself to be a 'feminist', you can't say it's a very virile house.

– Tila

I lived in other collectives, several squats including two big ones, pseudo-punk or artists in the mode of techno-travellers, *Mad Max* style. After a few years, I saw the limitations – as much on the level of perception as organization. Political questions weren't taken into account, or only in an identitarian manner, with a slew of paralyzing rules that weren't necessarily stated.

Here, it's different than what I experienced in the other collectives, there's a force that goes beyond us and that connects us. The culture of rupture is so present everywhere else . . . Here, we have no desire to return to the precariousness of isolation, and one of our objectives is to succeed in putting together many plans, constructing veritable relations of force, creating spaces, occupying them. It's this determination that can partly explain what holds us together and that makes our daily life have something fluid about it. We aren't going to risk separating when we're targeting the world!

Here, what makes the rhythm of the seasons, the deep cadence, is agricultural labour, and, beyond that, we want to be as available as possible to everything that might allow disrupting situations – whether these be events linked to the anti-airport struggle or through connecting from our base here with other movements.

As for daily life, we eat almost all our meals together. We meet together every Monday to do house-cleaning, with a discussion halfway through. We try at that point to determine the different meetings and organizational moments of the struggle that we think it important that we attend. There are always little or medium-sized events at our place, like a meeting with someone who has made a film, written a book, work sites, discussions, a grain-threshing party, soon a week on the theme of the Commune . . . obviously we talk about the struggle a lot amongst ourselves, in a place like this, it's necessarily linked to everything we are building, everything we harvest, the people we see . . . It's an infinite field of projection and there are always new plans to imagine in order to win. The zad has become the expression of the possibility of a permanent collective frenzy. It's a little bit like walking, where with each step you let one foot fall and you catch up with the other, and that's how you advance. You know that you will not necessarily be in that temporality for your whole life, but that is how it is right now.

Obviously, it's exhausting a lot of the time, because our dwellings remain fragile, the roofs leak, there are often people passing through, we are sometimes forty for a whole week confined to thirty square metres with rain non-stop and the mud that goes with it outside. But that's nothing compared with the effervescence, the force of attraction, the power created by living in such a historical moment.

– Sean, occupier since 2013, Saint-Jean-du-Tertre

Above and beyond the level of the dwelling places, the collective life of the zad is woven out of a criss-cross of diverse activities (gardening, construction, parties, discussions), material sharing (showers, internet) and affective ties. One need only walk a few dozen metres on the roads of the bocage to be struck by the contrast with the streets, so often empty in a good number of western villages, or with the indifferent, frantic hurry of metropolitan crowds. It is difficult to go from point A to point B without the encounters one makes along the way leading to getting lost in multiple conversations and detours. In daily walks, a few places constitute crossroads where one almost always ends up. At the Gere farm, there is a climbing wall, a hip-hop recording studio and a bike-repair studio. Further west, at the Wardine, there's a dance studio, a space for children, and a multi-purpose room where parties and reunions are held. In the office at Saint-Jean-du-Tertre, there is space for writers next to carpentry and mechanical activities of all kinds. At Fosses

Noires, the living room is often 'squatted' by neighbours while a dormitory is set up for people passing through. There is a trailer with an internet connection, a bakery and a café. These open spaces are important for the solidity of the territory – they allow something like a neighbourhood life in the middle of the bocage, and help to avoid everyone shutting themselves up in their own little collective.

> To accept to have a dormitory here means accepting to take the time to greet and welcome the people who pass through, eat with them, discuss, explain how things work on the zone. So we reserve the right to refuse people if there aren't enough empty beds. In that case, we send them to other places that have room. Even so, there are people coming by every day, sometimes as many as thirty. You find you have to stop what you're doing to show someone something, to lend a tool, to give directions. It takes a lot of energy. People have quit our collective because they couldn't do it any longer.
>
> – Lucas, occupier of Fosses Noires since 2012

At the time of the evictions, the medic group set up its trailer across from Fosses Noires. Ever since, people have gotten used to coming here when they have a medical concern. They know that I have nurse's training and that I never refuse care to people who need it, even if I have no affinity with them. It's not something that bothers me, it's just that it takes a lot of time. I could tell stories like when we're relaxing in the evening, it's getting late, we're about to start a game or go to bed and someone shows up who's cut himself with an axe chopping wood for his dinner . . . There, you know you've got two hours of care in the middle of the kitchen ahead of you.

> – Sophy, occupier at Gaité, then at Fosses Noires after evictions

People often think that we live in a community of 150 people, when in fact we mostly live in small-size collectives. But these collectives are connected to each other by links that include friendship, neighbourly proximity and camaraderie. Proximity means that your schedule is frequently interrupted when neighbours need a hand running after a pig that escaped, or because a tract has to be written right away after an unforeseen event, or when companions drop by with an empty seat in their car heading for the demonstration in Nantes, right away . . . You can find yourself among fifteen people harvesting tons of potatoes all day long, then among eighty stuffing yourself with French fries that evening during a concert at the Wardine. And if you need twenty people for fifteen minutes to lift a cabin frame or push a car stuck in the mud, you'll find them without any trouble and everyone considers this normal because it's reciprocated . . . And then, it's nice to know that all these people are there, somewhere, around you. You feel that living in a collective creates unbelievable strength.

– Mael

Out of the norm

The desire to invent improbable forms of life in keeping with the strange territory, the absence of coercive police forces, and the tufty hedges of the 'lawless zone' all make of the zad a refuge open to people on the margins.

It's fun sometimes to linger on the ways and appearance of the people who pass through this strange world, but one thing is sure: given the forms of life that get invented and embraced here, you are not going to be the most original one in the village. Here, there's room for 'freaks', people 'on the margin', it's a place on the margin where people who don't recognize themselves elsewhere can live a little more peacefully. That's something that's dear to me, that kind of liberty. In fact, we were always looking for that, shadowy zones, dead angles in a camera's viewfinder, the backs of signs to write something on or to glue a sticker to. Our life is largely made up of 'récup' [scrounging]: trash that's useless to most people becomes our riches. It's like when you're hitch-hiking, you realize immediately that the motorway is not supposed to be the hitchhiker's friend: you don't look like anybody, people are too clean, the road shoulders are inhospitable, the toll areas offer very little space between two barriers and are hostile territories. And yet, you manage to insinuate yourself into the space, fuck with the zone, create a zone, one that's apart. The people who pick you up in their car take leave of their everyday life and remember that it's possible to do so, at least for an instant. The zad is similar, but it's in a bigger arena and it's longer-term.

– Malala

As its name indicates, the zad is in fact a zone, one that, even though in circulation, possesses physical boundaries. As one enters and leaves the interior world differs from the exterior world in visible and geographic ways. If, in certain places, one can enter the zone without at first realizing it, a few observed details quickly signal a difference. And, along the big roads, the difference becomes more pronounced: barricades on the side, obstacles, paintings on the walls, signposts erased, cars abandoned with wild grass growing out of their trunks. The passer-by can no longer be mistaken: he is inside. And that interior carries within it the clandestine imaginary of the zone, the margins – in terms of both space and way of life – that attract and repel, a synonym of expansion and of violence, chaos and the overcoming of limitations, of boundaries. One can rest for a time there, away from an 'exterior' hostile to marginal and other unusual people, or build a world in the image of that originality: build, at your leisure, the cabin of your dreams, without needing a permit, finding most of the building material for free; mount a pirate radio station without worrying about the communication authorities; repaint a kitchen during a delirious party; learn how to suture a wound practicing on a pig's cheeks; grow spirulina in a greenhouse; wear a skirt though you're a guy; ride in a car that has only a skeleton left of its body. In the end, everything or nearly everything can be transformed to suit the most unscheduled desires. One can give form to one's desires, replacing economic or regulatory constraints with those that the territory imposes, or go beyond what a certain morality condemns.

The zad maintains the tensions that assure its strength: the tension between a space of secession and one taken up and involved with the world, between an enemy in front of us and one that traverses us, between a zone of experimentation and one of combat, between a secure, protected space and a space always at risk. It is this razor's edge that defines the richness of the zad. There is no choice to be made between these seemingly antithetical pairs, for the two propositions are always linked: a space of experimentation that was not in struggle would, quickly, fall into the realm of folklore; a space of combat without experimentation would be terribly cold; a territory incapable of enunciating from time to time a 'we' would rapidly dissolve; while a place protected from the exterior world would die, collapsing in upon itself and its supposed interior security. Here, precariousness merged with the possibility of projecting ourselves into a long future, opening up a space of liberty and imagination.

> In my life here, no one ever tells me what to do. Everything I do, I do because I want to do it. When I go somewhere else, I no longer know how to react when someone tells me what to do. I have a hard time read-justing to normal life! I can no longer live normally in society. Here, it's possible to change the conditions of the world in which you live by organizing yourself with other people. Elsewhere, I feel much more powerless.
>
> – Isabel, arrived 2010, grows medicinal plants

Pushing the limits

The zad acts like a magnifying mirror in which the usual social schemas, in all their weightiness, can be revealed and defied, to the point of having them break down completely. Tactfully, or with powerful hammer blows, women have thus ceaselessly made a place for themselves in the fields, on the barricades or in the assemblies, shaking up the customs of the rural world and those of some of the occupiers. And yet for all that, there is no time-worn utopia at the zad. Even in a moment as significant as the demonstration for reoccupation, female occupiers, builders of experimental cabins, had the tools taken out of their hands on the Chateigne work site by guys sure of their rights, and left the place, disgusted. The zad, nevertheless, offers a field of confrontation anchored in practices, sometimes open to backsliding, but that, little by little, raise questions and present new evidence about gender relations.

> Culturally, doing repairs or mechanical things or climbing trees are considered masculine activities. There are fewer girls who do that kind

of thing, there's no denying it. The zad is one of those places where you can set aside privileged moments to learn all that in a more restrained and kindly milieu, by organizing work areas just for women, for example. This allows you to find strength. Once you know how to do it, you're more confident and you can say to someone who tries to take the tools away: 'No, get out of here, I know what I'm doing.'

Things are evolving here. I forget about that when I stay here too long without leaving, but each time I go to the city, or even visiting my own family, I remember everything I'd forgotten about ordinary sexism: 'My son is very intelligent, my daughter is very beautiful', things like that. It's possible to be uneasy reacting on the zad when confronting a sexist situation, because people say, hey, it's worse in the exterior world. That may be true, but at the same time I'm less ready to accept it here. Because, perhaps, you might say that if people are here, it's because they are better prepared to ask questions, to understand things.

– Tila

One of the things that beckoned to me the most when I arrived in 2011 was the strength of women in the struggle, their presence in the meetings, speaking out, the actions. It made me ask myself questions I hadn't asked before. Situations I had lived came back to me where I felt uneasy without knowing why: remembering the way in which women, myself included, can have a lousy representation of themselves, or the condescending way certain people speak to women. Sexism is like a background, so incrusted that you don't even realize that it exists. Basically, I wasn't really comfortable with a radical vision of feminism, but here I wanted to open myself up to something like that.

– Malala

We had made a work site with some of my women neighbours on the zad. In my world, you make a work site and someone is busy cooking for us. Except here, friends said: 'Let's turn it around, and that way the person cooking also takes part in the work site.' It might appear very basic and idiotic when you present it like that, but there is still a strict division of tasks in the agricultural world, and that allowed me to have another vision of tasks and of life. Maybe it's just big words, but concretely, nowadays, I can go to the work site and come home and cook. I may prefer planting cabbages, but I tell myself that each task is as important as the other. And my women friends on the zad really helped me make progress in that area. Like one time I went to cut wood at one of the neighbours, to help out. We finished work and my neighbour asked: 'Stay for a drink?' Then, he called out to his wife, 'Letitia, make us a cocktail!' Three years ago that would certainly not have shocked me so much, but now it seemed very bizarre. Anyway, I'm not saying I'm perfect, I've still got a way to go, but it also made me make progress in my daily life, with my wife. I may never have turned into a real macho, but I surely would have remained within the classical schema. On the zad, we do many agricultural activities with lots of girls. Then again, I'm pretty accustomed to it because I happened to work a lot on the farm with my sister and other girls. But what I've experienced on the zad has made me pay more attention to language and even to written texts.

– Cyril, farmer, member of COPAIN

If the zad does not perform an instantaneous evaporation of macho education by the grace of Notre-Dame-des-Landes, it also does not completely eradicate other aspects of the social machine. Integrated differences of material and cultural resources, life experiences and trajectories, have an effect on ways of projecting oneself on the zone, of relating to assemblies and organizational efforts, or of imagining the exit doors in moments of confusion. But the unscheduled space in which lives in struggle are welded together opens onto an overturning of roles, almost to the point of disrupting sociological categories and their fatalisms. In the same way, camaraderie, and attention paid to sharing tools and making the diverse productions of the zad accessible to everyone, tends to erase lines and divisions held firmly in place there where the economy reigns.

Conflicts

The period after the evictions, from January to July 2013, was really the 'springtime of confusion'. Try to imagine a village that had tripled its population overnight, the community that was there before was largely dislocated. Lots of people arrived with a culture or a way of life even more different than the ones who had arrived on the zad the preceding years. There was less of a militant culture and more people who had come from the streets, rave parties. There was also the tension brought on by the police presence and the constant fear of new operations.

– Akim, occupier since 2011

For those who seek to break with the economic or the state sphere, the zad represents an attempt to invent an autonomous collectivity on a scale and a duration relatively unknown in the West these last decades. We are talking about a territory with a few dozen dwelling places scattered on a few hundred acres, traversed by thousands of people with multiple aspirations. This is a space undergoing constant pressure and major upheavals without being ordered by a customary and communitarian tradition that would establish an *a priori* common sense. If 'living together' on the zad was to mean something more than an advertising slogan or an injunction to submit to social pacification, nothing about how that might come to pass seemed evident. Besides, some people think that after the period of the evictions and the end of the military occupation, the authorities were betting that the zone could not survive in a complete absence of police and judicial institutions, and that a generalized chaos favourable to a general evacuation would develop. But three years later, if such a bet existed, it was lost.

And yet, it goes without saying that among the different ways of relating to the zad, certain ones are sometimes frontally contradictory. Subjects of conflict are varied. Conflicts over the use of the territory: inhabitants in the new cabins cause a decrease, by their presence, in the territory open for hunting. Ethical conflicts over how to defend the zone: by taking it back to 'wild nature', or by living in it, with all that this implies of anthropocentric activities. Tactical conflicts: maintain the zone preventatively barricaded or facilitate access to the land for farmers, as well as access to the roads for people living nearby? The violence of human relations: when street culture, with its hair-trigger sensitivity and its rapid flare-ups of aggression, meets up with militant practices of the slow regulation of dissension through dialogue, or when one or the other confronts the vigorous pragmatism of the agricultural world. All of this makes for lively

interaction, and the tensions surrounding access to land and the place
of agriculture on the zone perhaps offer the best illustration of it.

> The spring of 2013 was a time when you'd hear some people on the
> zone criticizing farmers and agriculture very strongly, along these
> lines: 'Don't touch nature! We want fallow land.' Or 'The zad belongs to
> all of us, so I'm at home everywhere, I can walk with my dogs unleashed
> wherever I please, I can cut through barbed wire if I want, in any case
> I don't want to see animals being raised on the farms.' And us, on the
> other side, maybe we were assholes too, but we stuck to the COPAIN
> line: 'All cultivated land should continue to be cultivated.' This was in
> continuity with the historic strategy of farmers in struggle on the zone.
> And there we had two clashing ideologies. We tried to have meetings
> to explain, but for the people living there, it wasn't working at all. So
> we ended up taking a position. We said: 'OK, we'll leave three
> parcels . . . ten acres where we won't plant any wheat, it will be a non-
> motorized zone, but the rest we're planting.' But, in the end, we didn't
> set out in our tractors right away to get to work but instead took up our
> walking sticks and went from cabin to cabin, with a map and an
> explanatory text.
>
> – Cyril

Whether it is about dogs, fields or seizing power, the different
'users' of the places were forced to experiment from day to day to
avoid having the zad implode. The first step: the formal structures of
organization, general assemblies and other weekly meetings of the
occupiers, were showing their limits, in terms of the serenity of the
debates, the capacity to represent the totality of people concerned and
the means for enforcing decisions. On the other hand, two determining factors opened the way to moving ahead: the need to, at a mini-
mum, defend against the project of the airport together, and the
impossibility, as time went by, of ignoring the presence of others when
one has chosen to live on the zone.

Among the techniques of reconciliation: mediation, which relies
on all the in-between types who blur the lines of fracture (occupier/
growers, farmer/barricaders, naturalist squatters or inhabitants who
have become squatters); the explanation of acts that may have been

perceived to be aggressions (why cut down the hedge or build a sound barrier?); generous listening; circulation of external collectives, who lend new energy when spirits lag; a strike of 'public services' – bread, radio, internet, infirmary – in response to the theft from the bakery collective in spring 2015; the capacity to adopt a certain level of violence in setting one's own or the collective's limits without becoming a bully. These different ways of responding to conflicts, more or less strong, apathetic or empathetic, are themselves frequently the sources of intense political quarrels.

But after a long peaceful spell, in the summer of 2015 a series of physically violent incidents and the fear of an endless sequence of settling scores led to the convocation of emergency assemblies. Before now unknown, these meetings met regularly for several weeks and were attended by almost all of the zone's inhabitants. To see so many people with such dissimilar political codes and perspectives on the subjects under scrutiny commit themselves to this kind of collective process was no laughing matter – and this despite the difficulty of the task at hand: taking precautions to establish several big, commonly desired 'limits', making them meaningful and possible, but without turning them into timeless moral rules. Thus, these sorts of assertions: 'We do not want personal enrichment or capitalizing based on narcotics – even in general – and we want the zone to be a favourable place to become free of our addictions'. We had to imagine how to go about holding these lines and transmitting them to the new arrivals. Some people expressed their worry over the idea of the emergence of a coercive and authoritarian police force, while others were fed up that rotten situations were remaining without any collective response. Some evoked experiments in collective justice in Mexico, but it became quickly apparent that we had very few models or examples of large communities that had tried to liberate themselves from the establishment of a police force or a system of punitive justice. What came into place, bit by bit, was above all the fruit of a combination of lessons learned from past conflicts and a real collective ingenuity, capable of rising above ideological blockages. A long tour of the different living spaces to discuss the project finally led to the creation of the 'cycle of the twelve', a 'group of mediation of the zad's conflicts'. One of the group's notable traits is its avoidance of any specialization, and its functioning through drawing names out of a hat. The group consists always of twelve people. Every fortnight during a meeting of the inhabitants, the names of three people out of all of the volunteers on the zad are pulled out of a hat, along with the names of three places out of all of the dwelling places, each place designated to supply one person. Six people are thus available for a term of one month for the task, which they share for two weeks with the six previous people and the rest of the month with six newly chosen ones. In an introductory text circulated on the zone, the 'cycle of the twelve' was presented in this way:

> A new creature has been born in the swamps of the zad. The child of our quarrels and of our desire to live for a long time together without police . . . it can be used for conflicts between any legal or illegal inhabitants of the zad in which one or several of the protagonists do not wish to stand alone. It is not an affinity group but a changing group . . . in which anyone may participate. It will not enforce a law, will not attempt to impose the interest of a group, but will refer to the meetings of the inhabitants, to the discussions over limits, to the 6 points for a future without an airport, all the while considering the specificity of the situation and that of the actors in the situation. Its goal is not to make order reign, nor to be a personal sounding board, nor to prevent conflicts from existing; its purpose is rather to prevent the behavior associated with our conflicts or our errors becoming unlivable, leading to inhabitants or occupiers leaving the zone, or the useless destruction of links with our supporters . . .

Deciding to react to certain situations was not supposed to have as a corollary stifling the different lines of political conflict essential to the vitality of the movement – much to the contrary. And even if, in the case of an emergency, a temporary removal of someone from the zone is necessary, the 'cycle of the twelve' mostly just offers attentive listening and multiple perspectives. Rather than thinking in terms of punishment or imprisonment, it reasons in terms of reparation: prepare a good meal for the people to whom one owes something, or help them build their cabin.

It is obviously too soon to draw any deep conclusions about this experiment, but already the capacity to tackle this essential set of problems has reinforced the conviction that it's possible to become free of habitual institutions without having to mimic them. On the path to the constitution of a 'free commune', taking charge of conflicts constitutes the first 'communal task' which the totality of the inhabitants of the zad had to come to terms with and continue performing.

Towards the Commune

It's really unbelievable to have such a large lawless zone, where the cops don't come, or no longer come. Even when they were still here, they had no control over what we were doing. It's a little like after the revolution, if there has to be one: We're getting organized. Here, anything is possible!

– Sean

The term 'lawless zone' has been used frequently by detractors to promote a frightening image of the zad. Some members of the movement, though, have embraced the term, literally, in an attempt to see what possibilities such a state of exception, won through combat on the 1,650 hectares of the bocage, might actually offer. Can what has been opened up by an 'absence', be it of the law or the state, give rise to forms of common 'presence' that could be substituted for them? Here, more than anywhere else, a vast field of possibility has emerged on the zone. Step by step, the movement develops collective infrastructures capable of going beyond the individualism that prevails elsewhere, projects a collective use of land, and begins to seriously envision ways to 'become Commune', reactivating as much the promises made by villagers in the high Middle Ages to bring each other 'aid and assistance', as the memory of the communes that sprang up in Paris and several other cities in France in 1871. If the 'state of law' is that which everywhere imposes its laws, its suspension may very well be what will permit, once again, the birth of the Commune.

Collective Infrastructures

A weekly 'non-market', pay-what-you-want bread four times a week, collective internet connections, meeting places, studios of all sorts, care spaces, free clothes depots . . . If the collectives and the inhabitants constitute the nervous system of the zad, the infrastructures are its skeleton. Sharing collective tools is an essential factor of living together. It is difficult to sort out at the heart of the infrastructures their material aspect, their organization, or what role is played by the texture of links between the inhabitants. They are both a necessity to the independence of a zone that seeks to free itself from the guardianship of institutions and the market sphere, and a guarantee of its cohesion. They indicate an intelligent and dynamic acceptance of autonomy, freed of the stereotypical myths of autarchy. Secession is not being thought here as a rigorous and moral rupture with everything that emanates from the exterior, but rather as a process. Dependencies are removed little by little, according to the rhythms of the movement, and the new means developed by the community are always concomitant with a growth in political power. The question of autonomy is thus no longer that of a utopia to attain, but rather that of a directing line.

Producing Food . . . and Fighting

> I see things that excite me a great deal about the agricultural dynamic on the territory. Experiments in collectivization. It's as if everything I read, all the old revolutionary myths, like the Spanish Civil War – I have the impression of getting near all that, touching it with my finger.
>
> – Jean

The question of the means of subsistence of the occupiers, frequently asked by people outside (with or without provocation), exacerbates all the fantasies and clichés. It would be pointless to try to come up with a single response, since the reality consists mostly in a hodge-podge of sources, including the RSA (a version of French social security), seasonal labour, regular employment, recuperation (scrounging and dumpster diving) and auto-production, all of this sometimes supplemented by small thefts from big box stores. A fragile equilibrium exists that the collective structures do a great deal to make secure: they allow the question of getting by to not be limited to a strictly individual sphere.

But, in the end, it would be unimaginable that a struggle that involves occupying hundreds of acres of arable land would not devote itself, in its own manner, to making the commune-in-the-making able to feed itself. In this bocage where agricultural activities are unavoidable, the political engagement of farmers has been a major point of reference for a long time. 'Never more will country people be Versaillais!' shouted Bernard Lambert in 1973 before a crowd of thousands of people, giving voice to the political path followed by the farmers of the Loire-Atlantique reunited in the heart of the Farmers'/ Workers' movement. And even if the image of a revolutionary figure from forty years ago, the worker-farmer, has been substantially eroded, with the re-emergence of the idea of the Commune on the zad, agricultural workers from the surroundings find themselves ready to help generate anew a collective and autonomous production, and to take part in the unfolding of a political adventure.

> In our group, we wanted to both find an agricultural form that made us dream and that was not too demanding, that, for example, did not require a permanent presence, because we were going back and forth a lot to Rennes, where we come from. We gave ourselves a goal: grow enough wheat for the zad and for the cafeterias at the 'Maison de la Grève', without knowing very well what that implied in terms of presence or technique. In any case, we had given ourselves the goal and the means to make it happen. It's only afterwards that we realized what it really meant! What interested us was not the agronomical, biological, or ecological optic, but the doing of it in common. So we envisaged fields whose hypothetical yields could cover our needs before even knowing how to plant them. We put the cart before the horse, you might say . . . But for us there was no need for prudence, we weren't in debt, we bought none of the land and very little of the material, and we've always managed to find a bit of money when it's necessary. Farmers who've been doing it

for twenty years find this a bit bizarre or risky. They think we haven't taken enough time to get to know the land, or to understand the techniques well. But it's not a serious problem. And it's also what makes them able to understand what we've been trying to tell them: that we aren't just farmers, that that's not what we want to be, even if we're deeply involved in cultivation and putting all of our energy into it, it's because we think it's important for what it reinforces materially here, for what it brings to the struggle.

– Raoul, in his 30s, occupier since 2013, 'cereal group'

CURCUMA is not a spice, it's the 'Collective for the Wear, Repair, Breakdown, and eventually Use of Agricultural Tools' . . . We have time, a little energy and we tinker with old engines so that we can use them for cultivation. Utilizing a mechanical engine collectively multiplies its wear-and-tear threefold. So even if at times we know nothing at all, with lots of patience and gentleness and the desire to do things together, we repair things, and they sort of work. It's through these activities that I started to have more connections to farmers. Deep down, I see being a farmer as a profession that's a bit individualistic, organized around a micro-unit. Here, for the first time I see farmers doing lots of things for each other, being of service to other people.

– Tom, ex-future pruner, occupier since 2013

It is important to remember the 1,650 hectares of the zad were divided before 2012 into 400 hectares (988 acres) cultivated by farmers who refused to sell out to the airport construction company AGO, subsidiary of Vinci, 400 hectares of forest, and 800 hectares (1,976 acres) that were supposed to be redistributed from one year to the next by AGO to farmers who had signed an agreement with them and received expropriation indemnities. For this last group, the airport was the chance to win in every way: in addition to the indemnities, they benefited from new land outside the zad while waiting for the beginning of construction. After 2013, in the wake of victories made by the struggle and the halting of the project, the movement decided it was no longer possible to allow Vinci to control those lands, nor to abandon them to the disposition of those who had sold out. The 220 hectares (543 acres) currently being used by the struggle against the

airport for various agricultural activities are thus the fruit of occupation and the relations of force that the farmers of COPAIN, supported
by the 'sow your zad' collective, have maintained with the Chamber of
Agriculture and with certain productivist farmers in the vicinity. In
the wake of victories and the provisional halting of the project, the
land is being used differently from the way it is usually managed.

> What's unusual here is to be able to experiment with setting up an agri-
> cultural project in an illegal manner, and I hope there will be others who
> come here with that perspective . . . In any case, given the amount of
> land in question, more people who are ready to move here seriously are
> needed if we want to win this fight and not have the land in the end be
> taken over by the big landholding, agribusiness farms nearby, not to
> mention that there will be retirements among the resisting farmers . . .
> What's clear is that you can't do this kind of work without having a rela-
> tion, a particular attachment to the land you're cultivating, which is not
> necessarily an individual relation, it can be done through a group.
>
> – Willem, occupier since 2014

Ines: I think what will make the defence of this place is not the fact
there's food production, that the cows give us forty litres of milk each
day, but rather that there is life being lived here, attachments are being
made, confidences and complicities that have been created or deepened.
For me, what's interesting has also been starting to understand what's at
stake with agriculture today, the whole problematic of the land, which I
knew nothing about.

Jeanne: I think it's a story of reappropriation: it's enormously complex,
working in milk production, but it's possible to do and anyone can do it.
You learn how to work with the cows, the milk, the prairies, to the point
of learning the names of the different grasses. That really changed how I
looked at the world here: I walk through a prairie and it doesn't evoke
the same things it did six months ago! You develop a certain sensibility,
you are thinking the living from one end to the other, from the field and
the plants to what's alive in the cheese . . . You learn everything on the
job. It's endless: if you don't want to stop you can go on learning for your
whole life. And we learned so much in such a short period of time and
in such a comfortable way! I'm talking about relational comfort. To

think there are people who go to Ag school, their ass on a chair, and that we found ourselves here with everything ready to hand, and farmers who were really available and happy to teach us things and happy we were doing it. We talked, we took walks, they invited us over, we had exchanges, these were precious moments. It's alive, it's part of a situation where it makes sense and it's completely involving. Learning should be like that and it could be like that more often. And then we went beyond questions of agriculture and discussed lots of things together, we talked strategy, struggle.

– Ines and Jeanne, members of 'cow group', Bellevue

Thinking the Future as a 'Lost Territory of the Republic'

Before, the 'against the airport and its world' was fluid, and now, with the question of the territory, we have a concrete grasp on things, we've moved from rhetoric to practice: if we are against the airport and its world, what do we want for here? That changes everything.

– Ulysse

Thirty years later, the Larzac struggle between 1970–81 remains a reference point for the inhabitants battling against large development projects. All the more so in that the victory against the project of the military camp was compounded in 1985 by the Civil Society of the Larzac Lands' obtaining of a long lease on the 6,300 hectares (24 square miles) that the state had purchased for its abortive project. Establishing a collective management of the land is a hypothesis that is very appealing to a large number at Notre-Dame-des Landes. But if the Larzac of the present looks above all like family farms integrated, for better or worse, into the local and global markets, the zad wishes to leave a large place open to other possibilities and the exploration of other shores.

For me the ideal would be that all these lands would be maintained as experimental projects. With small agricultural projects that protect the land, shared centres for instruction and exchange. That the zone remains open, that anyone might come and get involved. If the airport isn't built, but in its place, there's big construction developments or agribusiness, we will have lost the battle.

– Ariel, member of ACIPA

I'm afraid that the philosophy and the cultural side of the zad will be lost if there's no more struggle, and the only thing that's left is the agricultural side. I'm used to all the turmoil, because there's one big seething cauldron here, even if it is heated by several fires and they aren't all lit at the same time . . . I'd be pissed off if it stopped all of a sudden. We want to see something at the other end, to be able to say that the inhabitants were right about it. I want this place to remain a seedbed of alternative thinking and living, an experimental zone that remains open, uncontrolled, non-commodified, free of cops. No one wants to say: 'We won the airport fight, so let's clear out the zad and put back a world of farming.' Everyone would be frustrated that the fight could end like that, that we could erase all that and go back to some former state.

– Dominique, spokesperson for ACIPA,
native of Notre-Dame-des-Landes

In autumn of 2013, a series of discussions began about the question of the future of the 800 hectares corresponding to the agricultural parcels that were not being farmed by the farmers who had rejected an agreement with AGO. In the course of successive discussions, the quality of the reflections, still unthinkable a few months earlier, was nourished by paying attention to the precise technical, land-based and geographical realities of the territory, but also to the existential and political aspirations of one another. What made the discussions immediately meaningful was the reality of common practices, notably at the agricultural level, but also the will shown by some of the occupiers to envision a *permanent* future, with, for example, the production of wood to be used for collective buildings and long-term work sites. It became apparent that having come this far together, the abandonment of the airport only made sense to the extent that it allowed everyone to remain – historic residents and occupiers. A text of six points, long debated among the totality of the movement's components, took shape and states publicly the shared bases of a common future. It affirms that the lands of the zad must be taken in charge by an entity issued from the movement, and not by the usual institutions. Beyond the questions of land management, it is the legitimacy of what was invented during the struggle as a new life itself that is being defended. As the movement's large demonstrations began to announce from that point on, the struggle 'to abandon the airport' has become just as much a fight 'for the future of the zad'.

Yet if unanimity appeared to have been reached concerning the principle, the question of the means, and especially that of the relationship to institutions, divides the movement. The old polemic, 'revolutionaries versus reformists', which remains in vain so long as it does not go beyond the ideological positions of the two sides, can also be approached by both sides with some pragmatism. Autonomy is the opposite of submitting to regulatory principles imposed from outside: there is thus little chance that autonomy could be legalized. Inversely, short of a rapid evaporation of the French State, there are few chances the zone would remain entirely outside of the boundaries of the law in the years that would follow the abandonment of the project. Even without being a fervent defender of the law as the basis of social organization, it seems difficult to overlook this area. For those who perceive a way in which to confront these issues, a strategic relation to the law has been elaborated throughout the struggle: neither ideal nor capitulating, the legal arena is a marker of political force that can be utilized to sanction advances and manage the margins of manoeuvre, but that can never suffice in itself to uphold the relation of force. It also remains to be seen if the chaotic and liberating force of the Commune might undertake, without betraying, some relation to partial and paradoxical processes that aim to reinforce its own situation.

> It's good in principle, but afterwards there's just one small detail: how to make it work. That remains to be invented. On the one side, we farmers in place are part of the game of legal and solid structures. On the other hand, the occupiers don't want any kind of power that they would be obliged to obey. We're up against this dilemma, knowing that if we use different approaches, it will be very difficult to defend the 800 hectares

for the movement in its totality. Imagine that we manage to agree and that we manage to put into place an official structure that would guarantee our land and guarantee a space of liberty for the occupiers. It would be a perfectly legal structure inside of which legal and less legal activities would take place.

– Marcel

Beyond these complex polarizations, the Commune that could emerge in the twenty-first century remains uncharted territory. To enrich our imaginaries, we have dusted off the old notion of the *communaux,* which both reawakens the deep history of the bocage and has known a quiet surge of interest among theorists of post-capitalism. (Intellectual labour on the defence of the commons against privatized appropriations has generated important literary production in the last few years.) This can be summed up in a few words: use before property. Obviously, this raises more questions than it does responses: private use, collective or common, usage that is permitted or forbidden, conflicts over use . . . After the return of a delegation from the zad from a visit to the Zapatistas in Chiapas in the winter of 2015, occupiers talked about a traditional *communality,* still alive and transcended by a revolutionary movement, ritualized by festivals, with key functions taken in charge by changing personnel and communal tasks performed collectively – a communality in which each individual is nothing but what connects him or her to the land and to others. Other people have been inspired by the *communal luxury* extolled by certain artisans during the Paris Commune and by their conviction that any labour, whether it be the construction of a barricade or of a building frame, is accompanied by an enormous aesthetic ambition, with a central place left to pleasure. In this open quest, regardless of the inspirations, everyone is free to envisage horizons and share them with others.

There was that festival at Saint-Jean-du-Tertre to do the threshing. All afternoon, people of all ages were working in the dust around the old grain elevator to sort out the grain for the flour milling and to make bales of hay, while others were drinking beer or standing around ready to replace them. The idea was to bring people together like in the old days around agricultural moments, and, at the same time, it didn't look like a folkloric or nostalgic thing, because it was living. The next day after a night spent dancing, there was a banquet with three hundred people in the courtyard for hours. We sang songs about the struggle . . . I don't know what the Commune looks like, but this wasn't a bad beginning. It was during the time when Valls was saying every week that he would come in January to evacuate the zad. Frankly, when I realized that day what we were, I said to myself the state would never prevail.

– Justin, part-time occupier since 2012

The zad at Notre-Dame-des-Landes is in the process of becoming a political entity, in the double meaning of a territory – that which defines and operates for itself its modalities and its functionings – and a force ready to confront the world. What is at stake is the possibility of projecting itself beyond the borders of the territory and the struggle, and even beyond reasonable victories, those within sight. When the possibilities opened up by what has taken shape in the territory are taken seriously, enthusiasm and imagination are unlimited.

What's good about this place is that it's impossible to imagine ONE future: there's room for several futures, including the one that some of us here are trying to make. Some of the possible futures may end up as nightmares, like everything that tends toward creating an alternative ghetto. What we want here is something that doesn't exist, that has not yet existed, but that has inspirations. What we're trying to do on the zad is to allow situations that leave room for the unforeseen: it's pretty bizarre, because it's about allowing a lack of control . . . we refuse what exists already, everything having to do with assured futures, worlds already known. There are already things here that are completely unknown. Lots of people threw themselves into life in the zone, without a safety net. It's like we fell into it, and it engaged us completely. To be in that disposition completely transformed us, at the same time that it made us look into what our deepest needs and demands might be. It's a personal change, but also a political one. There's already something of a victory in it. It's what I always intimately imagined 'revolution' would be. There is something of that aspiration to what's happening around the zads right now.

– Kevin, occupier since 2014

The Six Points for the Future of the Zad

The purpose of this six-point text is to establish the common bases necessary for the zad project once the airport project has been definitively buried:

> We defend this territory and live here together in different ways in a rich mixture. We expect to live here for a long time and it is important for us to take care of this bocage, its inhabitants, the diversity of its flora and fauna, and of everything we share here. Once the airport project has been abandoned we want:
> - inhabitants who own or rent properties earmarked for expropriation or eviction to remain on the zone and regain their rights.
> - agricultural workers who refused to comply with AGO-VINCI to continue to freely cultivate the lands they are looking after, regain their rights, and pursue their activities in favourable conditions.
> - new inhabitants who came to occupy the zad to take part in the struggle to remain on the zone and what has been built since 2007 during the occupation in terms of creative agricultural experiments, self-built dwellings or temporary dwellings (cabins, yurts, trailers, and so on) and forms of life and of struggle to be maintained and pursued.
> - lands redistributed each year by the Chamber of Agriculture for the AGO-VINCI account in the form of short-term, precarious rentals to be put under the control of an entity issued from the struggle movement that would unite all its components, and the anti-airport movement, not the usual institutions, to be in charge of determining the use of those lands.
> - those lands to go to new agricultural and non-agricultural use, both official and non-official, and not to enlargement or profit.
> - these bases to become a reality through our collective determination. And, together, we will devote the attention necessary to resolving the eventual conflicts that arise when putting them into place.

5

To Make A Movement

I think our movement became well known because we said: let's also do things, I mean, let's stand in the way. If filing appeals and using all the laws in the world to try to get them to stop doesn't work, I'll stand in the way too, I'll stop the trucks. That's what we're trying to export – if from protesting we move to rebellion, that's a strong signal, even if it still isn't revolution!

– Guido, 70 years old, retired

Conflict and violence

The day after striking Air France workers tore the shirt off the human resources director during a scuffle, the shirt began its journey to become the most widely covered item of clothing in the French media in 2015; Prime Minister Manuel Valls declared the workers' actions to be that of 'scum', meriting heavy sanctions; and former president Nicolas Sarkozy, indignant, went one step further: 'We are not in 1793!' The extreme nature of the comparisons shows the hypersensitivity of an era that has made comfort its highest value, as much as it attempts to invalidate the very possibility of conflict by designating it an unacceptable excess of violence. The operation is initially instigated at the level of language: new synonyms appear that seem at first absurd, but that soon become integrated into common sense through repeated use. A strike becomes a hostage-taking of consumers, a lively demonstration becomes pillaging, while sabotage becomes once again terrorism like in the time of the occupation. The scandal is performative and establishes the limits of what is acceptable. For beyond the war of words, repressive judiciary operations are undertaken in a parallel fashion, making those presumed 'responsible', individually, subject to very heavy penalties. In this framework, each condemnation for 'violence' is not just a reaction to events, but a preemptive act upon the future, which delimits the field of the possible for the struggles to come. And it secures the future in advance against acts of disobedience and despair – acts that already we are being told to limit to a virtual or, in any case, inoffensive sphere.

The goal of these operations is the reconfiguration of the real, in an attempt to remove any demonstration from the realm of confrontation. By tightening the norms and lowering the thresholds of what is permitted, the idea is to circumscribe what are real and fundamental differences to the merely discursive realm of negotiation, set within the framework of existing legislation. It is certainly permitted to adopt an insurgent tone from time to time, and to threaten a social explosion, but only to conjure up its image. And when the line of what is politically acceptable is crossed, a sub-prefecture pillaged, a factory director sequestered, or gas carboys threaten to blow up the factory, the fever of the enraged workers gets reabsorbed through 'social dialogue'. Violence is thus returned to the rank of a simple device brought to bear during a negotiation; it is no longer anything but the demonstration – true, a bit excessive – of a search for compromise. In this way, any possibility of long-lasting confrontation, which is to say the constitution of a clear dividing line between irreconcilable visions of existence, is buried.

'We don't hold discussions with violent people' is the last resort of the promoters of the airport and the TAV, the final argument that is supposed to break down anyone's conviction regarding the absurdity of the two projects. In a way, they are right: it does seem that between them and us discussion actually is pointless and our disagreement is too profound to find common ground. And it's easy to see that without the drawing of a battle line, any opposition would have long ago been covered over by tarmac or mountain dust. The battle line, which is one of the foundations of politics, requires the periodic acknowledgement of an open conflict in which the use of force can rarely be avoided.

The term 'violence' in this context plays a particular role. If the dictionary defines it as 'the quality of that which acts with force', for the state its use is always tinged with a highly political import. The state reserves its use for those who act with force, but only those exterior to the state – enemies, insurgents having recourse to illegitimate or illegal extreme actions. For it's really the state, and it alone, that possesses the famous 'monopoly on legitimate violence', something which guarantees, paradoxically, to the police an exemption from the use of the term 'violence' in their regard, to the point of permitting mutilation and murder. Thus, the denunciation of 'police violence' has almost the effect of a pleonasm and runs up against a wall, the solid block that founds and supports the totality of state power and its authority. Inversely, without an effective link between the act and the name given to the act, ripping a shirt or merely calling a cop a *pecorella* (little sheep) is an act of violence, as one NoTAV was accused of in an absurd trial accompanied by a large press campaign. This capture of the term has had as an effect the almost total abandonment of any possibly positive acceptance. As though the word had been buried with the ending of the revolutionary movements of the 1970s, movements that embraced 'political' or 'revolutionary violence' in their tracts and more or less armed actions. This burial creates a void both in the designation and in the understanding of certain practices, and opens the road taken by the vehicles of hysterical communication after each eruption of social fever. The paralysis maintained around the use of force is compounded by the difficulty of providing an explanation for it. Nevertheless, to abandon it definitively to the state means depriving ourselves of the right to conflict. And contrary to what is claimed, such an abandonment has less to do with the art of living together than with a shared resignation.

Open a front and revive politics

And yet it was 'violence', along with the zad, that was all over the television in the autumn of 2012. The media, hungry as usual for spectacular clichés, mainly propagated the figure of a masked youth, covered in mud, vilifying the bourgeois press behind his makeshift barricade and throwing rocks at the forces of order there to destroy the cabins. But where such an image often has as its principal effect to depict a struggle by way of its radical fringe, in this instance the inflexibility of the practice, its intransigence, its uncompromising fervour had the opposite effect and produced a sympathetic reaction. The solid anchoring of the movement for years in the political land-scape, and everyone's shared determination to resist, a determina-tion that transcended the diversity of practices, played a clear role in this reversal of infamy against the depository of legitimate violence. A figure of hope was born, showing in action that one can still take hold of the real and oblige the French government and its riot police to back down. The 'rioter' aspect of the figure was certainly not shared by all the opponents to the airport or the TAV, but to the extent that the infrastructure projects have become more tangible, 'violence' has insinuated itself into the conflictuality of the move-ments and it has no longer been possible to overlook the use of rocks, tractor barricades and Molotov cocktails. The barricades and obsta-cles that lie on and along the side of the roads in Notre-Dame-des-Landes indicate clearly a refusal of any pacification or end of hostili-ties, for the minute combat has ceased, it comes back again for a replay. Even more remarkable is the fact that, far from making excuses for the radicality, the movements have learned to be proud of it, to hold positions and use practices that seemed no longer admis-sible in a popular struggle. It has given rise to various imaginaries that borrow just as much from Astérix and his unassailable village, as from the lightning raid actions of Italian *autonomia* in the 1960s and 1970s.

The NoTAV and zad conflicts are also part of the history of the last fifteen years, an era that has seen a spectacular return of conflict – often reduced in the media to the term 'black bloc' – in the heart of social movements, anti-globalization movements and the *Indignados*. In Italy, we saw it erupt during the anti-G8 demonstrations in Genoa at the beginning of summer 2001. The assassination of Carlo Giuliani by a policeman during a riot, and the hundreds of demonstrators injured in the street or during police raids of militant spaces in the nights that followed, were so many wounds that markedly traumatized Italian activists. Police repression was followed by a wave of nearly unanimous condemnations of the rioters on the part of the organizers of the event, who accused them at best of being irresponsible, at worst of being manipulated by the police. Any new discussion of revolutionary possibilities was definitively postponed for other tomorrows. It was the Valsusians who, ten years later, at the moment of the summer 2011 demonstrations at Maddalena, reopened the possibility by affirming 'We are all black bloc'. Several NoTAV demonstrations were introduced by Carlo's mother, Haidi Giuliani, who had become friends with people in the valley. On 15 October of the same year, perhaps as a consequence of the NoTAV activities that summer, a group of *Indignados* had a long confrontation with the *carabinieri*. In the midst of destroyed bank buildings and projectiles flying in all directions, a police van in flames, and on its side, a slogan could be glimpsed: 'Carlo lives'.

If the zad and NoTAV have contributed to reopening the possibility of confrontation, it remains no less true that, despite everything, the term 'violence' is prone to ambiguities that mean regarding it in all cases with circumspection. It enunciates the judgment of the state, leaving attempts to define one's own relation to the question, whether it be in the case of 'non-violence' or 're-appropriation of violence', very difficult. Whether one limits its meaning to physical impacts or extends it to include psychical impacts, one enters into the delicate – and often fallacious – question of determining who is defending and who is attacking, or trying to trace a dividing line between what is legitimate in terms of strategic, ethical, or political criteria. The definition will fluctuate, and is finally not conducive to thinking about confrontation. What is important has less to do with one's position vis-à-vis violence (embracing it or rejecting it) than the determination to not allow the possibility of being radically in disagreement with the decisions made by the authorities to be taken away. If the words used to talk about conflict without making it into a malediction being conjured up still cannot be easily found, these two struggles have actively contributed to enunciating a few syllables.

Conditions for an enduring front: asymmetry and equilibrium

To draw a line of battle and hold it is also to expose oneself to receiv-
ing blows. The state obviously does not passively accept that the
perimeter of its territory be put into question. If it regularly tries to
re-establish peaceful relations by holding a hand out to its least viru-
lent opponents, the persistence and the radicalism of the struggles at
Notre-Dame and the Susa Valley make it necessary at the same time
to harden and to militarize its presence a little more to retain a superior striking force. In so doing it, too, recognizes and endorses the
existence of an interior battle line. The deployment of the Italian army,
after it had just returned from Afghanistan, the establishment of
exceptional trials or the construction at the Maddalena of walls
worthy of the most impermeable border zones no longer leaves any
doubt as to the existence of a physical conflict in the heart of the
nation. The police alone do not suffice to hold the level of the conflict
steady, and its persistence constitutes a stain in the image of a suppos-
edly peaceful nation. The standards of war are raised in the valley, a
war with the state, but which is not a civil war, since no fraction of the
population is openly opposed to NoTAV. The forces of order defend
the authority of the state alone, its capacity to make its prerogatives
over those it administers be respected. This interior militarization
should not disguise the fact that if there is indeed a war, the belliger-
ent forces are not at all engaged in the same way.

It is only by envisaging the fundamental asymmetry of the conflict
that we can understand the fact that the mutineers can hold strong
and not be crushed militarily, despite the enormous disproportion in
means. This asymmetry does not simply derive from the difference
in strength between adversaries who, like David and Goliath, duel
with one another. It derives from their very nature: one part of the
social body confronts the institution that claims to represent it in its
entirety. A tear is thus made in the heart of the abstraction that legiti-
mates the state, through which a form of 'secession in action' escapes
and begins to take shape. At the same time that the rebel part of the
population, as it withdraws, becomes distinctly visible, its arena of
influence and its boundaries do not stop evolving. The identifiable

battle line, the one that is visible in the very places where the railway line or the airport is being built, is rejoined by a second one which, in this instance, is something very different from a straight line around which armies can position themselves. This line is fluid, mobile, difficult to make out, and the war can thus not be mistaken for the kind engaged in by two states or two similar forces whose positions can be clearly distinguished. It resembles more a 'cyst' that develops and metastasizes, as the French prime minister expressed so well. The fact that the conflict is interior to the nation renders the task very difficult for the repressive apparatus, which cannot allow itself to envisage a pure and simple annihilation. For by highlighting the existence of the battle line, it risks admitting that its own founding uniquity has been put into question. To engage in the conflict, it thus has no other choice but to try to circumscribe the adversary's limits, to freeze it into a subject that it can eject, the better to combat and triumph over it.

For this, it disposes of a method all the more reliable in that it hides its workings. By rendering each gesture more weighty and by giving rise to desires for vengeance, repression is not content to dissuade; it tries to attract its target onto its own terrain. By striking, the state pushes the opposing party into a kind of paranoia, or, depending on the degree of pride or bravura, into a counter-attack. In this way, it hopes to create a face-to-face confrontation where the opposing party has no chance. To produce the enemy in order to then destroy it is a truth of repression amply discussed in the counter-insurgency pamphlets inspired by the colonial wars. Only, the method doesn't always work, especially when, as in the case of the NoTAV and zad movements, the confrontation with power takes place in an extremely precise, situated point, and is profoundly integrated into the population. Even if their authority is seriously questioned, the French and Italian states can only with great difficulty accuse the movements in their totality of having attacked their security when it is only, after all, opposition to an infrastructural project. And their attempts to isolate a radical and offensive fringe ceaselessly come up against the reality of the links that unite the opponents to each other and their shared anger and determination, undivided by sectarianism.

Each time one of the parties tries to transcend the asymmetry of the conflict, it risks falling outside the battlefield, as when a former Socialist Party president of the Pays-de-la-Loire region suggested the zadists should be eliminated using methods applied to jihadists in Mali. Or, when a mysterious communication urged the NoTAVs to take up arms and enter into open battle with the state. The movement is careful not to go beyond certain limits. There were undoubtedly NoTAVs in the Maddalena woods on the night of 3 July 2011 tempted by the idea of taking extreme revenge on the *carabinieri*. And yet when the brigadier Di Matteo, abandoned by his colleagues after a raid, fell into the hands of the demonstrators, no lynching took place. In the woods where his fate was discussed, the arguments that saved his life were as much strategic as ethical. The consequences for the struggle which such a rise in conflict would produce were immediately evident. A political consideration can also be added to this, one that reveals the stakes of the conflict: it is not about physically annihilating the enemy, even if that were possible, but of freeing oneself from its hold.

The strategy of political aikido and its limitations

This withdrawal from the adversary's operations is not always the result of a conscious and skillfully undertaken calculation on the part of the opponents. Even if this kind of political wager enlivens fringes of the two movements, and was determinant at many moments, strategic options often emerge from a seething maelstrom of intuitions and impulses that can be contradictory in nature. It is difficult to take advantage of all opportunities, and some NoTAVs regret, for example, not profiting from the victorious surge after Venaus, when the Olympic Games were being prepared in 2006 in the valley – in brief, when the Italian state was in a position of weakness from which a definitive end to the TAV could have been forced. For when, four years later, the project was resumed, it was the state that imposed its rhythm, its intensities and its battlefields.

Their position of being the aggressed responding to their aggressor has an effect on the tactical possibilities of these movements. It is usually easier and more natural for them to react, or to anticipate the predictable gesture of the adversary, than to invent their own line of action as a political group would do with its organization, its program, its congresses. As such, they find themselves frequently having to undergo, rather than initiate, situations. But while this can be seen as a disadvantage, practicing a kind of political aikido by reversing the adversary's attacks is a way to take advantage of the position. It is in this way that they have achieved some of their most impressive victories.

Military strategists know this well: more than any other, the besieger runs the risk of being besieged in turn, especially when he operates in the heart of hostile territory. When the forces of order evacuated the Venaus *presidii* or the cabins of Châtaigne to strip the movements of their places of organization, it is they who were in the end forced to evacuate, overwhelmed by the popular pressure surrounding them. And when the police presence managed, with some difficulty, to install itself more substantially at the crossroads of the Saulce or at the Maddalena, the opponents, once again, gained the advantage by denouncing what was an illegitimate occupation force. A military defeat becomes a political step forward, a situation that stimulates the struggle's powers of invention, for a clear target becomes visible, a place to harass the enemy and to make the movement grow. The police checkpoint sectors in the bocage and the valley are now part of the patrimony of the struggle, contributing to the education of a whole political generation in the art of skirmishing and other sabotages. A reinvention of guerilla warfare without guns or clandestinity, adjusted, in this way, to the struggle, has opened new horizons. The practices are, from that point on, inscribed in very concrete experiences, and their rhythms, their meanings and their consequences must be analyzed and thought through.

Humour is also mobilized to turn enemy operations against themselves, spreading a derision that the sad characters who have to pay the price for it would never be capable of themselves. When the Loire-Atlantique prefecture fantasized that construction would resume by launching a call for bids to the companies of the BTP, occupiers responded with their own 'call for bids' to come build the zad – a call

answered by a thousand people who came individually or in collectives to help out at thirty construction sites. When the TAV promoters
proposed withdrawing their complaints and heavy penalties in
exchange for guarantees of peacefulness on the part of the NoTAVs,
the latter, in return, proposed an immediate evacuation of their work
site lest they risk new destructions of their machines.

Finally, and most decisively: the anti-airport movement could
never have imagined claiming territorial independence for the 1,650
hectares of the zad. It is this kind of objective that has proven so
elusive to regional autonomist movements, perhaps, precisely, because
their stated goal was such independence, which was not the case at
Notre-Dame-des-Landes. It came into existence incidentally, after the
failure of Operation Caesar, in the recognition of the impossibility of
maintaining order on the territory. It was only then that autonomy
became, in fact, and rather gently, a durable perspective for the struggle. And this to the point of obtaining the implicit recognition of the
people in power themselves, who periodically lament the existence of
this lawless-zone-where-the-police-can-no-longer-go. In the same
way, it was when confronting the threat of imminent construction
that the Free Republics sprang up – never were these communes
premeditated or formally prepared. They, too, were liberated after a
defeat inflicted on the forces of order: stopped at the Maddalena by a
barricade, and brought to a standstill by an unexpected siege at
Venaus. These are not victories won by a superior physical strength
on the part of the opponents. If the state did not counter-attack immediately, it wasn't because of a possible military defeat, but because of
the political impossibility of using the degree of force necessary to
take back the areas. That failure allowed the seeds of the free communes
to germinate.

Nevertheless, the strategy of reversal also finds its limits, notably in
the dreary chambers of justice. Offensives harden, judicial strategies
change. With the maxi-trial, the NoTAVs had a glimpse of a massive
repression touching the popular movement as a whole. The integration of the logics of the state of emergency into the French constitution augurs for new twists in the claims to democracy and an increase
in the means available to subdue the mutinous. There is no obvious

response to the mechanical rise of that friction. The Maddalena work site is – each day – the proof that it is possible for the TAV, despite a fierce opposition, to continue to advance.

The hypothesis held by some revolutionary theories that the augmentation of repression, by unmasking the secret workings of the state, will reveal to the people the intrinsically violent character of society and sweep them up into a generalized insurrection, is not many people's cup of tea these days. Hardening of repression is mostly perceived with anxiety in the valley and the bocage, and all the more so in that the exemplarity of these struggles increases by tenfold the symbolic reach of blows from the adversary. But if the situation 'causes us some headaches', in the words of a farmer on the zad, this has not led to a shirking of our historic responsibilities. We have followed all the strands of struggle that have emerged around the airport and the TAV to the point of unwinding the whole ball of yarn. The propensity to generalize the battle, whether by making links with sister struggles or by multiplying the fronts, shows that at the zad as in the valley, the physical, practical and also political dimensions of the conflict have been shouldered. The valley has heralded opposition to development projects throughout Italy, and what is fermenting in Notre-Dame-des-Landes cannot be conceived without tracing its connections with dozens of other sites that recognize themselves in the slogan 'zads everywhere'. On both sides of the Alps, a question arises about the forms a movement of movements might take.

RIP Rémi Fraisse

When it comes to the zads, the French judiciary system has not yet managed to match the obsessional zeal of the Italian courts. But when it comes to maintaining order, the French appear more advanced. When the NoTAVs were surprised by teargas inundating the Maddalena, we could not help but think to what point gas is used almost systematically in France, and for sometime, accompanied by the famous 'non-lethal weapons' that have not stopped mutilating people since their use began. And even if in the first days of Operation Caesar, the police held back a little, notably when it came to arrests, the riot police made up for their restraint. The confrontations during the deforestation in Sivens in the autumn of 2014 were a model of this kind: grenades thrown inside a van full of occupiers or the gassing of people trying to prevent the advancement of machines by burying themselves in their pathway. And then on 25 October 2014, among the seven hundred grenades thrown at the demonstrators, one of them, characterized as an 'offensive' weapon of warfare, took the life of Rémi Fraisse. This was neither tragic inadvertence nor a regrettable 'accident': it was the execution of the threat contained in any act of maintaining order. Jean-Christophe J., the killer, is still a working member of the riot police in the Gironde.

One of us is dead

In September 2014, preliminary work on the construction of a dam in the Tescou Valley began, providing the backdrop to a bad fantasy film, an *Avatar* where the bad guys win. Each morning, inexorably, the riot police arrived to clear away the occupiers, followed a few yards behind by immense machines that began to cut down the forest in the midst of clouds of teargas. A month after the beginning of the deforestation, a terrace of sterile clay was exposed, extended with shaded paths, and the developers were emboldened to leave their machines in the valley overnight, inside a military camp manned by police. Though there was only a miniscule fraction of the forest remaining to be cut down, it was in this context that the opponents organized a festive weekend on 24 and 25 October 2014, whose slogan now rings with a bitter irony: 'Bring life back to Testet.'

> The police had sworn they wouldn't be there that weekend, but . . . what's a cop's word worth? . . . It's important to understand that because there were a lot of people coming, the biggest machines were put in a sheltered area on the zone. But, who knows why, the 'police life base' was still there as everyone was arriving. I love that term, because it says every-thing about their vision of 'life': an earth platform as hard as concrete, surrounded by three-yard ditches and double layers of fencing . . . In the night, they were obliged to flee by a little group of demonstrators who set fire to the base . . . So later, when a demonstration arrived at the work

site, they were there, blockading the fencing that had been half torn away, around a smoldering pile of ashes. There was nothing else to defend but their presence. The confrontation began and lasted the whole day, with explosions every minute, without our being able to take back the zone or get the police to leave. And it ended up like that, around 5 p.m. – people with grenade shrapnel in their backs and legs.

– Alexis, militant, Toulouse, there that weekend

With nightfall, the situation was calm, fires were lit all around the police camp, and many demonstrators went back to their own encampment or to get a drink. It wasn't until a few hours later that the battle resumed – but with very little of the organization, protection or mutual attention that existed earlier in the day. At 2 a.m., an offensive grenade was shot at Rémi Fraisse; shortly thereafter, police dragged his body back to their 'life base'. 'The guy is dead. It's really serious. They can't know about it', said a cop. The body of Rémi Fraisse was then placed rapidly and discreetly in a 'transportation bag' and evacuated from the site. The forces of order left the area soon after. Confusion about the cause of death was maintained for several days, just as it was after the death of Vital Michalon in 1977, during the mobilization against the Superphénix nuclear facility. In that case they spoke of a 'heart attack'. In 1986, they asserted that without his 'renal weakness', Malek Oussekine (22 years old) would have survived the beating at the end of the hall of a building during a student demonstration. They count on forestalling rage in this way. Michalon was killed by the same kind of offensive grenade that was used at Sivens, causing Minister of the Interior Bernard Cazeneuve to come up with the following euphemism in the guise of an admission: 'No offensive grenade has brought about the death of demonstrators these last few years.' The evening of the death of Vital Michalon, Christian Bonnet, then interior minister, praised the forces of order: 'Thanks to their courage and devotion, the Creys-Malville centre, built with public money to assure France a portion of its energy needs would be met, was not damaged.' What was important then is what is important now. Even if the list of police murders gets silently longer every month, murders do not happen very frequently during a demonstration or a struggle. For many of us, it was the first time that we were confronted, in our bodies and our hearts, by the murder of one of ours, someone on our side, whether we knew him personally or not.

The four weeks that followed the assassination were marked by dozens of demonstrations in every French city, from Paris and Lyon to the smallest towns. The most impressive were those in Toulouse and Nantes, cities close to the two most famous zads in the country. It seemed as though a real movement was born in Sivens, strongly marked by hatred of the police and, from one Saturday to the next, produced a new rhythm. For the first time, the zad was in all the streets – in front of the Maddalena work site, the NoTAVs unfurled a banner: 'Rémi lives'.

In Toulouse, a way of taking back the streets was sought that was different from the traditional parades with their pre-established routes and identifiable organizers. Gatherings took place without a route or an objective, depending on the pressures and confrontations with the police. It had been a long time since the streets of the city had seen such animation. Sometimes the crowd took the only exit available to them and other times, the opposite: they gathered to confront the only blockade in their way. Very little destruction along the streets, the police themselves were the target. They received their dose of projectiles, insults and slogans expressing the disgust they inspired. As if the crude reality of the street had for a time overtaken the golden image put forward in cop TV shows.

In the Toulouse demonstrations, everyone participated in the confrontations, there was a solidarity, a commonality, even if it had the appearance of black bloc. Something powerful was happening. The cops could feel it and they behaved themselves. For sure, it didn't really reflect the zads, with their diversity, but the death of Rémi Fraisse left no room for indifference or silence, and that's primordial. We ran, we were as if in a trance, together, with that shared rage, and at the same time the euphoria you feel when you know the street belongs to you. We felt that it couldn't stop there. We shouted, 'everyone hates the police', and the people nearby smiled. The following Saturdays we started up again, but the cops were a little less taken aback!

– Bénédicte

Some people hoped here would be a deflagration similar to the one that followed the death of Mohamed Bouazizi in 2011 in Sidi Bouzid, or Alexis Grigoropoulos in 2008 in Athens, or Bouna and Zyed in 2005 in Clichy-sous-Bois. If there was a detonation, the charge was not of the kind that creates insurrections. Although the movement was substantial in its duration and determination to produce a frontal clash with the forces of order, it did not attract significant popular support, even from the allied forces within the zads. The whole citizen political sphere around the Testet collective and ACIPA distanced themselves from a population judged to be far too radical, and sometimes went so far as to urge people not to join their rallies. Beyond that, what people traditionally call the 'forces on the left' were careful not to claim this dead person as one of theirs or to urge people into the streets as they did after the murder of Malik Oussekine or more recently Clément Méric by neo-Nazis. For Rémi Fraisse had gotten killed at night, surrounded by masked people attacking the police. Risking any ostensible association with 'zadists', their satanic image and frontal relation to the police, was irreconcilable with the mainstream left and its panic over seeing a force it could not control take over. So much so that when the wave of anger passed, the persistent demonstrations had a hard time not limiting themselves to gestures that, while certainly sensational, were less and less able to be shared. A few weeks later, demonstrators applauding as vans of riot police went by after the attacks of 7 and 8 January in Paris cruelly reminded people that 'No, not everyone' hated the police. The sequence that followed the death of Rémi Fraisse thus revealed the first tensions surrounding the possibilities and errors of a 'zad movement': the capacity to appear everywhere as a force outside the 'zones to be defended' and yet finding oneself, finally, isolated there if the singular power derived from composition fails. But it was also, concretely, the moment when the gesture of occupying a space in order to safeguard it and to live there came to be diffused in a vivid way.

Zads and NoTAVs Everywhere?

How to extend struggles to other territories whose particularity lies in being anchored somewhere? Among the NoTAVs, the will to 'contaminate other situations' took root after the euphoric victory of Venaus. A caravan of Valsusians went as far as Rome recounting their experiences and discussing it with others in struggle. They made twenty stops: in Arquata, where the TAV line from Terzo Valico was already in the cards; in Genoa and Rosignano, where the waste from a chemical factory had whitened the sands of the beach, giving them a frighteningly Caribbean appearance. The NoTAVS also tried logically to extend their struggle by following the train line to Chambéry where a hundred buses joined a demonstration in January 2006. But despite the energy spent, the French side of the struggle has not at this point taken on the strength of its Italian homologue.

The French government has, of course, done everything it could to squash that bird in its nest. On 3 December 2012, only a week or so after the debacle of Operation Caesar, the two heads of state, François Hollande and Mario Monti, met for a summit in Lyon. Twelve Italian buses got en route to lend support to the French demonstration. With controls and blockages, the French police spent many long hours trying to make them understand what 'the suspension of the Schengen accords' might mean. The 'lucky ones' even benefited from a personal motorcycle escort to the Place des Brotteaux, from which the demonstration was to begin. *Was to,* for the crowd, kettled behind anti-riot fences, was never allowed out to march. The NoTAVs only finally left the square to get back into their buses, not without a few skirmishes, during which a bus and its inhabitants were lightly gassed, while a cop, struggling with a driver who refused to leave, took the wheel to drive the bus out of the city. 'We saw nothing of France except its police', summed up the participants of that unhappy excursion. And it must in fact be said that the reaction of the French authorities was completely disproportionate. Such disproportion bears witness to a psychosis of contamination, but also to the lack of strength of the anti-TGV mobilizations on the French side of the Alps.

The inspiration of a victory

In graffiti, on posters, at the bottom of tracts, circulated on the web, written on banners by hundreds of people (those who participated in the resistance on the zad and those on the exterior alike), the slogan 'zads everywhere' suddenly invaded the streets and the minds in the autumn of 2012. Undoubtedly, it aimed above all at showing the support that existed everywhere for the zad at the moment it was the most threatened. But at the same time, everyone could perceive in it a kind of mantra charged with a highly performative power. In a period of repeated defeats of social movements, the debacle of Operation Caesar could not help but have an enormous effect on those who had contributed to it. Some politicos and CEOs, half frightened and half menacing, declared that if the airport were abandoned, it would be more and more difficult to get a development project underway, and that it was, by that token, necessary to forestall any risk of contamination. The idea of 'spreading the zad everywhere' carried with it the suggestion that it was possible 'everywhere, as in the zad', to win again. And in fact, the slogan, when it works, functions a bit like a reconnaissance technique between allies. A rallying cry that becomes the catalyst of the desires and aspirations of all those who, sharing a political sensibility, have not yet found the form with which to give it shape. Such is the aggregating force of evocative ideas, open to multiple interpretations, capable of summoning up energies and transforming them rapidly into action, and then of writing the first lines of a shared history. 'Zad' had become the name of a battlefield and the path taken to rejoin it.

I had followed what was going on at Notre-Dame-des-Landes from afar, but I worked and was a student in Albi, so it wasn't possible to go there long enough to understand what was at stake. And there was something going on right here. So I got involved in participating in defending the territory they were going to destroy near where I live. That struggle allowed me to have a way of confronting things concretely.

– Hélène, former occupier of Testet zad

The 'zad effect' spread all the more quickly in that it benefited from the network of solidarity strongly stimulated by the mobilization that helped win the victory over Caesar. Supporting a cause metamorphosed little by little into a singular manner of embodying it. The zad support committee became the zad committee and sometimes then a zad, period. In so doing, it maintained living connections, it reinvented itself by proposing a local continuity to the political mobilization in which it was born. Some people ended up dreaming that a little bit of the hope of Notre-Dame would take root near them. As in Avignon at the end of April 2013, when opponents occupied land in order to prevent a four-lane motorway from destroying the green belt around the city, fallow land that once sheltered a major vegetable market. Behind an aged, sputtering tractor a banner that had once hung beside the road in the Nantes bocage could now be seen: 'Sow your zad – occupy, cultivate, resist'.

In the Morvan, opposition to an industrial mega-sawmill became a zad six months after Operation Caesar: a physical opposition to the arrival of the woodcutters onto the site and construction of cabins by the local opponents, some of whom had participated in the resistance of autumn 2012. In a few months the project was definitively annulled on the terrain where it had been scheduled, and postponed to an unknown date anywhere else. The choice of naming their combat a 'zad' was seriously thought through and discussed, the term having taken on a very particular meaning: that of a last resort and a firm determination.

Similarly, because of its fame, the slogan NoTAV began to connote more than the simple question of a high-speed train. Other struggles against development projects were inspired by the Valsusian fight as well as by some of its practices. 'NoTAV', in this sense, acquired a sometimes equivocal polysemy:

The word 'NoTAV' is very interesting. Recently I served time in prison for a few weeks after actions in Turin against the eviction of renters, and when I arrived, the inmates asked me why I was there. I told them: 'We tried to prevent evictions; we put barricades up in front of the doors.' 'So you're a NoTAV!' NoTAV, for many, has become a synonym for rioting, throwing rocks at the police – generically, whoever rebels for reasons, let's say political reasons, linked to struggles. It's become emblematic of the present that we are living, for better or worse, with all the limits that entails. It means that the other oppositional movements don't exist, because in everybody's consciousness, when you confront the police, you're NoTAV. It's the strongest movement, the principal movement.

– Gabrio

The possibility of a zad or the theory of the scarecrow

Will there be a zad at the Triangle de Gonesse?

– *Le Nouvel Observateur,* 7 January 2015

Are we heading towards 'the biggest zad in France' in the Gironde?

– *Rue89,* 20 October 2015

Zadiste (masculine and femnine noun): militant who occupies a ZAD to oppose a development project harmful to the environment.

– *Le Petit Robert* dictionary (2016)

And so, since 2012, the possibility of a zad made its disturbing entry into the insurgent repertoire, becoming for a time one of its most useful weapons. Shaking their noisemakers, French militants tried to make the zad into a scarecrow, in order to frighten developers and assure the protection of the earth and its riches endangered by their voracity. The media, hungry for images, symbols and novelties, rushed to see in any movement against a development project the seeds of a new 'zone to be defended'. The word's invocation seemed sufficient to protect such places – soon discovered to be numerous – and some-times even spared any real construction of a zad. It seemed then that magic, invocation and evil spells cast against the developers came to the assistance of many emergent struggles. The 'zad movement' even obeyed, for a time, the laws of magic: contiguity (part for whole) and similarity.

What is similar produces similarity. That was the intuition put to use, despite manifest differences between all the different territories and their vindications. The practices and methods used at Notre-Dame would fatally produce the same victory everywhere they were put into practice. The scarecrow was embellished not only with clothes from the 'original' zad, but with its power and its ability to prevail over any attack. It is true that autumn 2012 had something magical about it, and it is not surprising that some people hoped to make the charm last by concocting a magic potion bearing *apparently* identical attributes. This is how artistic associations and collectives in the Niort basin decreed a 'cultural' zad, but one without any physical dimension, an imaginary zad. The magic of the word alone, like an 'abracadabra', was supposed to be enough to grant all wishes.

The identification of the part for the whole informed this period of time as well. The cabin, an occupation of a few days or a collective vegetable garden: already these were signs of an emergent zad. Anything bearing any aspect whatsoever in common with Notre-Dame-des-Landes was granted its full force. The scarecrow was no longer just a straw mannequin, it *was* the zad. Planted in the middle of a desired space, it symbolized the ubiquity of the opponents, in the same way that an absent farmer creates a double to watch over his fields. Everywhere, threatened places were going to be easily saved, thanks to this gift, this 'zads everywhere', which circulated with an unheard of speed.

To make it work, the scarecrow, as a veritable projection of the self, is dressed with one's most frightening garments. A frightening and diabolical image is held up to the birds that steal the harvest so that, literally, they move on. A simplified image, simplifying, and, ultimately, an unstable one. For resorting to magic runs risks, in the same way that threats made when one does not have the means to carry through on them must be made with the utmost delicacy and circumspection. The Hérault opponents to the industrial windfarms of Escandorgue may well have baptized their blockade of the tree cutters a 'zad', but they did not fool the developers for long. Staging does not always hide what goes on backstage well enough. It shouldn't be forgotten that the round mirrors made out of ruined compact discs can be scarecrows, and turning in the wind they reflect a deformed image of ourselves that can be used by anyone – even our enemies.

The height of opportunism was reached in Rodez, when the FNSEA installed a 'zad' in front of the prefecture to protest against the strengthening of the law against water pollution caused by manure. The fog that was created around modes of action and the role of zads on the political chessboard helped empty the term of its substance, its complex history and, in the end, its power to sway. When magic becomes merely communication, its effect evaporates and the place is left free for the creation of a foil, no longer destined for developers, but for everyone. The violent and drunken 'zadist' could slip into the empty spot.

Long ago, scarecrows were periodically burned and their ashes scattered over the planted fields to assure regeneration. Once the ability to frighten disappeared, it had to be renewed and reinvented, without which the make-believe figure appears only as what it is.

But we cannot get lost in the contemplation of sorcery and forget that the diffusion of zads was also realized quite concretely. There were places where 'zad' came to mean a real change, a genuine attempt to obtain a victory inspired by practices. At Sivens, the launching of a call to occupy the valley led to an extension and a fanning out of the struggle that was truly significant. In the Tarn, Isère and the Morvan, the idea took root that the physical defence of a terrain threatened by a harmful project represents a truly effective blow, creating, in addition, a way to share a common territory, a front that is not merely symbolic, but open and material.

The lessons of Sivens

The fight against the Testet dam in Sivens is a highly interesting example of reproducing elsewhere the recipe that worked at Notre-Dame-des-Landes. It was the first of the struggles to take the name 'zad' to a national level of attention, but in a very different context and with a balance of power much less favourable to the opponents. The project, in effect, was supposed to benefit the farmers, the water retained being used to maintain the water level of the Tescou river, which in the summer did not allow the pumping of enough water for the vast grain cultivations situated nearby. Additionally, few people lived on its banks, and the nuisances generated couldn't be compared with those of a nearby airport or a TAV. The opposition focused, therefore, on the ecological impact of the construction of a dam in a swamp zone. The agricultural establishment, for the most part, was in favour of the infrastructure. Nevertheless, the Sivens forest was a place frequented by a number of Tarn inhabitants; it was a place where one could walk along bucolic nature paths lined with signs detailing the names of the particularly rich flora and fauna of the region. Walkers, neighbours and ecologists, grouped together in an oppositional association, joined up with a dozen or so activists who were occupying the abandoned farm of the Métairie near the little hamlet of Barat. Immediately, though, this occupation in an isolated area ran up against the presence on the territory of those who were, roughly speaking, 'pro-dam':

> They were always circling around, passing by several times a day to look at the least construction, the least thing. If there were cabins being built in the trees, whenever we left, even for a moment, they were on the ground. The first cabin we built was burned that very night. Suddenly, there was this very combative set of relations in the territory. For and against. And it wasn't an even fight, numerically, or in terms of organization. There was the attack on the Métairie in January 2014. That aggression surprised us and had a big effect. We knew that it was very organized, because they chose the moment when there were only two women at home. Twenty of them came, masked, with their license plates covered. They blew a hunting horn and in five minutes it was over: everything was destroyed, pulverized, cut through the shutters, leveling things with a buzz saw, they undid the electrical system, and flattened the tires of the cars that were there so as to not be followed.
>
> – Hélène

But the opponents did not buckle under the intimidations and even made use of their eviction from the Métairie to start an encampment not far from there, on the very site designated for the construction of the dam. They organized weekends, picnics and other initiatives there. A month later, riot police arrived to evacuate the zone.

Overwhelmed because of their small numbers and the need to protect their encampments day and night, the members of the collective, not without apprehension, launched a public call for new occupations, in the hope of bringing new energy to the movement. Even though the gesture may seem similar, the reasons for the call were different than those that brought dozens of squatters to Notre-Dame: at Sivens the movement barely existed. It was the absence of any popular movement of support that caused the harried activists to call for help; at Notre-Dame, an oppositional movement anchored locally lacked activists to reinforce its pre-existing troops. The arrival of nomad 'zadists' did not meet the need for local anchoring, and despite the illusion of number and the media coverage, the imbalance between local support and external aid became more accentuated. And yet, the echo of Sivens contaminated for a time the schools nearby, such as the Gaillac and Castres high schools, whose students went on strike to protest the deforestation. But on site, the reproduction of certain of the innovative practices tested at Notre-Dame – occupying, barricading, wearing masks – did not seem to be enough for victory.

> At Sivens, it was like cut and paste: a way of not taking into account that it wasn't the same scene, nor the same context as Notre-Dame. It's true that the 'model' of Notre-Dame gave us strength, but there was also a persistent, disillusioned rumor, that folks from there were going to arrive any minute en masse . . . There was the misguided hope that the big brothers were coming, and at the same time the recurrent disappointment that they weren't there . . . There were demonstrations of support that came from there, in actions, texts and even food supplies were organized. But we always felt it wasn't enough.
>
> – Oscar, former occupier of the Testet zad

Active solidarity from the 'mother of all zads' seemed to be taken for granted, whenever similar practices were used and the name 'zad' adopted. The zad effect produced the trap whereby material aid between those who claimed it would suffice for the construction of a material force, disguising sometimes the need to find one's own path, to build one's particular history. This generated many frustrations, as much among those who launched the appeal and who had a hard time organizing with their new comrades, as among those who responded and occupied the default position of being central to a fight they had planned on merely joining. This factor contributed to a significant turnover in occupiers that prevented any real sedimentation of experience and, therefore, any community of struggle, from coming into being.

> When it continued to get bigger, it really became complicated, because there were many people who were there for the occupation, but who wanted nothing to do with the General Assemblies, nor the battle plans, nor organizing collective life, or perspectives. It was really hard.
>
> – Hélène

Between the juridical actions of the "Testet collective" and the occupiers of the zone, a movement able to organize mobilizations materially and politically when severely attacked did not take shape. The permanent crisis of the repeated evictions and the construction's ongoing progress prevented any resolution of the problems. When construction was finally suspended with the death of Rémi Fraisse, it was perhaps already too late: the citizen component distanced itself from the real fight and the occupiers found themselves in a more and more delicate situation.

> At one point there were two hundred of us occupying the zone, but little by little we were reduced to fifty. We were in a kind of vicious circle of fear: the more the pro-dam pressure was strong, the more barricades we built; the more barricades we built, the more people became afraid and stopped coming here, and thus the more barricades we then needed to protect our little group.
>
> – Sébastien, former occupier of the Testet zad

Opening up a front says nothing about the capacity of holding it, and one runs the risk of seeing these kinds of forces emerge. Taking on conflict always carries with it the possibility of defeat. Its consequences do not end with the conclusion of an occupation or the building of a dam. Even if an active militant network remained in the Tarn after the last eviction, the barriers erected from that point on against any political possibility linked to the zad were not small. The zadist scarecrow still haunts the area: whether it be for a festival or an instructive evening, the pressures have not disappeared. For the anniversary of the death of Rémi Fraisse, the commune mayor shamefully decreed all commemorations to be forbidden, on the pretence of risks linked to threats by the pro-dam people. Only his parents were allowed to go to the site, and only accompanied by police. As for Thierry Carcenac, senator and Socialist Party president of the Tarn department council, he urged any people audacious enough to brave the decree to be prudent, since, 'in this hunting season, the woods are not safe'. The two-ton monument placed at the spot in homage to Rémi disappeared a few days after its installation.

This experience teaches us that a struggle is not just a series of gestures: the significance it acquires and that exceeds it means shouldering a responsibility that is often a heavy load.

> I think many people in Italy sympathize with us because they know that if they pave us over, if they flatten us, it will be awful for all the other movements that want to rebel. That's one of the reasons why we don't give in, we have a responsibility.
>
> – Guido

Holding out at any price can be a double-edged sword. If it is necessary for Notre-Dame and the NoTAVs to do so in terms of other struggles, it also requires a strong community, able to support fatigue and exhaustion. No occupation can afford to ignore the relation to the territory where it emerges, as well as to the inhabitants who live there and the movement that supports it. Nevertheless, the existential dimensions of the experience near the Tescou River cannot be summed up in the language of cold, tactical reasoning. The conclusions we can draw from that experience are not valuable for all time or for all places. The opponents to the Centre Parcs holiday village in Roybon knew the same difficulties, confronted local militias and had very little support from the village, and yet nevertheless managed to put an end to the project.

Taking off again from where one is

Despite the difficulties the Sivens struggle encountered, it was after
the death of Rémi Fraisse and the subsequent demonstrations that a
new wave of zads were born: the Cassine zad in Chambéry against
the construction of a business district, the Roybon zad, the Oléron
zad against the industrial farming of genetically modified oysters,
the zads of Échillais or Sainte-Colombe-en-Bruilhois against incin-
erators, the Agen zad against the construction of a high-speed train,
the ephemeral zads of Rouen, Marseille, Saclay. The phenomenon
extended even beyond national borders to the Haren zad near
Brussels against the project to construct a mega-prison. We may
wonder why this spate of urban demonstrations, sometimes riots,
went hand in hand with the most massive dissemination of a form of
struggle – territorial and usually rural – whose essence lies in being
anchored. It seems as though the reaction to the drama at Sivens
finally, for a time, allowed the paradox of 'exporting a territorial
struggle' to be resolved, without, of course, reproducing the popular
and massive aspect of the Notre-Dame struggle, nor replacing magi-
cally its long history.

And so, for the first time, a 'zad movement' exploded. It was marked
by three aspects: agitation or a spreading disturbance – in short, a
contagious social movement; the advance of troops exporting their
determination; and finally an artistic or philosophical movement,
imprinted with the novelty of its ways of seeing the world, its particular and recognizable practices that everyone could pick up and use for
themselves, modifying and reworking them. A pathway was opened:
a target (that of projected infrastructures) for all those who want to
combat this world, at the same time that the means (the practices
developed at the zad) were available to all those who were looking for
a model to which they could weave their local opposition and echo it
in that way.

This form of contamination did not, however, just resolve a paradox; it also generated a new one: as the contamination spread, the 'zad
effect' was emptied of its force. Zadism and its tenants, as images
shaped by government leaders and the media, became a screen hiding

the real force of Notre-Dame. Did the term have to become unusable for its true essence to be exported? Inventiveness was forced to replace the temptation to imitate. Experience could take on a certain depth, and avoid the big traps of the 'zad identity' at a moment when claiming a label had become a strategically dubious gesture.

In December 2014, at Saint-Victor-et-Melvieu in Aveyron, a struggle took on strength against the building of a transformer on seven hectares of agricultural land. This was an infrastructure that allowed the invasion of the region by hundreds of industrial windfarms. To stop this deadly project, the Amassada cabin sprang up right in the middle of the site desired by RTE, a subsidiary of EDF (Électricité de France).

There were a lot of people here used to being active together and who liked doing it, especially the networks of zad committees, the ones who built the Secadoz cabin that we moved to Notre-Dame-des-Landes. So l'Amassada came into being at a precise moment, when Victor, a young farmer cultivating the land of the Plaines threatened by the transformer, came to meet members of the zad committee. This farmer had gone to Testet to see what it was like, if it was possible to defend land in that way, and had come back with lots of enthusiasm, but also lots of questions, especially about what he described as a chaotic zone that made him relatively frightened, while at the same time the fear was mixed with an attraction for that kind of fight that seemed to him to be potentially victorious. After our meeting, where he saw his doubts and enthusiasm were shared, he decided very quickly, in the space of two weeks, to build l'Amassada on the Plaine. But broadcasting an affiliation with the zad was a sensitive issue. So we didn't call ourselves a zad, but we invited farmer-occupiers from Notre-Dame to come speak at our inauguration, for example.

– Estelle, opponent to transformer at Saint-Victor-et-Melvieu

From the first days of a zone to be defended at Notre-Dame-des-Landes, other similar experiences felt a closeness with its practices. This was the case in Dijon, where, since 2010, the threat that the ancient belt of vegetable markets around the city be destroyed to build an eco-neighbourhood caused the emergence of the 'free zone of the

Lentillères'. Four years after seizing the first stretch of land to start a collective garden, the neighbourhood housed a market farm, several lots cultivated by dozens of people, occupied houses and self-built houses, a party hall and studios.

> We had to ask ourselves the question whether to call ourselves a zad, even if the occupation of the Lentillères started in 2010, before the term was taken up by other struggles of that type. We decided no because there were some fears: the fact that it might accelerate things too much, that it would squeeze the time we needed to build something together and that it was harmful to our constituting ourselves as a coherent force. We also were worried about the kind of visibility it might generate, with ready-made images, clichés. And then, our struggle was built on the wager that to anchor ourselves we needed to know each other and under-stand each other progressively, and since all that had been happening in a pretty terrific way up until now, it made sense to continue that way.
>
> – Olivier, occupier of free zone of Lentillères, Dijon

The delicate media situation led to the search for, and enunciation of, what each place had that was its own: its filiations, name, manner of doing things, and so on. And so it was outside the slogan that a truth about the zad was discovered: the particularity of the connection it maintains with its territory and its history.

> Here everybody talks about the zad, but the situation is much more like in the Susa Valley with its enormous involvement of the people living there. This explains why there are not many people living on this zad, since the opponents are mostly living throughout a twenty-kilometre surrounding area!
>
> – Camille, opponent to industrial sawmill in Morvan

In the idea of a zad, there's the whole history surrounding the composi-tion of different groups. Here, you can't count on that. First, because there isn't a permanent presence in the cabin, because we don't need to occupy every instant. It's more of a presidio than a zad, if you will. And then, even the youth, we're all from around here or most of us, we were mostly born here, others moved here. And we're still a small-scale struggle . . . People who frequent the zads would show up here and ask: 'How is it going with the locals?' and that would make us smile because we are all locals.

– Estelle

The proliferation of zads also raises the question of temporality. Given the rapid advancement a project might take, one cannot expect a recent opposition to have the time to become rooted. How to do without years of struggle and information? How can the confidence necessary to solidarity be created? Where can the time and the occasions that produce such confidence be found? One of the keys to the combats of Notre-Dame-des-Landes and the Susa Valley is undeniably their long-term dimension that made it possible for the participants in the struggles to get to know each other, and for those who were not from the region to discover the customs and singularities of the place, allowing them then to welcome thousands of supporters without being overwhelmed.

We started to occupy the neighbourhood five years ago. It happened bit by bit. It was duration that allowed us to anchor ourselves in the city, in the imaginaries, and even as an inspiring struggle on the national level . . . The invitation to come share the fruits of the harvest through the pay-what-you-want market on Thursdays was a tool for connecting up with lots of people. There was real time for encounters and weekly discussions in the courtyard of the market garden, the occupied farm. There are people for whom the market is a major economic necessity, for whom it's really their only source for food and vegetables, and others who just prefer to buy here rather than elsewhere. In 2010 when we started to occupy, we had no projection of the sort 'in five years we want four hectares farmed, six houses, sixty gardens . . .' and yet that's where we are now.

– Olivier

But how can we federate, connect with each other, learn from the successes and failures – our own and those of others – given experiences differing in size, context, duration objectives? Forms of organization without Organization are sought on both sides of the Alps that take seriously the need for material inventiveness.

From occasional mutual aid to the network

One of the most obvious links between the different struggles is the occasional support they bring to each other, pooling their resources in common to confront an offensive from power. The NoTAVs go to Sicily in great number to demonstrate on the side of the No MUOs. Several cars leave Notre-Dame-des-Landes to participate in a Lyon demonstration in December 2012 against the Lyon–Turin line, or to help support the occupied neighbourhood of Lentillères. There are many such examples, and they contribute to creating a circulation between the sites of struggle. And yet, these sites do not all have the same capacity to help their comrades, something that reinforces a bit the centrality of the bocage and the valley, themselves limited by the number of struggles to reinforce and their geographic distance. It also raises the politically equivocal question of the existence of 'capitals of insurrection'.

Attempts at horizontal coordination that are supple and multifaceted have begun, like the interzad encounters at Notre-Dame in the summer of 2015, whose invitation was addressed to 'the different components of struggles relative to a territorial development project, with occupation as the point shared in common (ongoing, projected, or terminated)' and concluded with a call to 'form a network' to go beyond 'mutual aid from zad to zad'.

For several decades, the establishment of a network has been the canonical form of organization of most of the political movements that lie outside of the classical structures of party or union. The absence of constraints that preside over reticular aggregations fills a number of the needs of each individual point in the network: preservation of its own specificity, of its singular goals, of its discourse and autonomy of action. Some connections are activated, condensed or stimulated when an event occurs, and then disappear after the action, in an almost spontaneous and natural manner. In addition, the growth of the network, through mutual attraction of the parties more than through recruitment, gives rise to the thought that from one point to the next, it could extend infinitely.

But its particularity is that it is not itself anchored; the network is, in a certain manner, virtual, like the internet and the technologies of managerial capitalism that use similar terminology. It is easy to understand its popularity in the anti-globalization movement, which was expressed mostly during enormous rallies between which only an empty space seemed to exist. For the purpose of linking together grand moments in the way we link points together, the network appeared adequate. But struggles are sometimes more than punctual events, and this is particularly true of those that take root in a territory. When a real space continues to exist in all its subversive materiality, we need to construct relations that are more engaging than those, versatile and loose, of the network. The connections will draw from a different material, where the affective counts at least as much as the proximity of ideals or political practices.

Convergence or big bang

That affective connections, in their solidity and their entanglements, might be the best cement holding a vast conjunction of revolts together should not prevent our looking to extend that conjunction beyond the forcibly limited scale of personal acquaintanceship. To give the realm of emotion its part in political elaboration, against a militant tradition that, at best, relegated it to the back burner and at worst to the status of an impediment, does not mean the one can be content to subsume the other. To trace out a path in reality for 'zads everywhere', a path that would be more than a slogan, or a 'party of the No', that would indeed be something other than a party, we need imaginaries, images.

The idea of the convergence of struggles, frequently invoked these last years, has played the role of an incantation capable of overcoming compartmentalization and increasing power. But the part-timers did not join up with the salaried workers, who did not join up with the students, who themselves failed to 'join up with' the ghettos. These different worlds never succeeded in being reunited under the same banner. The ambition itself is dubious, and the idea of a convergence which presupposes all the struggles, each as a singular destiny, could tend, in the end, toward the same point, when they each have their own rhythm, objectives, contradictions, disturbances, and so forth.

Convergence conceived of as the search for the lowest common denominator means the only unity one risks ending up with is not one reuniting that which was divided, but one eradicating all differences instead.

Nevertheless, something of the ghetto riots of 2005 was evident a few months later during the anti-CPE movement, just as something of the 2006 agitation was taken up again in 2010 by workers on strike over their pensions – practices, ideas, and dreams too. The points in common are numerous, and not only conjugated in the future tense. They are fulcrums rather than a final end. Points of passage, passwords, through which may transit detours and shortcuts. Around each one, solidarities are reformed, and sometimes also divergences, opening up the field of possible transformations. Thus, the participation of some of the occupiers at Notre-Dame-des-Landes in support of the refugees of Calais and moving some of them to the zad creates a blueprint for a much larger junction between the anti-airport struggle and that of immigrants. Such a junction will not take shape because of some decree proclaimed at some zadist congress, but through the multiplication of contact points, as when in Angers, a Zone d'Accueil à Défendre (Welcoming Zone to be Defended) was invented to receive thirty Somali refugees.

The geography of struggles evokes in this way something more like a big bang, in its expansion and its proliferation of stars in formation, than a confluence of straight lines. And to find passageways between trajectories travelling towards unexplored confines, it is sometimes useful to identify what it is that seems to polarize them. The zad and NoTAV are poles around which the political lines of force of our era align themselves.

Index